Assisted Living Strategies

for Changing Markets

How For-Profits and Not-For-Profits
Can Still Prosper While Serving Seniors

21ST CENTURY SENIOR

Jim Mo

D0814272

Assisted Living
Pragmatic Strategies For Changing Markets

First Printing, April, 2001

Westridge Publishing
Fort Worth, Texas

Library of Congress Card Number: 00-111923

ISBN   1-893405-02-8

ALSO BY JIM MOORE:

Senior Housing – Co-Author
A Development & Management Handbook

Assisted Living
Pure & Simple Development and Operating Strategies

Assisted Living 2000
Practical Strategies For the Next Millennium . . .
. . . How to Survive and Succeed in This Large, But
Complex Market

Senior Housing & Assisted Living
The Contemporary Long Term Care Column Series:
1991 to 2001

TABLE OF CONTENTS

SECTION TWO - The Competitive Battlefield

CHAPTER

SECTION THREE - Physical Design Strategies

CHAPTER

SECTION FOUR - Financial Considerations; Capital Costs and Operating Expenses

CHAPTER

CHAPTER

SECTION SEVEN - Special Market Niches and "Carve-Outs"

CHAPTER

SECTION EIGHT - Strategic Considerations

CHAPTER

SECTION NINE - The Future is Not What it Used to Be

CHAPTER

Appendices

LIST OF FIGURES

SECTION ONE - Developing a Solid Foundation

FIGURE

SECTION TWO - The Competitive Battlefield

FIGURE

SECTION THREE - Physical Design Strategies

FIGURE

SECTION FOUR - Financial Considerations; Capital Costs and Operating Expenses

FIGURE

SECTION FOUR - Financial Considerations; Capital Costs and Operating Expenses - Continued

FIGURE

SECTION FOUR - Financial Considerations; Capital Costs and Operating Expenses - Continued

FIGURE

SECTION FIVE - Pricing

FIGURE

SECTION FIVE - Pricing - Continued

FIGURE

SECTION SIX - Affordability

FIGURE

SECTION SIX - Affordability - Continued

FIGURE

SECTION SEVEN - Special Market Niches and "Carve-Outs"

FIGURE

SECTION EIGHT - Strategic Considerations

FIGURE

SECTION NINE - The Future is Not What it Used to Be

FIGURE

Appendices

INTRODUCTION

This book is being released during a period when the industry is at a critical crossroads. There was plenty of bad news in assisted living in 2000 and early 2001: public company stocks were depressed, some major metropolitan markets appeared to be saturated, new project fill-up was slowing and pricing concessions were becoming commonplace. But don't be fooled about the industry's future. It's time to get back to basics - focusing on the senior consumer and their families while executing sound business strategies. That's what this book is all about.

Assisted Living Strategies for Changing Markets does not cover *everything* you need to know about assisted living. No single book can. But, the 42 chapters address the most relevant issues facing our industry in the first part of the 21st century. You will receive leading edge information on strategies, tactics, industry benchmarks, rules of thumb, current trends and future marketplace impacts. I've attempted to present pure and simple winning strategies and money making ideas communicated with sophisticated simplicity. Real world problems are identified and cost-effective, practical solutions are provided.

The table of contents is structured and sequenced as a series of relevant assisted living industry issues and strategies. I've written each chapter so that you can benefit from "random access". By that I mean you can scan the detailed table of contents and jump to the chapter addressing the issue of interest to you on any given day. I've also tried to strike a delicate balance between leading edge ideas and theories combined with proven experience and trends observed consistently in the marketplace. These observations are the culmination of a 20-year odyssey where I've traveled over 4 million air miles, working in an average of three senior housing markets a week. During my work, I've lived briefly in over 40 senior living communities in an attempt to get as close as possible to the residents, the front line staff and the local competition.

As in past books, I've profiled a typical 80-unit assisted living community; using detailed industry comparables and financial factors that are representative of existing projects in approximately 75 percent of the U.S. markets in the 2002 time frame. Financial factors are presented in 2002 dollars using the prevailing interest rates of this time period. A word of caution – each individual project in each market is unique; the quantitative examples in this book should be used for guidance purposes only and must be appropriately adjusted for each individual situation.

For the experienced senior housing professional and their staff, this book can be a useful checklist of appropriate strategies and initiatives. For those who are new to our industry, it can act as a strategic planning handbook. I wish you much success in your endeavors to better serve seniors and their families.

ACKNOWLEDGMENTS

This book reflects the consolidated input of literally thousands of professionals, industry colleagues and senior consumers. In *Assisted Living Strategies*, I merely acted as a facilitator to translate their collective knowledge and experience into a usable format. I felt it necessary and appropriate to repeat the following statement in each of may books. I am deeply indebted to the professional staffs at hundreds of senior living communities that have taken valuable time from their very busy schedules to allow me to both help them and to expand my base of knowledge and experience. I have tremendous respect for these professionals who provide endless love, care and patience to their residents; much of it accomplished in a time sensitive, stressful environment.

I've learned something new about our great industry every day for the past 30 years. I owe this valuable experience to over 10,000 residents and senior consumers, in formal focus groups and informal conversations, who took the time to share their personal experiences with me. They discussed both the good life and the challenges of growing older. Hundreds of clients, sponsors and owner/operators allowed me into their communities and boardrooms to exchange strategic ideas. Industry colleagues openly shared their ideas, experiences and strategies.

As with past books, my professional team at MDS played a significant role in creating this book. Each professional - in their own way - kept me focused and on target. I would especially like to thank Mary Ann Baltzer for manuscript preparation, Kim Jimenez and Virginia Bregenzer for proofing and editing, Jeff Moore and Roy Barker for technical consultation. Jeff Guinn provided final professional editing and Broc Sears created the cover design.

I'm deeply indebted to Sue Bregenzer, who as MDS' Business Manager, has always found the time to provide enormous assistance in coordinating my column for the past ten years and producing the manuscript for this book during one of the busiest periods of our company's 30-year history.

Finally, my long days and busy travel schedule were made much easier because of the understanding, support and patience of my wife Gerry.

SECTION ONE

Developing A
Solid Foundation

CHAPTER 1

THE ASSISTED LIVING INDUSTRY
IS *NOT* WHAT IT USED TO BE!

The Industry is Being Defined
by Ten Major Trends

In my previous book, *Assisted Living 2000,* published in July of 1998, I said:

> *"This book is being released during a period that could well be a major turning point in our exciting industry (July, 1998). History may record that from this point forward Assisted Living's Future Is Not What It Used To Be!"*

There was really no magic in that observation. That's because I saw the following ominous leading indicators on the horizon:

1. The relentless development by public companies of their assisted living product pipelines.

2. I knew development could not continue at the 1998 pace – and most public companies could not consistently deliver on other optimistic promises made at their Initial Public Offerings (IPOs).

3. The attendance at seminars and trade association conferences was swelling, in large part, from inexperienced parties ("wanna be's") seeking to jump on the assisted living bandwagon.

4. Stock prices and above average price-earnings (P/E) ratios of senior living public companies started drifting downward (before the free-fall for many of them).

5. Lenders and investors had started to raise the bar on their borrowing criteria.

6. Wall Street analysts, institutional investors and lenders incorrectly lumped assisted living and independent living under the skilled nursing peer group umbrella. This created a dark cloud of concern that, at the time, was largely misplaced.

We now know the senior living and health care business sectors will likely experience boom-bust cycles just like real estate, high technology, the Internet and other traditional businesses.

The Glass is Still Half Full

Notwithstanding the above trends, assisted living has a number of favorable attributes and solid business fundamentals. The concept is cost-effective, it serves a clearly defined need for a growing market segment, and it is generally "user friendly." As income qualified consumers exercise discretion and choice, assisted living – *proactively* communicated – could become the preferred sheltered living option.

Assisted living is also positioned well for future growth as managed care concepts still seek a solid, practical operating platform. There is considerable debate on how managed care will ultimately interface with long term care, but assisted living's cost-effective and efficient method of delivering services appears quite compatible with the fundamental cost containment philosophies and objectives of managed care. There is one big caveat; we've got to start thinking long term – HMO's must eventually think beyond their next quarterly financial report!

Ten "Unexpected" Trends

Despite favorable industry hype and market responsiveness, assisted living, as a mass market service delivery system, has proven to be a constantly moving target; and no one definitive success strategy has emerged. Investors and operators in this business sector have encountered some surprises in recent years, and there may be more to come. If you don't pay attention to some increasingly evident trends, you will pay a price. I would propose my personal "top ten" (refer to Figure 1-1). These ten largely unexpected trends are forcing sponsors and operators to constantly monitor their radar screens and re-evaluate their current operations.

FIGURE 1-1
TEN MAJOR TRENDS
IMPACTING ASSISTED LIVING

1. High acuity levels and resident turnover
2. Is there really *affordable* assisted living?
3. Cost creep and complex pricing systems
4. Entitlements are a moving target
5. Lenders becoming more selective
6. Potential for market saturation
7. Public companies experience boom-bust cycle
8. Threat of regulation?
9. A future market correction?
10. Overbuild not solved by demographics

---

1. *Increasing acuity levels and high resident turnover.* Many operators had visions that their residential/social model of assisted living would attract the moderately frail elderly; they hoped these residents could be cared for with relative ease and at modest cost. However, changing entitlement systems and managed care market forces are bringing higher acuity level patients into nursing homes, and the effect is filtering down through the continuum of care to assisted living. Add to that the natural effects of aging in place and it's not surprising that assisted living communities are finding themselves with an unexpectedly high number of residents in need of complex and expensive care. As a result, most assisted living sponsors are experiencing annual resident turnover rates of 40 to 50 percent. This translates to an average length of stay of approximately two and one-half years.

Many operators have responded by providing higher acuity services such as incontinence management and dementia care; services that weren't considered a few years ago. In fact, some organizations are becoming increasingly concerned about drifting into "gray areas" concerning nursing-type licensure. They are (or should be) keeping close watch on their state and local licensure requirements, which vary considerably from state-to-state. The licensure issue is one reason why nursing homes themselves, rather than fighting assisted living, are starting to join in; some 60 percent of existing nursing home operators are estimated to be at least considering the assisted living alternative.

2. *Truly affordable assisted living is a moving target.* There is a lot of talk about "affordable" *assisted living*. Well intended individuals are making erroneous comparisons with the concept of affordable *senior housing*. Clearly, such federal programs as Section 8 and 202 have been very good for the economically disadvantaged Senior needing basic housing. But unfortunately, assisted living operates in an altogether different economic arena.

Let's look at the elementary costs involved in providing basic assisted living; shelter, food and reasonable assistance with ADLs. These operating expenses come to at least $50 per resident day (if you're fortunate). Multiply this by 30.4 days per month, and the basic outlay for just operating expenses – with no debt service allocation is $1,520 a month.

There is simply no escaping this. Even if someone were to *give* the developer or sponsor the land and the building, which seems unlikely, the basic operating costs must still be covered each month – just for the operator to break even. Tax credit programs help the land and building cost challenge, but are certainly not the total solution to the affordability problem.

I wish there was a way to resolve this, because there are certainly large numbers of seniors in our society who need and deserve affordable assisted living services. But, as a practical matter, assisted living is and probably will continue to be largely private pay. From society's standpoint, that is our challenge – and dilemma – for the future. Chapters 25 through 30 cover these critical affordability issues.

3. *Cost creep – an insidious economic disease.* Residents want high ambience, non-institutional residential settings, but they will also need increased assistance in activities of daily living. These needs must be met through a strong, albeit largely invisible, medical structure. Satisfying these needs may not entail the significant expense of high-acuity nursing services, but increasing levels of care in assisted living are resulting in subtle increases in operating costs. These cost increases "trickle" through your financial statements in the form of overtime and additional staffing requests; and one day you may get a significant financial "wake-up" call. Implementing price changes with existing residents to compensate for the newly discovered cost creep is not a pleasant experience for front line professionals to initiate. Chapter 15 addresses cost creep impacts and strategies in detail.

Complex pricing systems are emerging. In response to cost creep, operators are implementing tiered, multilevel pricing policies. While these policies may seem rational, they can sometimes cause marketplace confusion.

Suddenly your community's nice, simple, easy-to-understand basic service fee schedule has evolved into a multi-level pricing structure. You start by increasing fees $200 to $300 a month for increasingly intense levels of assistance with the activities of daily living. Or perhaps you charge $8 to $12 for every 15-minute increment of additional hands-on care daily.

4. *Entitlements Are a Moving Target.* There used to be the argument – and it still exists in some quarters – that since assisted living provides a less costly alternative to nursing home care, it will be very attractive to managed care organizations as they infiltrate into long-term care. Today I am less certain that this is true.

Acuity levels in nursing homes have increased to such an extent that relatively few nursing home residents today also fit the ideal profile for assisted living. Two years ago one might have argued that at least 15 to 20 percent of nursing home residents could be appropriately relocated to assisted living (assuming, of course, that they could private-pay). Now, the overlap has narrowed. I think that we essentially have two separate populations in these settings, with very little overlap: 1) a very high acuity nursing home population that the government largely supports but can ill-afford to pay for, and 2) a moderate acuity assisted living population who, if they were to become Medicare- and/or Medicaid-qualified, are far too large a population sector for our government to support. I would love to see assisted living become a major player in the entitlements arena, but how can this work given the current numbers and budgetary restraints?

I don't see Medicare HMOs going beyond covering basic Medicare benefits anytime soon. Meanwhile, private long-term care insurance, which might be expected to use managed care philosophies to keep costs and premiums under control, is still only a relatively small player in the market and is growing perhaps a little less rapidly than some might have anticipated five or six years ago.

For these reasons, we counsel all our clients that assisted living must be viewed primarily as a *private-pay business*. If there is ever an entitlements breakthrough, that will be a big plus for the industry – but don't count on it.

5. *Lenders Are Becoming More Selective.* Lenders have raised the bar and are on "a flight to quality." That means they are focusing on refinancing vs. start-ups, dealing only with experienced operators, requiring more equity and taking far less financial risk.

6. *Potential for market proliferation and possible saturation*. The current consumer demand that is assisted living's greatest strength has also proven to be a major weakness in the late 1990s. Unrealistic and inaccurate industry hype on both Wall Street and Main Street attracted inexperienced and/or aggressive developer/operators who were eager to cash in on what they perceived as almost unlimited demand. A worst case scenario involved the concern of the possibility of a serious glut of poorly planned facilities and a significantly tarnished reputation for the industry, as people unfamiliar with assisted living would grossly underestimate the complexities of resident care and the true dynamics of the competitive marketplace. This did not happen – except for some isolated examples.

7. *Public Companies Experience Boom-Bust Cycle.* Many large, public companies initially felt that they must have a multi-facility presence in most major metropolitan areas such as Atlanta, Boston, etc. Starting in 1998, a number of public senior living companies launched a relentless pursuit of growth – trying to keep Wall Street happy by establishing enormous development pipelines of new assisted living products. They were trying to report favorable Earnings Per Share (EPS) growth quarter after quarter; hopefully in the double digit range when viewed on an annualized basis. Like tax sheltered real estate in the 1980s, the *deal* appeared to be more important (at least initially) than ultimate *product performance* in the marketplace. These companies booked significant development fees as revenues and looked forward to dramatic increases in management fees, operating profits and earnings per share.

It quickly became apparent that this geometrical growth could not continue and, in 1999 and 2000, most public companies either curtailed or significantly reduced their development pipelines. In doing so, they took a significant downward adjustment in earnings.

As this book goes to press in early 2001, this major market activity has not yet resulted in definitive and significant market saturation. But in assessing whether saturation is approaching, there are some important "vital signs" to watch for and questions to ask. Are occupancy levels in various neighboring communities starting to sag? Why? And what about new project fill-up rates? Today, projects fill up, on average, at a rate of five-to-seven units a month, net of turnover. Anything slower than that over a reasonable period of time is cause for concern.

Market area overlap is already occurring in some cities. This is the ultimate marketing challenge for assisted living developers. Interestingly, in some market areas there is primary market area overlap occurring within the *same* company's operations. Marketing manager A is competing with marketing manager B to fill units for the same multi-facility operator. And they are confronting savvy consumers who are smart enough to attempt to make deals by pitting one sales manager against the other. The headquarters office, of course, just wants to see units filled, and may not be aware that the company is actually competing with itself to accomplish their objectives!

With firms that compete with one another, the situation resembles having two new service stations opening on opposite corners of a major intersection. It's not that there isn't sufficient market size and depth to *ultimately* support both of the competing businesses, it's that they're both going through their critical market introduction and launch phase at the same time. This phenomenon, coupled with my view that we've been largely order takers rather than proactive marketeers, characterizes many assisted living markets today.

8. *Threat of regulation*. As acuity levels rise, assisted living care may well cross the line into the domain of licensed nursing. If this happens, the types of assistance offered, staffing levels, and resident care outcomes are likely to trigger competing trade association debates, accreditation issues and a barrage of new state and federal regulations.

There is concern that the nursing OBRA experience not be repeated with assisted living. The question arises, though, that if Medicaid eventually becomes a major third party payor for assisted living, what sort of strings will be attached? How much regulation will be federal, how much state, and what will the regulation be like? For now, the most practical approach to the issue is to make sure that your community is built in accordance with anticipated basic regulatory and fire/safety requirements. Special emphasis should be placed on fire doors, appropriate corridor widths and sprinkler systems – that, while not required now, may well be issues in the near future. In short, make sure that at least your "bricks and mortar" are prepared for future government oversight.

9. *A Market Correction in the Future?* In 1998, my firm calculated that if all the projects announced by major companies in a particular market came on line during the following 18 months, the area's assisted living inventory would increase by over 23 percent. That was viewed as a huge increase, especially given current resident turnover rates. The combination of companies going public and the past availability of capital fueled the recent boom. Is there a "boom/bust" potential here? The marketplace is slowly providing answers.

Achieving a demand vs. supply balance in assisted living is somewhat like the Federal Reserve attempting to stimulate economic growth and employment without triggering inflation. In both situations, there are many variables to understand and control. Figure 1-2 summarizes what I believe are the current (early 2001) top four supply vs. demand issues.

10. *You can't necessarily rely on future demographics to solve current overbuild problems.* In some respects, current assisted living growth assessments are analogous to the 1990's real estate sound bite, *"if you build it, they will come."* Even if you're not filling up now, you might rationalize that, surely with the highly publicized aging boom you'll have no problems in 18 to 24 months. This summons up memories of the 1980s, when inflation was supposed to cover up many a real estate mistake. Unfortunately, tomorrow's demographics will not likely cover up today's serious assisted living project overbuilding mistakes. Keep in mind that, because of resident turnover every year, we must refill an average of 40 to 50 percent of the *existing* assisted living unit inventory.

Sponsors and operators seeking to respond to some or all of these trends must first understand the numbers associated with assisted living development. These numbers include demographics, capital costs, operating expenses, and the financial dynamics and consequences resulting from existing and future competition. I've attempted to address all of these important issues and much more in this book.

FIGURE 1-2

CURRENT ASSISTED LIVING SUPPLY-DEMAND BALANCE ISSUES - 2001

Supply Trends

1. The public equity markets have essentially dried up - curtailing the availability of new risk capital.

2. Public companies have made significant cuts in their development pipelines.

3. Lenders have tightened credit costs and borrower criteria.

4. Annual resident turnover will require re-marketing of up to at least 35% to 40% of the existing assisted living units in the market.

Consumer Demand Variables

1. Truly proactive marketing can result in deeper market penetration.

2. Age 80+ senior prospect growth over the next 5 years will be significant; averaging approximately a 12 percent annual increase or 135,000 households per year from years 2000 to 2005.

3. The adult child/decision influencer has significant untapped potential.

4. Modest breakthroughs in providing affordable assisted living can dramatically increase demand.

CHAPTER 2

THE CHANGING CONTINUUM OF SENIOR LIVING OPTIONS
Responding to a Multiple Product Spectrum

The Total Continuum of Living and Care

There are two major forces at work that are shaping a new and different continuum of care and senior living options. The *business sector* is shaping more efficient service delivery systems, while the *consumer market* is advocating quality, choice and affordability. These forces are sometimes compatible, but frequently they are in conflict.

As senior consumers are pushed down through the vertical continuum, more comprehensive living arrangements and levels of care are emerging on senior housing campuses. These include a sophisticated residential/social model of assisted living and special care units dealing with dementia and Alzheimer's care. In addition, rehabilitation, home health care, and community-based service delivery systems are also becoming better defined and more sophisticated.

Why Assisted Living Will be the Catalyst of the Continuum?

There are actually two continuums of care/living options:

- ***The Horizontal Continuum*** – The consumer's perspective (Figure 2-1).

- ***The Vertical Continuum*** – The way business and managed care professionals view their strategic situation (Figure 2-2).

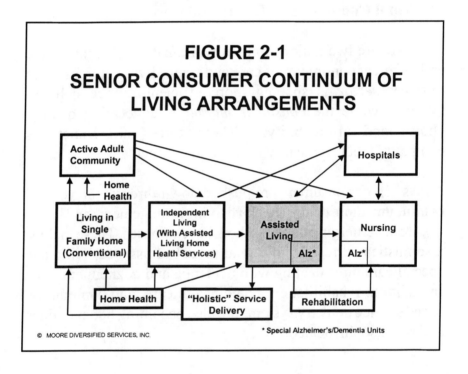

FIGURE 2-1
SENIOR CONSUMER CONTINUUM OF LIVING ARRANGEMENTS

© MOORE DIVERSIFIED SERVICES, INC.   * Special Alzheimer's/Dementia Units

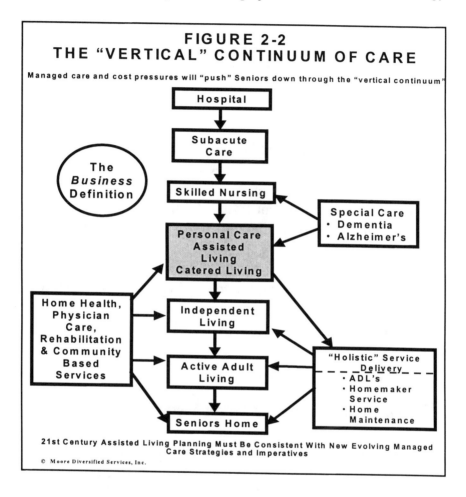

FIGURE 2-2
THE "VERTICAL" CONTINUUM OF CARE

Managed care and cost pressures will "push" Seniors down through the "vertical continuum"

The *Business* Definition

Hospital

Subacute Care

Skilled Nursing

Special Care
• Dementia
• Alzheimer's

Personal Care Assisted Living Catered Living

Home Health, Physician Care, Rehabilitation & Community Based Services

Independent Living

Active Adult Living

"Holistic" Service Delivery
• ADL's
• Homemaker Service
• Home Maintenance

Seniors Home

21st Century Assisted Living Planning Must Be Consistent With New Evolving Managed Care Strategies and Imperatives

© Moore Diversified Services, Inc.

Current Trends Shift the Continuum

In the past, senior housing and health care professionals thought of the continuum that influenced their strategies as a *horizontal structure* with essentially exclusive emphasis on the senior consumer. This relationship is depicted in Figure 2-1. At the left side was the senior's current home, while the other end was typically anchored by a hospital; the ultimate in health care service delivery. But with the evolution of managed care, industry consolidation and aggressive cost containment strategies, a new *vertical* continuum is now emerging as illustrated in Figure 2-2.

In the new structure, the hospital or other major health care provider is the gateway. After the acute care hospital comes subacute care, skilled nursing, special care/dementia units, assisted living, independent living, home health, community-based services, active adult housing and finally the senior's home.

Owner/operators now have two moving targets on their radar screens to track; the *horizontal* continuum in the consumer market and the *vertical* continuum in the business/managed care sector.

The Four Assisted Living Market Models

There are four fundamental assisted living market models: 1) integrated with independent living, 2) freestanding communities, 3) integrated with nursing and 4) assisted living as an integral part of a hospital campus. Each model offers unique marketplace opportunities and challenges. Figure 2-3 illustrates these four models.

Actually a *fifth* market model may be emerging. I call it the "holistic" approach to assisted living. Some major sponsors and operators are considering offering assistance in living into the senior's private homes – before they need full-scope sheltered living. They're hoping to create a relationship or "market umbilical" wherein the senior's future choice for permanent assisted living will hopefully be their community. Operators also hope to leverage their existing resources across a larger service delivery system.

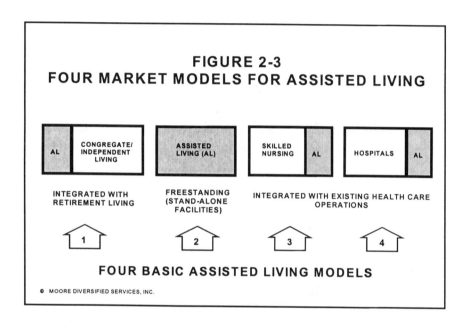

FIGURE 2-3
FOUR MARKET MODELS FOR ASSISTED LIVING

FOUR BASIC ASSISTED LIVING MODELS

© MOORE DIVERSIFIED SERVICES, INC.

Assisted living, integrated with independent living - The first market model has proven to be one of the best "cures" for a slow-moving independent living retirement community. The reasons for this are quite simple. In reality, most seniors do not want to move into even the nicest retirement community until a truly need-driven circumstance gives them a "wake-up call" and pushes them over the decision threshold. Faced with moving out of their homes, seniors want to avoid two other *future situations:* 1) having to move again and 2) facing the nursing home as their only other future option. Seniors are more willing to make the difficult move to independent living – as long as they know there is still another acceptable living option on the campus.

In competitive markets, those retirement communities offering either a full continuum of care, or at least a combination of independent and assisted living, have consistently performed better across the United States. In the 1980s, many owner/operators, and particularly those in the for-profit sector, initially hedged their decision about getting into the complexities of assisted living. For the most part, they paid a heavy price for this procrastination. The ultimate addition of assisted living was frequently one of the top three corrective action strategies for a slow-moving or severely distressed retirement community that previously offered only independent living.

Freestanding assisted living – The second market model was really the new product of the 1990s – offering unique challenges and opportunities. Assisted living integrated with either independent living or health care allows the sponsor's marketing flanks to be covered and provides some inherent cross-referral potential. This allows some maneuverability and hedging of risks in the marketplace. But *freestanding* assisted living sometimes becomes the lost patrol of health care marketing warfare. It is either right on target and takes the market by storm, or it flounders and gets lost due to marketplace ambivalence, rejection or confusion.

Assisted living integrated with nursing – The third market model provides nursing home operators with enhanced economies of scale, diversification and marketplace flexibility. For these operators, expanding into assisted living draws a wider pool of potential patients and residents while providing increased efficiencies and economies of scale from their existing base of operations. These benefits include expanded utilization of the "back of the house" core operations such as the commercial kitchen, laundry and maintenance functions. There is also the possibility of some staff sharing and the co-mingling of other resources between the *separated yet integrated* nursing and assisted living operations.

Assisted living on hospital campuses – The fourth market model – Due to managed care trends and forces, many hospitals are now being measured by the *vacancy* of the acute care beds. Most are experiencing shortened average length of stay and a decline in total patient-days. Revenue enhancement from other related sources is now the name of the game for many organizations. Hospital CEOs and CFOs are asking the pragmatic question, ***"Why should we continue to make courtesy assisted living referrals when we could be in the business?"***

Nursing homes and hospitals can now respond to a broader spectrum of health care needs, while serving more patients (residents) in a less intense, lower cost medical service delivery environment. They will be able to do this while maintaining optimum resource utilization (increased revenue producing census-days). Intracampus transfers between subacute care, nursing and assisted living are becoming quite commonplace. Chapters 6 through 8 provide more insight into the current trends of health care providers getting into assisted living.

The Four Major Components of Assisted Living

Twenty-first century assisted living service delivery is comprised of four major components:

1. Real Estate (bricks and mortar)

2. Hospitality Services (shelter)

3. Restaurant (meal service)

4. Health Care (assistance with ADL's)[1]

To be truly successful, you must execute each one in an integrated, *seamless* manner. And each component is now significantly different when applied to assisted living as contrasted to the strategic operations within their historical and traditional market sectors.

"Carve-Outs" or Market Niches

Any of the four assisted living models can be further modified or enhanced by adding specialized services offering diversification and revenue enhancement. These additional market niches include, but are not necessarily limited to, the following:

- Special Care (Alzheimer's/Dementia)
- Respite Care
- Adult Day Care
- Rehabilitation
- Home Health
- Community-Based Services

Many of these are discussed in other chapters.

---

[1] Activities of Daily Living

Special Care Alzheimer's/Dementia "Carve-outs"

These market sector overlaps are further complicated by the rapidly emerging trends of special care carve-outs. Special care Alzheimer's/dementia is being addressed by special purpose-built living options within traditional assisted living communities. See Chapter 32 for additional details.

**Special Care Alzheimer's/Dementia "Carve-Outs"
Are Being Defined as Two Distinct,
But Overlapping Market Models:**

- **Residential/Social Model** – Seniors with dementia but in *relatively good* physical health

- **Medical Model** – Seniors with dementia and *complex/deteriorating* health conditions

---

Two Basic Service Delivery Models

There are two basic service delivery models:

- *Service Provider* – Typically, the owner/operator's permanent staff provides meals, housekeeping, laundry, activities, direct care ADL assistance, health monitoring and medical emergency response activities.

- ***Home Health Agency Satellite*** – In this model, the owner/operator generally provides "shelter" type services and a licensed home health agency focuses on medically related services such as ADL assistance, case management and general health management.

Market Sector Overlap

Unfortunately, the discreet blocks illustrated in Figures 2-1, 2-2 and 2-3 do not do full justice to the real complexity of the continuum which is, in reality, blurred and overlapping. Figure 2-4 shows how assisted living clearly overlaps with the traditional business sectors of independent living and nursing.

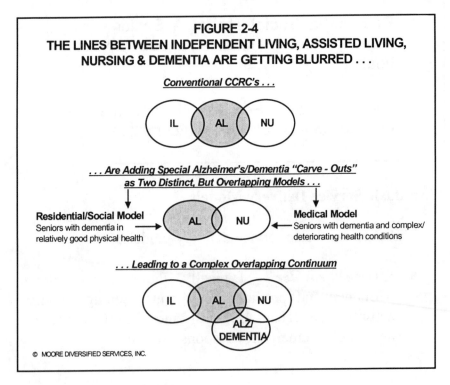

FIGURE 2-4
THE LINES BETWEEN INDEPENDENT LIVING, ASSISTED LIVING, NURSING & DEMENTIA ARE GETTING BLURRED . . .

Conventional CCRC's . . .

IL AL NU

. . . Are Adding Special Alzheimer's/Dementia "Carve - Outs" as Two Distinct, But Overlapping Models . . .

Residential/Social Model
Seniors with dementia in relatively good physical health

AL NU

Medical Model
Seniors with dementia and complex/ deteriorating health conditions

. . . Leading to a Complex Overlapping Continuum

IL AL NU
ALZ/ DEMENTIA

© MOORE DIVERSIFIED SERVICES, INC.

Home Health and Assisted Living

The relationship and roles of home health in an assisted living setting are appropriately addressed throughout this book. Many operators are using licensed home health agencies to deliver the care component of assisted living. Some are doing it because it solves some state regulation dilemmas; others do it so that they do not have to get into the complex health care business. Some sponsors carefully integrate *both* shelter and care services and cost to the consumer, while others seem to be looking the other way – hoping they can charge their basic fees for shelter and services and assuming the consumer will also pay the separate home health bills.

Figure 2-5 shows the major components of service delivery, while Figure 2-6 depicts a *seamless* approach to developing a win-win relationship with a quality home health agency. Home health agencies will be placing a *very* high priority on improving their private pay mix. And providing the care component of assisted living could be their new, significant market niche for the future.

As a sponsor, you *must* create a seamless relationship. I'd like to offer my four top success imperatives:

1. The resident and their family should feel like it is all one operation.

2. All services should be consistent, coordinated and seamless.

3. Your total cost should ideally come in as close as possible to an all "in-house" staffing model – with total operating expenses per resident day competitive for your market area.

4. The pricing to the consumer should be a consolidated charge wherever possible – or at the very least; fair, understandable and competitive.

Finally, you must always develop your home health partnering strategy from a consumer-driven perspective.

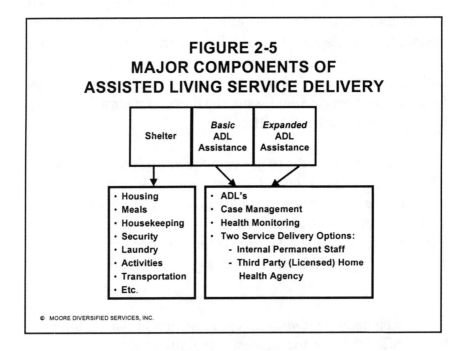

FIGURE 2-5
MAJOR COMPONENTS OF
ASSISTED LIVING SERVICE DELIVERY

Shelter	Basic ADL Assistance	Expanded ADL Assistance

- Housing
- Meals
- Housekeeping
- Security
- Laundry
- Activities
- Transportation
- Etc.

- ADL's
- Case Management
- Health Monitoring
- Two Service Delivery Options:
  - Internal Permanent Staff
  - Third Party (Licensed) Home Health Agency

© MOORE DIVERSIFIED SERVICES, INC.

Figure 2-6 depicts these two basic service delivery models. A word of caution; the *combination* of service provider and third party home health agency should appear *seamless* to the senior and their families. Cost recovery and pricing must be equitable, understandable and reasonably affordable.

The future of assisted living appears bright, but not without continuing marketplace and regulatory turbulence. Astute operators will discover they can frequently expand their market penetration by expanding their continuum and by communicating more effectively with adult children who are geographically separated from their aging parents. More and more hospitals and nursing homes will get into assisted living as they look for ways to expand their continuum – moving away from heavier concentrations of acute care while experiencing product and market diversification.

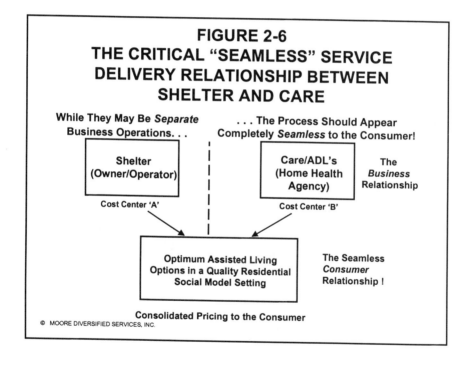

FIGURE 2-6
THE CRITICAL "SEAMLESS" SERVICE
DELIVERY RELATIONSHIP BETWEEN
SHELTER AND CARE

CHAPTER 3

MARKET POSITIONING FOR THE 21ST CENTURY

The Marketplace is Speaking – Are You Really Listening?

A senior once told me, *"Jim, you know life is what happens to us while we're making other plans!"* In spite of over 10 years of advertising and public relations efforts, seniors and their families still know very little about assisted living. It's true seniors think about their health *everyday,* but it's not until they get that inevitable wake-up call creating a crisis that they – or their children – search for viable options. Let's hope that many get to consider your assisted living community as one of the most appropriate alternative living options for many family dilemmas. The reasons are very simple – especially when effective market positioning strategies are deployed.

Market Positioning for Assisted Living

Assisted living responds very effectively to the need-driven, health-related concerns of the senior. It is also a cost-effective and emotionally acceptable alternative for many caregivers; adult children faced with a growing family dilemma (sometimes a crisis) involving complex emotional and financial decisions. For both seniors and their adult children, I have a simple but very powerful assisted living market positioning statement:

> ## "The surprisingly affordable living alternative offering ambience, dignity and maximum independence for many seniors in their later stages of life"

There's also a subliminal message jumping out of this position statement. The message is, *"It's not a nursing home, it's not a nursing home."* Let's clarify a very important point. These messages are not an indictment of thousands and thousands of fine nursing homes and their dedicated staffs. Nursing homes will continue to play a vital role in caring for very high acuity seniors. But make no mistake, assisted living has quickly become the preferred option for private pay seniors who fit the appropriate admission criteria.

In spite of the significant potential for very favorable market acceptance, the concept of assisted living is still largely misunderstood by the consumer marketplace – and surprisingly by many assisted living sponsors and owner/operators. While effective market positioning has proven to be very successful for some sponsors, others seem to either ignore or are not aware of the value of positioning strategies.

Many experienced owner/operators are still attempting to explain assisted living as another form of independent living or a vague but favorable variation of nursing care. These positioning strategies are lacking from two major perspectives:

1. If you are attempting to explain *assisted living* as a variation of *independent living,* this will likely result in consumer confusion in most markets. This is because the

concept of independent retirement living is largely misunderstood by many seniors who have not yet decided to seriously investigate <u>any</u> form of *sheltered* living arrangements.

2. Relating assisted living to nursing stirs up the *dreaded nursing home syndrome* in the minds of seniors and their families. Regardless of how nice a nursing home might be or how high the last inspection scores were, it is still the highly institutional *dreaded nursing home* to most senior consumers and their caring, guilt-ridden children. This is not an indictment of the nursing home industry – it is a marketplace fact of life!

Your ideally conceived assisted living community is not just bricks and mortar. It is also far more than just shelter, quality food service, housekeeping and health care. Guilt-ridden adult children and professional referral sources (doctors, discharge planners, etc.) need to hear another powerful market positioning statement:

"Assisted living must have a strong, but largely invisible, medical basis as the solid foundation for its internal resident care and operating philosophy."

The strategic advantages of assisted living may be subtle, but your messages to your target audiences must have high impact.

Assisted living gradually became the senior consumer's decision option by-pass of the 1990s (refer to Figure 3-1). One of the most common marketing objections heard by independent retirement community sponsors is *"I'm not ready yet."* Astute marketing professionals have responded to this objection by reminding prospects that, by procrastinating, they may fail the stringent health and frailty admission requirements of the independent living retirement community they're considering. The marketers urge them to be "pre-planners" – making timely decisions *now*.

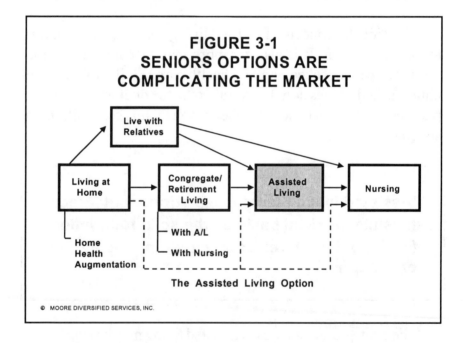

FIGURE 3-1
SENIORS OPTIONS ARE
COMPLICATING THE MARKET

The Assisted Living Option

© MOORE DIVERSIFIED SERVICES, INC.

Seniors and their caregiver children are now realizing that they do have a legitimate hedging option that can stretch this difficult move decision even further out in time. In many markets, seniors need not worry about qualifying for acceptance under independent living and CCRC admission criteria because some can wait and still qualify under more frail, high acuity conditions for entry into state-of-the-art assisted living communities.

Three Classic Market Positioning Mistakes

Unfortunately, there are three fundamental positioning mistakes being made consistently in the business:

- *"We're not sure what we have – but you're going to love it."* Many owner/operators do not recognize (or understand) what they have or how to effectively communicate their community in the competitive marketplace.

- *Is it a hotel?* – Owner/operators focus too heavily on real estate, food and hospitality services; failing to recognize that they are truly in the sophisticated sheltered living and health care business.

- *Too institutional?* – Health care providers and many not-for-profit sponsors are creating a health care or institutional assisted living model when the market really wants a residential/social model.

Remember: The marketplace is speaking – are you really listening?

Assisted Living Will Erode
Nursing's Private Pay Bed Ratios

Assisted living can frequently be positioned as a surprisingly affordable, more attractive alternative to nursing. Obviously, not every senior who might otherwise opt for nursing can be accommodated in assisted living. In the 1990s, there was strong evidence that anywhere from 10 to 15 percent (sometimes up to 20 percent) of existing *private pay* nursing home patients might be accommodated in various levels of well-conceived assisted living. However, the potential of this transfer alternative is now trending downward as patient acuity levels in nursing homes continue to increase due to emerging managed care market forces and subtle changes in Medicare and Medicaid entitlements and admission criteria. Many states now give little recognition to the original definition of *intermediate* level nursing care.

Assisted living operators are now dealing with incontinence, early to mid stages of dementia and relatively high medical acuity levels hoping for lower resident turnover while fighting harder for their share of the lower acuity, private pay nursing market. So the private pay ratios of most nursing operations will slowly erode as a consumer marketplace with purchasing power exercises choice.

Assisted Living is Primarily
a Private Pay Business

With the exception of some experimental Medicaid waiver programs and local entitlements, there are currently very few third party payors for assisted living. Long term care insurance may bring a new wave of benefits to fund at least a portion of future assisted living service fees. Insurance underwriters and actuaries are gradually recognizing assisted living as a cost-effective payor benefit. But they're having difficulty developing a universally accepted, actuarially sound insurance product. Today, assisted living is still fundamentally a private pay living option.

Double Barreled Market Positioning

Properly conceived, assisted living has two important – and relatively rare – *combined* product positioning points:

ASSISTED LIVING IS BOTH:

● *NEED*-DRIVEN (SENIOR CONSUMER)

AND

● *MARKET*-DRIVEN (DECISION INFLUENCER)

The marketplace <u>is</u> speaking – we need to become better listeners as we shape 21ˢᵗ century market positioning strategies.

CHAPTER 4

EFFECTIVELY ADDRESSING
AGING IN PLACE

Should You Embrace or Avoid a
"Naturally Occurring Assisted Living Community?"

A particularly human drama is unfolding in senior living communities across the United States. It will have an enormous impact on the future of the senior housing industry in general, and on assisted living in particular. "Aging in place" has become a commonly-used term. Most consumers feel they basically understand what it means. But do they, really? Frankly, aging in place has more serious implications than most consumers realize – and it's the task of professionals to help them grasp every facet of this concept. We have to also make certain we are fully prepared to help seniors and their loved ones deal realistically and gracefully with what nature has made inevitable.

Aging in place really involves the gradual deterioration of the health of seniors in senior living communities. It is one of the most predictable trends in senior housing today, and also the one that is most difficult to deal with effectively *and* compassionately. Annual resident turnover rates range from 15 to 25 percent for independent living, and 40 percent or higher for many assisted living communities. Yet practical, effective and consistent responses to this dilemma have often eluded even the most experienced sponsors.

It's necessary to take a sobering look at the implications of aging in place from the real world perspective of four very involved groups:

- *Existing residents* experiencing the growing complications of aging are not only trying to cope with their physical afflictions. They frequently experience fear, confusion, frustration and insecurity. Many refuse or fail to understand the implications of their changing condition. In other words, they're acting human.

- *Families* generally fall into one of two broad categories. They either deny the changes in their loved one's condition, the senior's recognition of the changes, or else hope their loved one will miraculously cope with it. Some, but not enough, also recognize it's time to make some very difficult decisions.

- *Peers of ailing Senior living residents* who have not yet experienced serious aging complications themselves don't want to be constantly reminded of the inevitable.

- *Professional staffs* frequently find themselves facing four aging in place challenges. They must provide love, patience and compassion while addressing the changing needs of the residents. They must effectively work with family members who simply will not realistically deal with bad news. The community's top management must strike a necessary delicate balance between high standards of care and complex and costly business issues.

There's always the special challenge of responding to the growing concerns of other residents who see their peers experiencing the sort of ominously gradual health deterioration they hope and pray to avoid themselves.

This book primarily addresses "purpose-built" assisted living, but there are many alternative ways to deliver living assistance to seniors. During the past ten years, the senior living industry has learned that the key to success is being market-driven; responding to the wants and needs of the senior consumer. Most owner/operators and sponsors now recognize that one of the most urgent challenges they face is effectively addressing the aging in place of their residents. But meeting this enormous challenge is more than many initially bargained for when planning to accommodate older, frailer seniors.

Two Fundamental Health Conditions of Seniors

A relatively high level of confusion exists between the two fundamental conditions involving the health and aging of seniors:

• *Chronic Condition*, which is the natural changing health status of seniors as they age. The need for assistance with the activities of daily living (ADL's) gradually increases with time – including addressing the special needs of those seniors experiencing various levels of Alzheimer/dementia. The *process* is generally predictable. It's harder being certain of the appropriate ways for care providers to *respond.*

● *Episodic Condition*, which is a sudden change in health status due to an "episode" such as a hip fracture or stroke. This usually triggers an abrupt increase in ADL needs, and sometimes a permanent change in the need for sheltered living arrangements. Here, treatment and procedures are well defined, with recovery outcomes that are reasonably predictable.

Medicare and Medicaid entitlement programs attempt to define these two conditions, with each offering unique entitlement benefits, challenges and opportunities.

Seniors age in place and eventually develop chronic health conditions. This chronic aging process has caused many older, conventional apartment buildings and condominiums to gradually transition into what is called a "NORC"; a Naturally Occurring Retirement Community. This same aging process can cause an *independent* living retirement community to evolve into a marginally efficient, defacto a*ssisted living* operation.

The Assistance in Living (AIL) Concept

Dealing with aging in place is, at best, extremely complex. There is a strong temptation to either procrastinate or to make shortsighted, short-term decisions. Many astute operators have created distinct living and care continuums that include active adult housing, independent living, assisted living, special Alzheimer/dementia units, and nursing. But others are implementing Assistance in Living (AIL) *strategies*, which offer as-needed assistance with residents' activities of daily living (ADL) in their existing independent living units.

In the short run, providing such services is good for the residents being served. It solves immediate, significant aging-in-place problems and, if properly priced, can provide the sponsor with a hedge against operating expense cost creep. But this short-run solution frequently triggers serious long-range problems.

Some sponsors are using licensed, third-party home health agencies to deliver the "medical component," while they continue to focus on the "shelter component." Properly executed, this can be a viable concept. However, the strategy is frequently not market-driven or resident-centered. Inevitable additional charges to the resident may appear fragmented, excessive, inequitable and/or confusing (see Chapter 2).

Deliver this assistance into your *independent* living section long enough, and most of your seniors will become *assisted living* residents, with many experiencing various stages of Alzheimer's. To compound this challenge, the profile of new residents moving in will likely change. New prospects visiting communities that offer AIL services in their independent living units increasingly judge all residents there as "older, frailer people." We know prospects and their families tend to make move decisions based on their observations of the existing resident population, so in this scenario it is almost inevitable only the frailest will feel that particular community is right for them. Thus, new move-ins tend to be the result of a *self-selective process*. They compound and accelerate the cumulative aging in place of the community's resident population.

You Must Ask and Answer Five Tough AIL Questions

Let's assume you're planning to provide assistance in living as needed to residents in your independent living community.

To avoid getting in trouble down the line as a result of delivering AIL services in existing independent living units, ask yourself five tough questions **now,** and answer them from the perspective of the year 2005:

1. *What is my optimum resident profile, for both existing residents and new move-ins?*

2. *What will be my future business posture and market positioning – moderately need-driven independent living or fully need-driven assisted living? Or both?*

3. *Will I be able to properly measure care levels and cover my increasing service delivery costs?*

4. *Will I be fully market-responsive if I charge residents for incremental increases in the assistance with ADLs as they age in place?*

5. *As service needs intensify, can I still deliver assistance with ADLs cost-effectively to randomly distributed independent living units throughout my community?*

If your long-term prospects look dim under your current operating scenario, consider adding an *integrated but separated* assisted living section to your campus. With less personal living area and more services compared to the typical independent living community, an assisted living section is frequently the most cost-effective way to deliver optimum service to your residents for a reasonable, affordable price. This can also be accomplished by converting existing space.

If you've responded to these five questions objectively, you probably recognize some potential problems.

The Separated, Yet Integrated, Concept

Does *separated,* yet *integrated,* seem like an oxymoron? Can the concept really be seamless? Consider this brief concept overview:

- Independent and assisted living *integrated* under one roof

- A common core area including commercial kitchen, laundry, maintenance, etc.

- Two *separate* dining rooms supported by a common kitchen (like many hotels offer)

- Properly sized and separated public spaces (lounges, etc.)

- Two separate residential "neighborhoods" (independent living and assisted living sections connected and integrated – under the same roof)

Before deciding which strategy is right for you, ask yourself three key planning questions:

1. *What is likely to be my least costly way of serving residents' varying and growing needs for assistance with ADLs?* For the most realistic response, make a detailed cost comparison between providing a dedicated assisted living section and delivering assistance with ADLs randomly distributed within your independent living units. Consider the likely impacts on cost and your resident profile now as well as five, seven, and ten years into the future. This is a tough, but very important, decision. The most attractive short-run option may not be the best long-run strategy. Look at several scenarios, such as providing ADLs for 10 percent of residents now versus the possibility of 70 percent in several years.

2. *How will three very important senior consumer groups and their adult children feel about the strategy you're about to adopt?* These three groups are your existing residents who need assistance with ADLs; residents who are still relatively healthy; and potential new residents. The obvious challenge is finding a service delivery system that will satisfy the first group without driving away the other two.

3. *Will your residents actually move to the appropriate living arrangement at the appropriate time, if you develop a state-of-the-art residential/social model assisted living section?* Despite the best of intentions, a multi-level, full-service senior living community can experience mediocre performance because of resident noncompliance. To help ensure that residents are willing to move when the time comes, you must develop very specific resident admission and discharge policies – and they must be tactfully, yet consistently, enforced.

Moving residents through your continuum will continue to present significant challenges. These could be further complicated by three initiatives currently in play: Fair Housing, Americans With Disabilities Act (ADA) and Negotiated Risk. The last initiative can work in your favor, since you can structure your negotiated risk terms to be reasonably compatible with resident transition through your continuum.

The Top Seven Strategies For Dealing With Aging in Place

Whichever route you follow, you must adopt certain strategies now in order to effectively plan for the future. These seven strategies are *imperative* when dealing with the aging in place issue:

1. Deal with the problem *now,* because it will surely intensify, rather than diminish, with time.

2. Resist simplistic "politically correct" approaches that accommodate individual residents in the short run, but create extensive community problems in the long term.

3. Clearly define the circumstances under which a resident must move to another living arrangement – using your Residency Agreement and Negotiated Risk contracts.

4. Clearly communicate policies, procedures, and admission criteria to new residents and their families.

5. Get your resident leadership involved in the acceptance of this difficult, but necessary, policy-making process. This helps your residents feel they are part of a positive solution, rather than representing a major *problem* within your community.

6. Closely monitor each resident's health status on a continuing basis.

7. If you operate an older community, consider developing a second-generation (new) independent living section that will replace the existing one as aging residents gradually (and inevitably) convert the initial community into a "Naturally Occurring Assisted Living Community".

Senior housing sponsors have an obligation to provide appropriate, cost-effective assistance with ADLs for their residents. But besides the satisfaction of knowing they're doing the right thing, there could be other significant payoffs for those who do so effectively. For instance, communities offering either full or modified life care contracts could lower their health care benefit costs by substituting assisted living and home health services for higher-cost nursing home admissions, where applicable.

CHAPTER 5

DEVELOPING A NEW
ASSISTED LIVING COMMUNITY

Successful Outcomes Require
Correctly Answering Ten Key Questions

When developing new assisted living communities, many owners and sponsors have been tempted to make situation-driven decisions, offering whatever they have to sell and hoping the marketplace will respond favorably. With luck, this method sometimes leads to success. But, far more often than not, inadequate planning results in either complete failure or a seriously distressed project. An example would be some of the independent senior living communities of the mid-'80s, in which the wrong products and services were offered, or else the right ones were improperly positioned or aimed at the wrong market.

The Ten Planning Questions

A better approach is to study the market and learn what is really needed both now and in the future; only then can you be certain you are providing the most appropriate products and services. This requires answering at least ten questions with the answers developed from a *market-driven* perspective rather than from an emotional *situation-driven* position.

Here are the ten important questions:

1. *What is your anticipated resident profile?* A classic example of situation-driven thinking involves planning for residents who are old, but need only minimal assistance with ADLs. Many well-intended, but naive, developers say, ***"You just don't understand, we are going to be different."*** This is a philosophy that inevitably leads to failure. Seniors who are responding to the market and opting for assisted living generally have relatively high levels of need for help with three or more ADLs. As many as 30 to 40 percent may have symptoms of early dementia. This profile is evident when you experience annual resident turnover rates of 40 to 50 percent.

2. *Which assisted living market model will you provide?* The market currently favors a *"residential/social"* model developed within local building code restraints and current or anticipated state licensing regulations. This trend reflects a dramatic contrast to the older institutional *"medical model."* But because of high resident acuity, appropriate medical care and significant assistance with activities of daily living (ADLs) must be made available to your residents. So, in responding to this question, you should review the description of market models covered in Chapter 2 and the market positioning points addressed in Chapter 3.

3. *How will your project interface with the total continuum of care?* When planning freestanding or stand-alone assisted living, consider whether the local competition offers a superior response to the *total* concerns of seniors and their families.

Most respond favorably to communities offering a total continuum of living arrangements. Review Figure 2-2, the "vertical (business) continuum" and Figure 2-1, the "horizontal (consumer) continuum" shown in Chapter 2. Ask yourself two important questions, *"Will I be a legitimate player in this continuum?" "If not, how will other players impact my game plan?"*

4. *How will you deliver assistance with the Activities of Daily Living (ADLs)?* Underestimating residents' current and increasing ADL needs is the most significant situation-driven mistake made by far too many operators and sponsors. Some inexperienced sponsors assume residents will satisfy their own needs through individual relationships with home health agencies, but this oversimplified approach can frequently lead to fragmented care, uncoordinated service delivery, or a la carte costs that residents cannot afford. Some experienced operators are successfully combining a basic shelter product with options for residents to buy additional services from licensed home health operators. But such plans must be carefully conceived and coordinated. They should appear relatively *seamless* to the senior consumer in terms of both service delivery and costs. For more details, review Chapter 2 on market models, Chapter 15 on cost creep and Chapter 9 dealing with home health care.

5. *What will be your overall design philosophy and strategy?* This complex issue has at least three major components:

Living units have evolved from modest "shotgun" studios of 275 to 300 square feet to slightly larger studios and alcove units of approximately 350 square feet. In the early 1990s, up to 20 percent of the assisted living units in new projects were modest one-bedroom units with average living areas of 450 to 550 square feet; accommodating either single residents who can pay higher prices, or couples in which at least one spouse needs assistance with ADLs. But recent trends indicate a growing market acceptance of an even larger concentration of one-bedroom units. Chapter 10 addresses this important issue in more detail, demonstrating that currently 60 percent or more of the assisted living units in some new projects are of the modest one bedroom design.

Elaborate common spaces are nice, but they can be expensive. For example, an 80-unit assisted living project design can have either conventional corridors and public spaces or several innovative "pods," also called "neighborhoods" or "clusters." These design features can increase common space in a typical community by up to 5,000 square feet. With hard construction costs currently averaging at least $100 per square foot, your project costs could increase by $500,000. When you include the additional cost of furnishings, soft costs, utilities, and debt service, the result is approximately a $60 to $80 increase in monthly service fees for each resident[1].

---

[1] Considers added debt service or return on investment for the additional cost.

Optimum project size involves a delicate trade-off between maximizing the number of units to optimize revenues and spread capital and operating costs efficiently, while avoiding unacceptable marketplace risk by overbuilding. Industry experience indicates that the *minimum* size for a highly efficient stand-alone assisted living community should be approximately 60 to 80 units. Earlier minimum size criteria of 45 to 60 units has not consistently met current day cost-effectiveness tests. The unit count can be lower if your assisted living units are integrated with other independent living apartments and/or nursing beds, thereby creating acceptable operational efficiencies by spreading fixed costs across other revenue producing units. **Keep in mind the project size decision involves the classical trade-off between the cost-effectiveness of your internal operations and external marketplace risk.**

Other considerations include building heights, exterior elevations and interior design features. These are addressed in Chapter 10.

6. *How much staffing will your project require?* Underestimating ADL requirements can lead to underestimating staffing needs. Remember that labor costs represent over 60 percent of total assisted living operating expenses. The universal worker concept has not resulted in significant staff reductions. However, there are benefits in cross-training direct care aides in areas such as food service delivery and housekeeping. Industry experience indicates that an 80-unit assisted living community generally requires between 36 to 44 total Full Time Equivalent Employees (FTEs) – or approximately 0.45 to 0.55 FTEs per resident.

7.   *What will it take to develop and operate your community?* Probably more than your initial estimates! Here is a summary of industry benchmarks from my proprietary database of over 8 million resident-days.

- Typical *all-in* development costs:
  $95,000 to $125,000/unit:
    - Includes *all* hard and soft costs
    - Your total project cost divided by number of units

- Typical operating costs: $55 to $60 per resident-day

- Operating profit margin: 32 to 40 percent

- Operating expense ratio: 60 to 68 percent

Chapter 13 deals with establishing a detailed development budget while Chapters 14 and 15 address operating costs.

8.   *How will you price your project?* Pricing must be competitive, market-driven, reasonably affordable, and compare favorably with the nursing alternative. Most importantly, pricing must be flexible to compensate for inevitable "cost creep" that results from residents' increasing chronic conditions and intensified ADL needs. More details are contained in Chapters 23 and 24. Above all, remember this: You cannot price your project in a vacuum! Seniors and their families are fast becoming sophisticated, value-oriented, educated consumers.

9. *What are your initial fill-up/absorption expectations?* The early announcement of a new project may generate significant initial enthusiasm, but little of this actually translates into future move-ins! While there might be an initial in-rush of move-ins of 10 to 15 percent, it is the *average net absorption over the life of the fill-up period that really counts.* A net absorption rate of between five and seven units per month is a realistic goal, and should be programmed into your financial pro formas (refer to Chapter 35 for more details).

10. *What will be the magnitude of your start-up losses?* There will be significant negative cash flow in the early months of a new project, as most of your costs are fixed and only about 20 to 25 percent of your operating expenses are truly variable (raw food, some utilities, housekeeping, some staff, etc.). A typical 80-unit assisted living community normally takes nine to eleven months to reach break-even cash flow. Break-even cash flow (after debt service) typically occurs at approximately 80 to 85 percent occupancy. During that fill-up period, the project may experience cumulative negative cash flows of $350,000 or more. See Chapters 13 and 35 for a more detailed analysis.

The Assisted Living Industry is Maturing

As the assisted living industry continues to mature, two new trends are emerging:

1. The market is gradually becoming more educated with respect to alternative living arrangements and health care options.

2. The senior consumer and their families will give you very little credit or compassion for your mistakes and unacceptable trade-offs.

State-of-the-art assisted living can be a surprisingly affordable living arrangement, and a viable alternative to nursing facilities. But your project won't succeed if you fail to answer these ten questions fully and honestly during your planning phase.

Perhaps the most important question of all should be saved for last:

"When, and under what conditions, would my own mother willingly, and with my support and blessing, move into this community?"

THE TOP TEN QUESTIONS TO ANSWER WHEN PLANNING ASSISTED LIVING

1. What is your expected resident profile?
2. Which assisted living model type will you provide?
3. How will your project interface with the total continuum of care?
4. How will you deliver assistance with ADLs?
5. What will be your overall design philosophy and strategy?
6. How much staffing will your project require?
7. What will it cost to develop and operate your community?
8. How will you price your project?
9. What are your initial fill-up/absorption expectations?
10. What will be the magnitude of your start-up losses?

SECTION TWO

The Competitive Battlefield

CHAPTER 6

THE LANDSCAPE OF THE
COMPETITIVE BATTLEFIELD

Everybody is Getting Into
Everybody Else's Business

The assisted living industry has truly entered America's free enterprise system. In the early stage of its life cycle, assisted living encroached on the nursing home industry as a more desirable alternative for many discriminating consumers with the ability to private pay for services. The market appeared to have almost unlimited potential.

Meanwhile, hospitals' economic survival is being seriously threatened by managed care and tightened government and private insurance reimbursement policies.

But both hospitals and nursing homes are fighting back. And both industries are placing assisted living right in the middle of their radar screens. Many hospitals and nursing home operators are seeking ways to enhance revenues by offering new services, achieving higher operational efficiencies and responding to evolving managed care initiatives. At the same time, they are being pressured to reduce costs by both the consumer private-pay marketplace and third party payors. In their search for a solution to this dilemma, some sponsors are finding assisted living a tempting, yet perplexing, business opportunity. Both

54

nursing home operators and hospital CEOs are asking the complex question, *"Is the assisted living service delivery system competitive or compatible with our future business strategies?"* A number of traditional health care sponsors see the opportunities, but many do not yet truly understand the challenges.

Positioning for Success and Synergy

The hospital and nursing home industries can position themselves to benefit from assisted living operations synergy and market opportunities. This synergy can best be defined as *increasing* your offerings, enhancing revenue and improving your position in the marketplace while *decreasing* your total operating costs on a per resident-day basis. But to do so successfully, many management philosophies, operating policies and organizational cultures must change dramatically.

For these health care providers, assisted living can be a synergistic diversification strategy by allowing their operations to expand or complete the continuum of care as they enhance revenues by serving a broader sector of the market. In addition, they can realize significant operational economies of scale; primarily in the areas of staffing, food service, housekeeping, laundry, maintenance, operations, and health service delivery. Assisted living also appeals to health care providers because their traditional subcontracting, outsourcing and patient referral philosophies are gradually being replaced by seriously considering revenue enhancing, internal service delivery strategies. But before they can diversify into assisted living, health care providers must adopt appropriate management philosophies, operating policies and create new organizational cultures.

Future Impacts of Reimbursement Systems

Age 65+ Medicare and Medicaid Risk HMOs and other managed care professionals are fine-tuning their strategies, hoping to play a larger, financially viable role in long term care. If this happens, a third-party payor system for assisted living may eventually evolve. Providers and payors would be taking on increasing financial risks for the total health care of seniors, which means they would seek the common objective of an integrated health service delivery at the lowest possible cost.

For Medicare and Medicaid policy makers, assisted living could *eventually* prove to be the cost-effective missing link between existing entitlements involving significant institutionalism (acute, subacute, skilled nursing) at one end of the continuum vs. some inefficiencies of delivering home health care at the other end.

A word of caution; don't count on significant third party payors for assisted living in the short run. The existing Medicare and Medicaid budgets are being strained and *cutbacks,* not new *entitlements,* are the current topics of discussion with policy makers.

Economies of Scale and Synergy

Both hospitals and nursing homes can realize significant economies of scale as they consider entry into the senior housing market. There are four major areas of potential economies of scale that could lead to synergistic growth opportunities. These include:

1. Staff and Management Resources – Some of the human resources that are already in place for a hospital or nursing home can lead to synergistic economies of scale when considering adding either independent living and/or assisted living arrangements on or near their campus. Contrasted with a new assisted living community that may be entirely "stand-alone," there are the benefits of inherent economies of scale if assisted living is integrated (but separated) within a comprehensive campus.

2. Food and Beverage Operations – Hospitals and nursing homes already have extensive commercial kitchens and mass purchasing power. While the food service menus and meal preparation and delivery are certainly different in senior housing and assisted living, there are some potentially significant dietary economies of scale that can be realized.

3. *Delivery of Health Care Services* – This is an obvious extension of a resource that most health care providers do quite well. Staff depth and the ability to rotate health care personnel can alleviate burnout and employee turnover.

4. *Housekeeping, Laundry, Maintenance and Security Operations* – In many instances, these existing operations have some additional capacity and underutilized resources.   Cost-effective, synergistic expansion can frequently be implemented with relative ease.

The key strategy is to spread your fixed and semi-variable costs across more revenue-producing units.

A Synergistic Diversification Example

Let's get quantitative about this very important strategy:

1. You now operate a 90-bed nursing home @ 90% occupancy.

2. You have 29,565 resident-days (90 x .90 x 365 days) available for spreading your fixed costs.

3. You now add 80 assisted living units and realize 93 percent occupancy, so you're adding another 27,010 resident-days for a total of 56,575 resident-days.

You can now spread both your existing fixed and at least some of your semi-variable costs more effectively. Here's an example:

1. Let's say your food service director's total payroll cost is $45,000/year.

2. With only the 90-bed nursing operation to spread those costs, the burden would be $1.52 per resident-day (PRD).

3. Now that you've added assisted living and implemented an *integrated* (common) kitchen function yet *separated* (two) dining rooms, you can spread that cost over 56,575 days resulting in a cost of only $.80 PRD.

4. Considering raw food costs at approximately $5.00 per day and total dietary costs (with labor and other supplies) at $10.70 to $14.40 per day, these types of savings on a per resident-day basis can be significant.

This dietary example is but one of many areas of potential financial synergy that you could enjoy.

Diversification Pitfalls

All of this diversification sounds easy, but it should be emphasized that implementation of these growth strategies involves significant challenges. There are a number of pitfalls regarding health care providers entering the senior living market sector.

One of the pitfalls involves the inability of providers to adjust their philosophy of service delivery. Health care providers sometimes have difficulty recognizing that offering independent and assisted living is really a new and different business culture for them.

The differences center on several important areas critical to the overall success of a health care provider's strategy: market positioning, marketing approach, physical and aesthetic design, interior finish-out, furnishings, and day-to-day operations.

Changing Business Culture
and Technology Differences

One of the most serious tactical errors that experienced (and successful) nursing home owner-operators can make when expanding into assisted living is to ignore the very important business culture and technology differences. Here are some considerations:

Design of the Physical Plant – Your new assisted living add-on, conversion or freestanding community must not appear sterile or institutional in any respect. But don't get carried away – state-of-the-art assisted living should look like a *"Buick"*; not necessarily a *"Cadillac"*, *"Mercedes"* or *"Lexus"*. The exterior should have attractive roof lines, window treatments and interesting (not plain) elevations. The interior of both the public spaces and individual living units should be carpeted, draped and have aesthetically pleasing wall coverings or other quality "residential" treatments. Residents will typically bring their own personal furniture and accessories.

Staffing – The images and performances of the professional staff should strike a delicate balance between efficient, compassionate, resident-centered *health care* professionals and user-friendly, high ambience *hospitality*-oriented service workers. Wherever possible, your staff should wear street clothes with ID badges – not uniforms. If your staff and management are shared between nursing and assisted living, it is imperative that these staff understand the philosophical differences between the two settings. Otherwise you risk alienating your assisted living customers and programs.

Market Positioning – Chapter 3 addresses, in detail, the optimum assisted living market positioning as contrasted with traditional nursing home positioning. The people who influence the decision to move into an assisted living community are frequently different than those who traditionally make nursing referrals. There is far less influence on the part of doctors and hospital discharge professionals – and far more on seniors' sons and daughters. Chapter 8 deals with changing referral patterns.

Two assisted living positioning statements discussed in Chapter 3 bear repeating because they are so important:

> *"The surprisingly affordable living alternative offering ambience, dignity and maximum independence for many seniors in their later stages of life."*

> *and . . .*

> *"Assisted living must have a strong, but largely invisible, medical basis as the solid foundation for its internal operating philosophy and external market positioning strategy."*

Market Models – Chapter 2 addresses the various assisted living market models.

Five Major Areas of Transition for Nursing Home Owner-Operators or Hospital Sponsors

You must pay close attention to the following cautions when diversifying from traditional nursing and hospital services into assisted living:

1. Professional staff may be too driven by a nursing home or hospital regulation mind-set:

- In nursing and hospitals, regulatory compliance frequently becomes the top priority as opposed to individualized customer service.

- In assisted living, government regulations do not (yet) drive operations; rather internally mandated standards of care, quality of life and safety are key concerns.

2. There is the potential for staff to do too *much:*

  - Inappropriate care planning
  - Excessive social services documentation
  - Nurse and hospital-type charting vs. contemporaneous case management record keeping
  - Too much assistance for the resident
  - Staff performance results in too much dependency by the resident
  - Premature transfer of residents to nursing facilities

3. Potential for staff to do too *little:*

  - "I thought assisted living residents were supposed to be independent."

- Ignoring a resident's unique and individual medicine management needs and shortcomings

- Improper screening for potential health problems

- Deficiency in providing meaningful social and activity programs

- Less than optimum encouragement of interaction between resident and family

- Not observing the resident's *individual* daily schedule and routine

4. Staff initiates practices that are not necessary or financially cost-effective:

   - This results in unnecessary rate increases for the resident

   - Patterned too much after nursing facility and hospital operations (involving artificial regulation restraints)

5. Lack of understanding of appropriate staffing patterns:

   - Inappropriate staffing *types* (too many RNs, etc.)

   - Excessive FTEs (full-time equivalent employees)

6. Lack of understanding of the community's overall philosophy of assisted living:

- Denial of admission of higher acuity residents by marketing or administrative personnel

- Premature transfer to nursing facility

Striking a Delicate Balance

While a touchy subject, it is important to note that the key assisted living philosophy known as "aging in place" is not always synonymous with "dying in place." And, if we're not careful, some owner-operators may be inviting future federal regulations. Chapter 37 deals with the critical distinction between resident satisfaction and quality of life.

Despite these challenges, the spin-off benefits for providers can be significant. For example, a hospital that develops a strong image by responding effectively to the senior market is more likely to enhance their capture of their traditional business: acute care admissions of seniors.

Like it or not, assisted living will be a major player in the overall health care arena. Many hospital and nursing home operators may still resist entering the fray. But, in response to marketplace forces and the changing policies of third-party payors, astute providers are revisiting their five-year strategic plans to see where assisted living might fit in. Chapter 7 addresses some specific strategic assisted living diversification issues for hospitals and nursing homes.

**ASSISTED LIVING
OPPORTUNITIES AND CHALLENGES
FOR HOSPITALS AND NURSING HOMES**

<u>Opportunities</u>	<u>Challenges</u>
1. Synergy of operations	1. Changing culture
2. Economies of scale	2. Mind-set of staff
3. Revenue enhancement	3. Serving different markets
4. Favorable response to managed care	4. Different cost structure
5. Expand the continuum	5. Creating a residential vs. institutional market model

---

Think of it this way, if you are either a hospital or nursing home provider currently *giving away* courtesy referrals to assisted living, should you rethink the process?

CHAPTER 7

NURSING HOMES AND HOSPITALS COMPETE FOR MARKET SHARE

The Real Turf Battle of the New Millennium

Nursing homes are being battered on two economic fronts; hospitals are creating swing wings and getting into skilled nursing, rehabilitation and subacute care on one front while many assisted living operators are crossing the line offering quasi-nursing services on the other. Some industry analysts feel that assisted living could eventually replace hundreds of thousands of the 1.7 million nursing beds in operation today. I feel there will be *private pay* impact on future nursing bed absorption, but the actual impact is currently difficult to quantify.

Nursing bed supply/inventory has seen only modest growth over the past five years. This is because Medicaid, Medicare and prospective payment system impacts coupled with the introduction of assisted living has changed the basic demand structure for new nursing beds. An indication of relative nursing bed demand-supply balance is a ratio indicating the number of beds per 1,000 seniors age 85+. This ratio has declined from 650 beds per 1,000 85+ seniors in 1980 to approximately 400 beds in 2000. The changing ratio is the result of increasing numbers of age 85+ seniors (the denominator), while the nursing bed supply (the numerator) has remained essentially flat. Current nursing bed occupancy in 2001 is approximately 87 percent. Meanwhile, industry estimates of *quality* assisted living units total between 400,000 and 500,000, reflecting the dramatic growth in recent years.

New assisted living initiatives being considered by the nursing home industry typically involve two primary groups of existing nursing facility operators.

1. *Traditional nursing home operators* who are seriously considering either expanding or diversifying into assisted living while developing sharpened competitive strategies for operating their nursing homes in the future.

2. *Nursing home operators currently involved in assisted living* or those contemplating the development and operation of new, freestanding assisted living communities with the possibility of a special care dementia unit.

For traditional nursing home operators, assisted living involvement is a two-step strategic process:

1. Carefully evaluate a number of qualitative and quantitative assisted living diversification factors.

2. Make an informed project go/no-go decision.

Hopefully, this process will guide you in making an objective evaluation of your relative strengths, weaknesses, opportunities and threats.

Nursing Home Operator Growth Initiatives

For nursing home operators, reimbursement and third party payor programs are becoming very complex. High bed census/occupancy rates no longer automatically lead to a strong financial position. The threat of increased litigation and regulation has made long-range planning a difficult task. Approximately 70 percent of the total age 65+ nursing home patient-days are Medicaid reimbursed; private pay nursing patients are becoming a relatively rare resource. In addition, nursing homes in many markets are struggling to sustain a strong presence as a myriad of competing consumer-driven health care options emerge. Many nursing facilities have room to grow, thanks to underutilized resources and excess land, but many operators wonder whether simply adding new skilled nursing beds is the best business strategy to pursue.

Three Market Model Options for
Existing Nursing Home Operators

There are three primary options available for existing nursing home operators who are considering diversification into assisted living:

1. Add assisted living to your existing nursing home campus. This could involve a new addition to your existing building. Generally, the new assisted living section should be *integrated,* yet *separated,* from your current nursing operation. This simply means that the public spaces should be *separated* (dining rooms, lounges, etc.), while the core, back-of-the-house functions (commercial kitchen, laundry, maintenance, etc.), should be effectively *integrated* for operational efficiency.

2. Retrofit all or a portion of your existing building(s). This could be a "swing nursing wing conversion" with interior space either totally gutted and reconstructed as assisted living units or with the conversion of existing nursing rooms to assisted living units.

One word of caution with this approach: assisted living is typically viewed as a residential/social model with very high aesthetics rather than a nursing home-type medical model which frequently tends to look more institutional in nature.

3. New construction of a freestanding assisted living community. This community could be developed on your existing campus or at a new site. The design configuration should represent the latest innovations and trends in assisted living. It should be a market-driven, consumer-focused market model that has a residential design flair – but with a strong but largely invisible medical foundation.

Some nursing home operators may have the need and opportunity to execute a combination of the strategies outlined above. The market model ultimately selected will most likely be influenced by your unique situation, existing restraints and necessary trade-offs. But you must not allow your *past* nursing home operating philosophy or business culture to impair the market's favorable response to your *new* assisted living option. More about this caution later.

Chapter 10 details market-driven design strategies for assisted living communities while Chapter 11 addresses existing facility conversion and adaptive reuse.

Comparison of Resident Profiles; Nursing Vs. Assisted Living

In order for nursing facility operators to successfully develop and operate assisted living communities, it is important to observe and compare the contrasting resident profiles of the nursing and assisted living market sectors (refer to Figure 7-1).

Some Inevitable Trends Facing Nursing Providers

The assisted living alternative is very popular with today's consumer. Nursing facility operators will likely face some *unavoidable* and *unfavorable* trends in the very near future. Here are three big ones:

FIGURE 7-1

COMPARATIVE RESIDENT PROFILES

		Typical Patient/Resident	
		Nursing	Assisted Living
I.	**Average Age of Resident:**		
	• Upon Entry	83 Years	84 Years
II.	**Payor Concentration**		
	• Private Pay	Less than 30%	97%+
	• Medicaid Reimbursement	68%	Less than 2%
	• Medicare Reimbursement	8%	None
III.	**Typical Average Length of Stay:**	12-15 Mos.[1]	30 Mos.
IV.	**Annual Resident Turnover**	75% - 100%	40%+
V.	**Average Number of ADLs[2]**	3.7	3.1
VI.	**Percent Female**	72%	75%

Sources: Nursing Facility Source Book, AHCA
Assisted Living Source Book, AHCA/NCAL
Overview of the Assisted Living Industry, ALFA

---

[1]Length of stay has a wide distribution; *Medicare* patients – relatively short stay, *Medicaid* patients in chronic care – relatively long stay.

[2]Assistance with the Activities of Daily Living (assistance with bathing, dressing, transferring, toileting and eating, etc.).

1. *Private Pay Census is Eroding* – Seniors and their families with the ability to private pay will exercise discretion and choice – seeking out their best options. In a growing number of cases, the option selected will be assisted living; often at the expense of private pay nursing. This is occurring with increasing frequency for Seniors with the ability to private pay who need sheltered living but have low-to-moderate acuity levels and ADL needs when compared to today's *skilled* nursing. In terms of acuity levels, the typical assisted living resident of today looks a lot like the nursing intermediate care level resident of yesterday.

2. *Nursing Patient Acuity Levels are Increasing* – Most nursing providers report sharply increasing patient acuity levels compared to the early 1990s. This is causing the *private pay* nursing prospect with lower acuity to aggressively seek out other options like assisted living.

3. *Nursing Referral Patterns are Changing* – Hospitals are getting into short-term nursing care via new subacute units and some are even adding long-term care nursing beds to their campus. And the growing assisted living industry has "intercepted" many potential nursing patients who previously would move from their private homes directly into intermediate or, in some cases, skilled nursing care settings. As a result of these changing trends, referrals to nursing facilities are declining.

Favorable Assisted Living Trends

Many nursing home operators who have expanded into assisted living have also discovered and benefitted from four *favorable* trends:

1. *Discovery of a New Feeder Market* – Assisted living provides a new feeder market into their traditional nursing home. Approximately 35 to 40 percent of assisted living residents ultimately experience a transfer to a nursing facility.

2. *Enhanced Private Pay Mix* – Private pay patients might initially be lost to the assisted living market sector in the future. But assisted living residents transferring to nursing are, at least initially, private pay nursing patients. And if they were in *your* assisted living community, they are likely to eventually become your nursing patient.

3. *Increased Average Lengths of Stay* – Because of the previously described assisted living and nursing "integrated feeder network", the average length of stay on your campus can be extended.

4. *Assisted Living Promotes Independence* – Appropriate case management, effective programmatic content and the favorable assisted living *residential* environment tends to foster and optimize a Senior's relative independence. This improves the resident's quality of life and can enhance your image and reputation – while expanding your revenue-producing capacity within your campus.

Each situation is unique, but the favorable and unfavorable trends outlined previously could provide the motivation and foundation for a sound assisted living diversification strategy for many nursing facility operators.

In terms of nursing vs. assisted living supply/demand balance, we're experiencing shifting trends as we enter the new millennium:

1. Nursing homes will generally face a challenge when attempting to sustain acceptable stabilized occupancies above 90 percent.

2. Some assisted living communities in selected markets are experiencing slower fill-up and are fighting to prevent sagging occupancy – with their objective being the achievement of stabilized occupancies of 93 percent or higher.

If we assume, as a hypothetical situation, a reasonable degree of supply/demand balance, we can attempt to answer the question, *"What does the future hold for both the nursing and assisted living industries?"*

Nursing Home Growth Outlook

Let's look at a five-year time horizon starting in 2000 through the end of 2005:

1. Growth in the age 80 plus households:

    - Total Growth from 2000 to 2005:   675,000
    - Annual incomes of $30,000 +:   37%   ⎤ Approximate
    - Incomes of $15,000 - $30,000:   26%   ⎬ Income
    - Incomes of less than $15,000:   37%   ⎦ Brackets - 2003

2. Nursing bed absorption required to increase *current occupancy* from 87 to 95 percent: 128,000 Beds Absorbed

        but . . .

3. The nursing bed market over the next five years will likely be flat to declining and bed turnover (requiring replacement) exceeds 100 percent annually in many situations.

Assisted Living Growth Outlook

The total future growth potential for basically private pay assisted living is contained within a pool of approximately 425,250 age 80+ Seniors who are either fully income qualified to private pay or marginally qualified – subject to some spend-down. This gross potential is reduced to approximately 13,000 when screened for factors such as the incidence level of actual *need* for assistance with the Activities of Daily Living (ADLs) and the *propensity* to opt for assisted living (market share actually captured). But the true future market potential for assisted living is significantly impacted by a large *challenge* – the re-filling of existing units vacated due to annual turnover and a big *opportunity* – deeper penetration into the existing pent-up demand for assisted living in selected markets.

Nursing vs. Assisted Living Growth Conclusion: The prospects appear much brighter for new *net* growth (after turnover) in assisted living than for nursing.

Special Care Niche Markets for Nursing Home Operators

Chapter 32 addresses special care Alzheimer's/dementia as a special care "carve-out" market niche. The chapter identifies two market models:

1. *Residential/Social Model* – For those Seniors with early stages of dementia who are in relatively good physical health, but need sheltered living combined with low to moderate level assistance with the activities of daily living. The physical product is typically a special design variation of assisted living.

2. *Medical Model* – For Seniors with more advanced stages of Alzheimer's and other related dementia who also have more complex health problems; experiencing higher acuity.

Special care dementia units represent special opportunities for nursing home operators:

1. *Synergy* – By adding a special care residential/social model to your community, you can increase your operational efficiency (by adding more revenue-producing units) while optimizing your market responsiveness. These living units are typically smaller with fewer amenities when compared to conventional assisted living.

2. *Nursing Bed Conversion* – You can reduce your number of traditional nursing beds (if desired/necessary) by creating a swing wing conversion to a special care/dementia unit. But beware of hidden challenges. You could be subjected to some "grandfathered" building code variances that will trigger new code requirements and operations licensure issues.

Both of these market models should have purpose-built physical plant designs with strong, appropriate programmatic content. The expected outcomes include enhancing resident cueing to compensate for cognitive and memory impairment coupled with an environment that lowers excitement levels with a minimum use of physical or chemical restraints.

Chapter 6 contains additional considerations for nursing home operators as they plan to enter the assisted living arena.

Hospitals Are Getting Into Assisted Living

Who would have thought that a hospital's financial success would be measured by the *vacancy* of their acute care beds? That is exactly what is happening to some hospitals who sponsor and become the *risk payors* of 65+ Medicare HMOs. They are taking the financial risk and are under pressure to lower the health care costs (within the defined Medicare benefit structure) for those seniors who joined their HMOs.

Why Give Away Referrals You Can Service?

Hospitals are realizing that expanding the spectrum of health related services to seniors is a natural and sometimes necessary step. Not only are more than 50 percent of hospital patient days related to seniors, but hospital average lengths of stay are declining and competition for outpatient services is intensifying. This makes assisted living an attractive revenue enhancement option for many progressive hospitals as they plan for the future; especially for those in suburban markets. In the past ten years, an increasing share of our company's assisted living feasibility studies and strategic planning engagements have directly or indirectly involved hospitals.

Expanding into assisted living is a relatively new initiative for hospitals, and one that usually remains a closely guarded secret during the exploratory phase. Typically, hospitals consider three options:

- The first option would be to convert existing space, which is generally best suited for the more institutional personal care, or a medical model of assisted living.

- Secondly, they can construct a new facility on the existing campus, creating a more residential/social model that can also benefit from the hospital's operational economies of scale.

• Thirdly, they may develop a facility off-campus at a "satellite location." The latter is a popular option for joint ventures between a hospital and an assisted living developer or operating partner. It also allows an inner city hospital to create a high-quality satellite presence in other suburban areas for both marketing visibility and selected service delivery opportunities.

Nursing homes and hospitals share a number of assisted living diversification opportunities and challenges. They are covered in Chapter 6.

CHAPTER 8

CONTROL THE
REFERRAL PIPELINE

If You Don't, Someone Else Will !

I've often used the sound bite, *"The assisted living industry is **not** what it used to be."* That statement is especially true when it comes to resident referral trends.

As in any successful business, we often become complacent, and take our clients and customers for granted. In assisted living, this can be a fatal flaw in an otherwise well-conceived business plan. Figure 8-1 depicts typical assisted living resident referral patterns. Each community and market area would obviously have a unique resident origin referral profile.

Potential Changes in the Referral Pipeline

Your referral pipeline may change dramatically in the future for any of six reasons:

1. Hospitals are getting into the assisted living business. Just as they have rapidly encroached on the nursing home industry by developing special subacute care units, many hospitals are now diversifying into assisted living. Since hospitals represent about 10 percent of traditional referrals into assisted living, it is reasonable to assume that an owner/operator's referral pattern could change in some markets in the future. Hospitals will probably have an even larger impact on referrals. Discharge planners and social workers counsel marginally stable seniors who may *try* to remain at home after discharge from the hospital. But many end up in assisted living. Astute marketing and prospect tracking by hospitals clearly gives them an advantage in attracting those seniors to *their* assisted living communities.

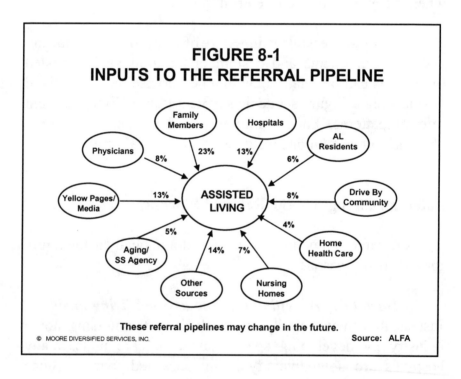

FIGURE 8-1
INPUTS TO THE REFERRAL PIPELINE

These referral pipelines may change in the future.

© MOORE DIVERSIFIED SERVICES, INC.   Source: ALFA

2. Nursing homes are creating a turf battle for assisted living residents. As outlined in Chapters 6 and 7, both hospitals and nursing homes are impacting the traditional referral patterns of assisted living. Nursing homes are integrating, but separating assisted living operations within their campuses. Many of these same nursing homes also have substantial cross-referral relationships with other hospitals and independent assisted living operators. Another significant trend is emerging. Consider this scenario:

- The private-pay bed ratios of many nursing homes are eroding as income-qualified seniors opt for the assisted living option.

- Approximately 36 percent of seniors exiting assisted living have to go on to nursing homes. They go, at least initially, as private-pay residents.

- So, nursing home operators are getting into assisted living for a double-barreled advantage – shoring up their declining private pay ratios and extending the average length of stay of a resident within their integrated operation.

These dynamics could have a dramatic impact on future referral patterns.

3. Independent living and continuing care retirement communities are expanding their assisted living emphasis. One of the most common growth strategies of both for-profit and not-for-profit campuses is to add assisted living, either within their community or on an adjacent/near-by tract of land. In the past, many residents would be discharged from their independent living communities and referred to other assisted living options in the immediate area.

4.   *Managed care and Medicaid waiver trends will undoubtedly alter referral patterns in the future.* While the jury is still out on the true role of managed care, Medicare and the evolving Medicaid waiver system for assisted living, it is certainly reasonable to assume that some changes will take place in the future. Under those circumstances, communities would enter either a "preferred provider network" or a "Medicaid approved" status. Some existing assisted living operators could be part of the scenario, while others might be excluded. This is best depicted in Figure 2-2 of Chapter 2; the vertical integrated network or continuum of care.

5.   *Many home health care agencies will be fighting for survival.* As Medicare and Medicaid reimbursement changes and other competitive forces continue to emerge, home health care agencies must develop new initiatives to serve their clients – and to survive themselves. This would, at the least, delay the entrance of some potential residents into a permanent sheltered living arrangement within assisted living communities. Chapter 9 addresses the role of home health in the future.

6. *Emerging competition will change traditional patterns.* As major markets become active with new assisted living projects, referral patterns of the past will not be projectable into the future. Competition involving price, value, benefits and unique designs could dramatically alter the future referral patterns of an existing assisted living community developed by yesterday's competitive standards.

Couple all of these trends with the significant overlapping of sheltered living and care options that have been outlined in Chapter 2, and it is easy to see that predictable referral pipelines for assisted living may well be a thing of the past. Referring to Figure 8-1, it is conceivable that between 30 to 40 percent of "traditional referrals" may, in fact, be up for grabs in the near future.

Progressive assisted living sponsors must carefully evaluate each element of the referral pipeline, and develop appropriate hedges and counter-strategies to ensure that the negative impacts of these potential trends are minimized in the future.

CHAPTER 9

HOME HEALTH CARE MUST BE RESTRUCTURED
It's Time for Extensive Re-Engineering

This chapter outlines what I believe to be imperative changes to the home health care service delivery system. These changes can be extremely beneficial to home health care organizations and will also materially benefit the needs of seniors. Conceptually, home health service delivery is a good system. But it has been too situation-driven in two diverging areas: 1) by governmental reimbursement programs and 2) by the increasing needs of seniors. In my opinion it *has* to be restructured.

Episodic Versus Chronic Needs

Most seniors would like to stay in their home full of love and memories until the day they die. But life is not that simple. Home health care as a service delivery system offers the hope (and frequently the reality) of staying in one's home longer. But there is growing evidence that we have crossed the line from cost-effective, quality, *episodic* or *temporary care* to providing fragmented, expensive, long term *chronic* care to many seniors who should not be living alone in an unsupportive environment 24 hours per day. Many seniors are living (sometimes just

86

existing) in a very high risk situation – as they struggle with the human drama of trying to stay in their home as long as possible. Many have irreversible long term *chronic* ailments - they are not recovering from a short term *episodic* event.

The Home Health Cost Issue

In recent years, up to 74 percent of total home health costs were paid for by Medicare, while 26 percent were from private pay or other sources. Medicare cost growth has been significant. This has masked the two sobering realities:

1. Many seniors receiving home health assistance might be better served in a service-enriched, seamless sheltered assisted living environment.

2. For the cost of just a one-hour home health visit (approximately $80), a senior can be provided *both* complete shelter (housing, meal and housekeeping services) and professional assistance in living (care) 24 hours per day.

Some Oversimplifications That Must be Addressed

I want to reiterate that home health care is a viable service delivery system. In my opinion, it has drifted off of the mark due to demands of the consumer and the Medicare reimbursement program. Summarized below are two over-simplifications that must be realistically addressed as we re-engineer the home health service delivery system.

1. ***Chronic Vs. Episodic Care*** – In the past, a home health professional would typically visit a senior in their home for one hour or less, including travel, two or three days a week. The Medicare reimbursement program appeared to be reasonably straightforward. However, now that same professional is frequently spending additional hours per day attempting to service seniors with complex and growing chronic ADL needs. While this is happening, the Medicare program is tightening the screws on reimbursement. Something has to give.

2. ***Community-Based Initiatives*** – Many of the Medicaid waiver programs from various states are addressing "home and community-based" services. The big qualification is frequently that the recipient of the entitlement must be "nursing home qualified." Well, with the rapidly escalating acuity levels of the nursing home, it is frequently difficult to conceive a "nursing home qualified senior" who could safely live alone in their own home with only sporadic community-based services delivered via home health. Policymakers have, again, oversimplified a response to a significant human need with inadequate and unrealistic public policy.

A Look to the Future – Some Possible Solutions

We need to lay all of the components of today's home health service delivery system out on the table, along with an accurate assessment of the true needs of seniors. As we re-assemble the components of a viable home health care service delivery strategy, we will likely come up with the following outcomes:

1. A more *holistic approach* to providing care for seniors. I've addressed this in detail in Chapter 33.

2. Home health care providers can team with assisted living sponsors in a seamless, win-win situation. This is where certain assisted living owner/operators and sponsors would provide the shelter component while a licensed home health agency would provide the care component. I've outlined this strategy in Chapter 2.

You might consider this business relationship concept similar to how third party management companies currently team with sponsors and owner/operators.

3. An additional opportunity may surface as assisted living operators objectively answer the question, **"What business are we *really* in?"** Some may realize that there could be a viable additional strategy in doing what they do best – (providing care for seniors) as an in-home delivery system. This would be an enhanced variation of the home health concept: serving those seniors who don't yet need full 24-hour a day sheltered living. Astute sponsors and owner/operators would, in effect, be creating an "umbilical" to their community when the senior's more intensified needs arise.

Market Positioning For The Future

Figure 9-1 summarizes the evolving (and inevitable) market positioning on this very important issue.

FIGURE 9-1
MARKET POSITIONING PLATFORM IN 2005

"It is far more efficient to delivery 24-hour *home care* into 80 residences on one five-acre campus (assisted living) than it is to provide the *fragmented, intermittent services* into 80 randomly distributed single family homes throughout a 400 square mile metropolitan area."

An example of cost-effectiveness:

- **Home Health:** $60 - $90 per *one hour* visit
- **Assisted Living:** $70 - $90 per complete *24 hour day*
  (Offering Full Service: housing, meals, ADL's, etc.[1])

---

[1]Basically all living expenses (real estate taxes, utilities, food, housekeeping, maintenance, home insurance, etc.).

Moore Diversified Services, Inc.

This positioning is not an indictment of the home health industry or an insensitivity to seniors' desires – it is an economic and health related fact of life. The economics and definition of the current home health delivery system will require significant restructuring and change. Our government and society needs and deserves a more efficient delivery system for seniors who do not require very high acuity institutional care. And we need affordable, viable sheltered living options for seniors who should not be living alone.

Eventually health care cost containment efforts will likely result in a total restructuring of home health care entitlements – possibly placing more emphasis and priority on assisted living. Despite the changing trends that are complicating assisted living, the concept can still be positioned to be one of the most practical solutions to long term care in the future; containing costs while successfully responding to the comprehensive needs and desires of the senior consumers and their families.

The re-engineered home health service delivery system can provide a key role in the seamless delivery of services to seniors. Properly restructured, it can retain its original leadership role as a financially viable service delivery system to seniors.

SECTION THREE

Physical Design Strategies

CHAPTER 10

MARKET-DRIVEN
DESIGN STRATEGIES

In Conceiving New Assisted Living Communities, You Get Only One Chance to Do it Right!

In Chapter 5, I identified 10 key questions which must be answered as you develop your new assisted living community strategies. Three of those 10 questions related specifically to market-driven *design* initiatives: 1) Which assisted living market model will you provide; 2) What is the optimum project size, and 3) What will be the overall design philosophy?

The Residential/Social Market Model

More than ten years of research in the competitive marketplace overwhelmingly indicates that a "residential/social" design model is clearly preferred by seniors and their families. This concept reflects a highly residential structure developed within local building code restraints and state licensing regulations. There is major focus on a design offering comfort, ambience and the perception of good value. This means providing benefits, features and amenities such as:

- Carpeting in all areas
- Drapes and window treatments

- Aesthetically pleasing wall coverings in public spaces
- Traditional artwork
- Non-institutional furniture (seems to belong in a home, not a motel)
- Significant millwork (door frames, moldings, baseboards, etc.)
- Ceiling heights consistent with total size (area) and volume of a particular space
- Responding to the trend of softer incandescent lighting fixtures (vs. fluorescent)
- Hallways with reasonable width and design techniques to minimize the "tunnel effect"

While the overall community is certainly positioned as the senior's new home and legal residence, the "look" of the public spaces should take on the impression of a well-conceived country club by sending subtle signals of comfortable, moderate luxury. As indicated in Chapter 3, this market model must also be positioned as having *a strong, but largely invisible, medical basis.* For example, the traditional *nurses' station* now looks like – and is positioned as – a *concierge desk* (solid wood vs. laminate, etc.).

The Medical Market Model

There is also an obvious role for the medical model assisted living design concept. The most common application today is providing an alternative living arrangement to nursing for seniors with more complex health care needs, or to serve advanced stage special care Alzheimer's/dementia residents. These seniors have complex, high-acuity health care needs as well as requiring a special Alzheimer's/dementia sheltered living environment. The development of this medical model can be realized by:

- *Conversion/adaptive reuse* of existing space such as a nursing wing

- *New construction* on a comprehensive senior living campus that is expanding the overall continuum

However, new development and construction of the medical model of assisted living as a freestanding facility is relatively rare.

First Impressions are Critical

The first visual impression of your community, the senior's as well as their loved ones, could well be the primary deal maker or breaker. Of course, your total offering must pass four competitive and consumer preference tests:

1. Superior *product*
2. Affordable, reasonable *price*
3. Perception of high *value*
4. Optimum resident *quality of life*

In over 900 focus groups, and in my personal "mystery shopping" in over 600 markets in 48 states, certain favorable attributes are common themes of successful communities:

A Strong Sense of Entrance – From the time they first turn onto your campus roadway, seniors and their families start forming both conscious and subliminal impressions. Ideally, the first entrance into the campus should be a mini-boulevard with a small island and perhaps a "monument" – a well-done sign indicating the name of your community.

After the prospect enters your campus, the next sense of entrance impression will be your main front entrance and porte cochere. Properly designed, the porte cochere should provide shelter from precipitation and the hot summer sun.

Building Elevations and Roof Lines – A well-designed community should have "breaks" in its elevation, and interesting roof lines. This means that the vertical walls of your community will, hopefully, be accented with balconies on the upper floors and other breaks in the elevations, rather than a flat vertical surface lacking interest or appeal. Roof lines should ideally have peaks or gables.

Exterior Window Treatments – One of the best ways to avoid the impression of institutionalism is to have interesting window treatments. This can be done with blinds, shutters or other design treatments influenced by your part of the country, utilizing attractive architectural themes that are prevalent in your area.

First Impressions of the Interior – When a prospect walks into your vestibule/lobby area, he or she wants to get a warm feeling of quality and ambience. Be careful of overdoing the impressions of "luxury." Depression Era seniors are concerned by opulence. They perceive too many "extras" as the potential basis of inflated prices. Always remember: Most prospective residents and their families will be on the lookout for signs you might charge them too much. Your public spaces should convey warmth and ambience, but not extravagance.

Approaching the Individual Living Units – Senior living communities will typically offer units that are "double-loaded" off of interior hallways. It is important that these hallways be at least six to eight feet in width and have breaks rather than long, extended, tunnel-like flat walls. The doorway to the individual living units is the entrance to the senior's <u>new home</u>. Where possible, it should look like a front door. This can be accomplished with solid-core paneled doors, and a reasonable amount of millwork (wood trim) around each door. In addition, the doorway can be "notched" rather than part of a long, extended wall. Direct and indirect lighting, colors and wall coverings can add the final quality accents to this portion of the design.

Individual Living Units – Studios or alcove units of approximately 350 s.f. are obviously modest in size, but should have full-function bathrooms with roll-in showers (for wheelchairs, if needed). Most now have a "Pullman or tea kitchen" consisting of a small (wet bar) sink and a small snack refrigerator. The refrigerator should be elevated from the floor so that the top is basically in line with the counter top. Typically, there are no permanently installed cooking units or burners. These would certainly not be appropriate for seniors in a nursing home, and the case is very similar for most assisted living residents. Provisions for portable appliances such as a microwave can be made to residents on a case-by-case basis.

One-bedroom units of 450 to 550 square feet have similar design features, plus a walk-in or walk-through closet between the private sleeping room and the bath. For shared accomodations of unrelated individuals, I've described a unique "equal turf" design concept in Chapter 24.

Living unit configurations involving *neighborhoods, clusters* and *cul de sacs* show very nicely, and may be recommended by your design team. That may be very appropriate. But you should have a <u>full</u> understanding of the initial capital and ongoing operating cost impacts before making this very important design decision.

Optimum Size of an Assisted Living Community

Once you've decided to build an assisted living project, one of your most critical decisions will be how many units to develop. Overbuild, and many of your units will remain empty. Underbuild, and you doom yourself to marginal financial performance – or worse.

The optimum size decision represents a classic trade-off between optimizing operational efficiency (more units) and prudent market feasibility (avoiding too many units).

Financial sensitivity analysis indicates that a well-conceived freestanding assisted living community should contain at least 60 to 80 units. In fact, many of the current industry models encompass 80 to 100 units. While it will be more difficult to reach the financial break-even point with a small project compared to a medium sized or large one, you can't just arbitrarily increase the unit count to make your operations more efficient.

From a market feasibility perspective, you generally should not assume an individual project market penetration rate of more than five to seven percent. That means your project should not require more than seven percent of the age- and income-qualified households that need assistance in living within a properly defined primary market area – and that's *after* allowing for important factors such as existing and announced competition and resident turnover. There must be a pragmatic balance between optimizing financial viability and avoiding excessive marketplace risk. Market and financial feasibility is addressed in more detail in Appendix A.

Another challenge in realistically assessing market demand is to keep your monthly service fees high enough to stay in business, yet low enough to be competitive and attract residents. That means focusing on how much you spend in two major categories: Initial capital costs, and ongoing operating expenses.

Both these financial areas have significant design implications.

Capital costs represent the money spent to design, develop, and furnish your project. They also provide funds for an effective sales and marketing program to bring the project to an initial stabilized occupancy of 93 percent. Currently, the total (all-in) capital costs for developing assisted living in most areas will typically range from about $110,000 to $140,000 per unit. This includes land, hard construction and soft development costs, and all other costs to bring your project to stabilized occupancy. A common definition for this cost-per-unit index is the total or all-in project costs divided by the number of living units or beds. This cost per unit range mentioned above probably encompasses approximately 75 percent of the current marketplace experience. The remaining 25 percent would experience total costs per unit either lower or higher than the range indicated.

Many of these costs are fixed, and do not change in direct proportion to unit count. This makes it harder for small facilities to come up with an affordable monthly rate while properly covering all development costs. For example, spending $200,000 on landscaping, enhanced common areas, or funding a construction overrun could increase each resident's monthly service fees by about $25 for 60-unit community, but up to $50 for a 35-unit community. This illustrates the challenge of spreading fixed capital costs to satisfy resulting debt service costs. Chapter 13 provides guidelines for developing a realistic capital budget.

Operating expenses are the funds needed to run the community on a continuing basis, not counting depreciation, interest, taxes or amortization. Assisted living operating expenses at stabilized occupancy typically range from $50 to $55 per resident day or about $1,520 to $1,670 per unit per month. These operating costs fall into one of three categories:

● *Fixed costs.* Examples would be certain salaries such as your executive director, and some "core operations" such as your kitchen or laundry.

● *Semi-variable costs.* These costs do change with project size, but not necessarily in *direct* proportion to changing unit counts. Utilities, maintenance, and transportation, for example, may vary somewhat depending on how many occupied units you have, but a significant portion of these costs are included in the basic operations of the project (fixed) and do not vary <u>directly</u> as a function of unit count.

● *Variable costs.* These costs generally change in direct proportion to the increases and decreases of the number of units. An example would be raw food expenditures. In a typical assisted living community, only about 25 percent of the operating expenses are truly variable.

Larger projects can more effectively spread fixed or semi-variable costs over more units, keeping individual residents' monthly fees lower. Labor costs, for instance, are a semi-variable cost outlay representing more than 60 percent of most assisted living communities' total operating expenses. This is why smaller new projects experience more significant negative cash flow during fill-up, and have a relatively high break-even cash flow (after debt service) of approximately 85 percent occupancy. This negative cash flow must be funded by your project's initial capital budget, as indicated in Chapter 13.

Project Size Versus Financial Performance

It is worthwhile to make cost sensitivity comparisons between a moderately efficient 60-unit project and a marginal 35-unit project. The purpose of the following analysis is to demonstrate the desirability of operating between a *minimum* of 60 units and a *marginal* project of 35 units.

Note: While a size of 60 units is acceptable, your financials won't enter the truly <u>optimum</u> zone until you develop and operate about 80 units.

To see how labor costs can affect various sized communities, let's assume that you decide you need two additional entry-level employees (perhaps because of the cost creep addressed in Chapter 15). With a direct compensation of about $9 per hour and a 22 percent fringe benefit factor, your cost per employee is roughly $22,840 per year. The two employees will cost you about $45,680 per year. To recover that expense over the *occupied* units in a 60-unit project, you'd have to raise each resident's monthly service fee by $70. In a smaller, 35-unit project, the increase would be about $115 per unit per month.

A typical community could have a number of other cost considerations that must be passed on to residents. When evaluating a typical detailed financial pro forma for both the 60-unit and 35-unit assisted living prototypes, two sobering observations emerge: Typical average total cost per unit is $115,000 versus $130,000, a 13 percent differential, with operating expenses per resident day standing at $50 versus $60, a 20 percent differential.

More importantly, the 60-unit project will require an average base monthly service fee of about $2,500 per month to maintain acceptable (not optimum) operating margins/financial ratios in a typical market, while the 35-unit project will require approximately $2,900 per month. This differential also increases a resident's required annual qualifying income before any spend-down from approximately $44,000 to $51,000, assuming he or she can spend approximately 80 percent of *after-tax cash flow income* for the service fee.

The 21st Century Design Decision – Studios or One-Bedroom Living Units?

In the first half of the 1990s, conventional wisdom indicated that a 300 to 350 square foot studio or alcove unit was both adequate and appropriate for assisted living, especially when compared to the alternative 200 to 225 square foot semi-private nursing room. But design criteria changed rapidly throughout the decade, as consumers exercised their private pay clout and articulated their product preferences. Many providers now offer one-bedroom units with living areas of 450 to 550 square feet in addition to a mix of well-conceived studios and alcoves.

The pace of this changing trend has been surprising. In the past five years, I've seen the average mix in new assisted living facilities change from about 85 percent studios and 15 percent one-bedroom units to more of a 40 percent mix of studios and 60 percent concentration of one-bedroom units (Figure 10-1). And it's not unusual for a CCRC to design its new assisted living section entirely of modestly-sized one-bedroom units.

Fueling this development trend are consumer demand preferences, and the resulting potential for financial gain to sponsors and owner/operators.

FIGURE 10 -1
TYPICAL UNIT TYPE/SPACE
ENVELOPE SCENARIOS

Unit Type	Size (s.f.)	Three Scenarios		
		"A"	"B"	"C"
• Studio/Alcove	325 - 350 s.f.	80%	60%	40%
• One Bedroom	450 - 550	20	40	60
		100%	100%	100%
		↓	↓	↓
• Special Care	325 - 350			
Alzheimer's/Dementia		Early 90s	Late 90s	Now

Moore Diversified Services, Inc.

Consumer considerations for the various unit types involve three key factors:

1. *What seniors and their families prefer* – Seniors want to maintain their independence and dignity. Their families are coping with guilt and economic concerns. One-bedroom assisted living units help to satisfy many of these concerns, assuming value and affordability expectations are also met.

2. *What consumers can afford* – The primary financial components of an 80-unit assisted living community with a base monthly service fee of $2,500 for studio units are comprised of approximately 60 percent operating expenses and 40 percent debt service and cash flow/profit. A one-bedroom unit might cost $2,800 per month, a $300 per month increase. Assuming a resident can spend approximately 80 percent of her *after-tax*, disposable income on a monthly service fee, she needs to gross approximately $5,300 more per year for every $300 monthly increase in fees. One-bedroom units are currently very popular, but this economic reality of relative affordability will put bigger units beyond the reach of many seniors.

3. *Health and acuity level* – Some seniors would have difficulty in dealing with even the modestly larger space of a one-bedroom unit. As long as the assisted living industry attempts to slow its relatively high turnover rate by accommodating higher acuity levels, including the early stages of Alzheimer's, studio units will continue to play a key role for many high acuity seniors.

Sponsor and Owner/Operator Considerations

From the sponsor or owner/operator's perspective, the studio vs. one-bedroom design considerations tend to focus heavily on marketing and financial issues. The financial issues include development costs, operating margins, cash flow and, for many public companies, earnings per share, which impacts stock price and price-earnings ratios.

Incremental Financial Impacts of One-Bedroom Units

• *Capital costs* – Your new, *incremental* costs in going from a studio to a one-bedroom will be an additional wall, door and window. There will also be expanded ceiling and floor space in both the living unit and the adjacent corridor. You will add approximately 175 square feet of space to the larger one-bedroom unit, which will increase your capital costs. Assisted living project hard construction costs in many areas of the U.S. average about $100 to $115 per square foot (2001 dollars). This cost index includes certain relatively expensive basic items found in every unit, such as the bathroom, small tea/Pullman kitchen, front entrance and the heating and air conditioning system.

These incremental additional space costs will probably total about $55 per square foot in hard costs, adding around $9,600 in hard costs to the unit. (Refer to Figure 10-2.) Note that the *incremental* costs per square foot for the extra room will not be as high as the *base* cost, because certain relatively expensive items mentioned previously (bathroom, Pullman kitchen, etc.) are not repeated.

- *Soft costs* – Certain soft development costs, including architectural, engineering, development and general conditions also vary as a percent of construction costs. Adding these increased soft costs to the hard costs results in a total additional development cost of about $10,000 for a modestly-sized, one-bedroom unit versus a studio unit. At nine percent interest plus principal, this yields an additional debt service cost per occupied unit of about $85 per month. This, of course, must be passed on to residents.

- *Operating expenses* – For an assisted living community opening early in the new millennium, these expenses will probably be $50-$55 per resident day, or $1,520-$1,670 per month at stabilized occupancy for a studio unit. The incremental increase in operating expenses for a one-bedroom unit versus a studio is represented by elements of cost that make up approximately 25 percent of the operating expense statement: housekeeping, maintenance, utilities, taxes, insurance and an incremental management fee assessment. These expenses vary largely as a function of building square footage, and will likely add approximately $5 per resident day, or about $150 per month, to the cost of a larger one-bedroom unit (versus the studio).

Adding the increased operating expenses of $150 per month and increased debt service per unit/month brings the total cost increase of a 500 square foot one-bedroom over a 350 square foot studio to $235 a month. But due to increased perceived value, operators can usually charge substantially *more* than just the basic direct cost differential for the larger units. As mentioned earlier, in many markets a one-bedroom unit commands a monthly service fee of about $2,800, while a studio goes for about $2,500. This gives the resident the luxury of a larger unit and allows the sponsor to realize higher financial returns. This positive financial synergy is demonstrated in Figure 10-2.

There is clearly a trend toward effectively designed one-bedroom assisted living units. But even this apparent win-win solution must be approached with caution. Don't forget, not every prospective resident can afford that monthly bump. But for those who can, larger one-bedroom units can be a very appealing option.

```
+------------------------------------------------------------------+
|                        FIGURE 10-2                               |
|                                                                  |
|                   RUNNING THE NUMBERS . . .                      |
|                . . . ASSISTED LIVING STUDIO VS.                  |
|                  ONE BEDROOM UNIT SYNERGY                        |
|                                                         Percent  |
|                             Studio  vs.    1-BR        Increase  |
| ● Living Area Square                                             |
|   Footage                       350         500          43%     |
|                                                                  |
| ● Typical Cost per Unit      $115,000    $125,000         9      |
|                                                                  |
| ● Monthly Service Fee        $ 2,560     $  2,770         8      |
|                                                                  |
| ● Operating Expenses                                             |
|   per Resident Day              $53         $58           9      |
|                                                                  |
| ● Cash Flow:                                                     |
|     - Before Debt Service   $ 11,200    $ 11,900          6      |
|     - After Debt Service    $  2,500    $  2,800         12      |
|                                                                  |
| ● Resident's Qualifying                                          |
|   Income                     $45,170     $48,880          8      |
|                                                                  |
| Moore Diversified Services, Inc.                                 |
+------------------------------------------------------------------+
```

How Many Stories?

The decision involving the number of stories in a new assisted living building is typically a function of a series of restraints and trade-offs. These can include local building codes, optimizing internal "flow", overall operational efficiency, optimizing resident walk distances from the furthest assisted living unit to the dining room (the higher the *vertical* building, the shorter the *horizontal* walk distances), relative cost and available land leading to resulting unit density. Another important factor is providing for safe, practical emergency evacuation of the residents.

Usually, all of the above factors and restraints dictate the ultimate configuration of a new assisted living building. Note that overall development and construction costs can vary as a function of the number of floors. As the number of levels increase, some costs go down (land, foundation, etc.), while other costs tend to increase (elevators, type of construction, etc.). For very preliminary planning purposes, you can typically count on the density (approximate number of units per acre) to range from 15 to 25 units per acre for a two- to three-story building. This includes not only the building structure, but roadways, parking spaces and the overall site infrastructure.

Building Efficiency

Figure 10-3 summarizes the general space profile for an 80-unit community. This profile obviously must evolve from your unique and detailed design and space planning effort. However, the ideal "envelope" might look something like that summarized in Figure 10-3.

FIGURE 10-3
A TYPICAL 80-UNIT ASSISTED LIVING
COMMUNITY SPACE PROFILE

- **Studio/Alcove**   **32 units @ 350 s.f.**   **11,200 s.f.**
- **One Bedroom**   **48 units @ 500 s.f.**   **24,000**
  Totals   **80**   **35,200 s.f.**

Weighted average *living area*: 440 s.f.

Common/public space @ 45%   **28,800 s.f.**
Total area under roof   **64,000 s.f.**

Weighted average *gross* area per unit   **800 s.f.**

Livable areas typically represent approximately
55% of the total area under roof.

Moore Diversified Services, Inc.

Note: If your overall building efficiency differs dramatically from those shown in Figure 10-3, stand by for some continuing financial challenges.

Special Care/Alzheimer's/Dementia "Carve-Outs"

Unique designs are evolving for special care units. We are rapidly progressing up the learning curve with respect to helping seniors and their loved ones cope with these dreaded diseases by pushing the state-of-the-art in the following areas:

- Lowering excitement levels and optimizing security, while minimizing the use of chemical and physical restraints

- Providing visual cueing to compensate for loss of memory and cognitive skills – reducing some confusion and disorientation

- Offering higher levels of ambience in a secure, user-friendly environment

- Developing a more *holistic* approach to dementia care and sheltered living

Purpose-built special care units with *strong programmatic content* are quickly becoming a separate, yet integrated, portion of many new assisted living designs. This very important "market niche/carve-out" is addressed in more detail in Chapter 32.

Five Effective Design Planning Strategies

There are five design concept considerations that can lead to a successful project:

1. Accurately determine the size and depth of your market, so that you know how many units you can realistically fill in the competitive marketplace.

2. Value engineer your project with a passion (see Chapter 13). A small project usually can't tolerate "Cadillac" designs, cost overruns or inefficient operations.

3. Be aware that future operating expense cost creep can be a very fatal disease for a modestly-sized community (see Chapter 15).

4. Consider the practical financial economies of scale that might be realized if your new assisted living project is an integral part of an existing continuing care or health care campus. This results in more total revenue-producing units to spread both fixed and semi-variable costs.

5. Study the possibility of orderly, prudent project phasing. This means master planning your community for additional units in the future, assuming a favorable initial market response to your project. Small-scale projects do work. But they require realistic planning and laser-sharp focused attention to detail.

Finally – the Rule of "10" for Designers

I often tell designers that if their designs can save $9,000 in annual operating costs, the value of their client's community is increased by over $85,000. That's because potential buyers and appraisers will "capitalize" your net operating income at about 10.5 to 11.0 percent.

Example:

- Increase in Net Operating Income
  (NOI):   <u>$9,000</u>
- Capitalization Rate: .105
- Indicated Increase in Value: = $85,715

See Appendix C for a full explanation.

When it comes to design, you have only one chance to get it right. Cost-effective design of assisted living units represents one of the biggest challenges – and opportunities – for the future.

CHAPTER 11

ADAPTIVE REUSE FOR
ASSISTED LIVING

Conversion Dreams Can Turn Into Nightmares

Adaptive reuse or conversion of existing structures to assisted living has emerged as a commonly-considered strategy. Typical initiatives involve conversion of apartments and moderately-sized hotels and motels into assisted living projects. But the conversion of existing real estate into other uses involves delicate trade-offs, objective evaluations and a clear understanding of marketplace risk. You must walk a very thin line between being emotionally influenced by inappropriate, *situation-driven* building and site limitations and realizing the significant *benefit-driven* opportunities that can exist through the cost-effective conversion of appropriate properties. Unfortunately, the underlying motivation of the developer in many cases is, ***"I have this old property (that I'm in love with) – now what do I do with it?"*** A common, but frequently deadly, rationalization is that, ***"Surely the market will understand what I went through to pull off this conversion!"*** It probably won't.

Recent examples of adaptive reuse clearly indicate that while many successful conversions were based on a sound rationale, other projects experienced an agony not unlike that of a homeowner "fixing up that old house." Serious problems continue to emerge as you get deeper and deeper into the conversion activity. You quickly pass beyond the point of no return.

The Existing Owner-Operator's Perspective

Many existing owner-operators face the difficult decision of adaptive reuse through the modification of a building in order to accomplish the following:

- Expansion and upgrade of existing, probably aging senior living structures on their campus

- Conversion and combining of smaller studio units into either one-bedroom independent living units or more functional assisted living units

- Addition of more cosmetically pleasing and functional public spaces

But in spite of laudable end objectives, we frequently fail to initially ask the defining strategic question, **"Should this structure be saved in the first place?"**

Addressing this question is often postponed when sponsors find themselves receiving *standard* and sometimes *premium* market rates for *substandard* structures. The sponsors know this can't last forever – but there never seems to be a good time to bite the bullet.

The Potential Buyer's Perspective

There are some economic and market realities which make adaptive reuse a very valid concept. From time to time, sectors of our real estate markets become overbuilt – or, as some say facetiously – under-demolished. Some properties become obsolete for their original intended use. These properties are frequently sold by lenders and owners for deep discounts. These market situations can lead to some interesting adaptive reuse opportunities. But along with these opportunities come significant risks.

The Rules of the Adaptive Reuse Game

I have four fundamental rules of successful adaptive reuse. If these rules are broken or inappropriately fudged, your project may fail.

First, *the site characteristics* of the adaptive reuse candidate should be essentially irreplaceable in the immediate primary market area. If someone else can build a new, state-of-the-art product on a similar nearby site, the new project is likely to be far more competitive than your converted existing/older property.

Second, *the building structure* should be truly unique – with innovative, practical and cost-effective adaptive reuse potential. It could be a historical landmark, or one with a past that is memorable for *positive* reasons.

Third, *the total turn-key cost* of acquisition, renovation and conversion should be somewhat less than the cost of a newly-designed and developed state-of-the-art assisted living community. But keep in mind that debt service cost recovery makes up only 25 to 30 percent of the resident's total monthly service fee. Saving on capital costs certainly helps, but be sure to totally quantify the real benefit in the competitive marketplace. With adaptive reuse, you must offer *very* competitive pricing. If the price/value relationship is not competitive, the cost vs. value perceptions in the consumer marketplace will inevitably focus on this important economic issue, highlighting the trade-offs you've made rather than the benefits you've delivered.

Fourth, *the consumer* will give very little credit for some of the inevitable tradeoffs and compromises in the end product that typically result from adaptive reuse of an existing structure. The only thing that counts in the consumer marketplace is the perceived value and tangible benefits of the end product or service. Just as homeowners fall in love with the "quaint old home" that appears suitable for fix-up, some operators get involved in irrational love affairs with their newly acquired "bargain real estate."

The key to successful adaptive reuse is to facilitate a value-oriented match between the realistic adaptive reuse opportunities that are present in the conversion property and the benefits and demand-driven needs of the marketplace.

The Scoreboard: Product, Price and Value

This means that the rework of a current site and building through adaptive reuse efforts must deliver an end product that is totally compatible with marketplace needs. The acid test of adaptive reuse feasibility is whether or not the fully converted community can effectively compete in terms of product, price and value with new state-of-the-art products that do not involve the potential stigma of conversion trade-offs or compromises.

Three Traps to Avoid

There are three major traps into which developers and owner/operators typically fall when implementing adaptive reuse:

1. *Inappropriate design configuration* – Significant flaws frequently exist in either the basic building footprint, floor layout or the configuration of the existing living units.

2. *Mediocre Location* – The project location was not really unique and ideally situated. Determining site location suitability is very similar to site selection for a completely new project. The margin for error is very narrow – and major compromises will likely lead to a troubled project.

3. *Undesirable Perceptions or Misconceptions of the Past* – Sometimes the history of the structure or site casts a permanent negative perception on the new community. If this is the case, all the renovation in the world won't make a difference.

Figure 11-1 summarizes the delicate trade-off: Conversion dreams or economic nightmare!

Many different structures can offer good conversion options as long as the "footprint" and overall design configuration is compatible with current state-of-the-art. Schools, hotels/ motels, nursing homes, hospitals and religious facilities have been successfully converted under the right conditions.

Schools

Many elementary schools in mature neighborhoods are now "demographically obsolete." The neighborhoods are aging. So the demand for large numbers of elementary classrooms has long since passed. These schools are sometimes located in good "in-fill" locations that can now serve seniors within high quality, mature neighborhoods. From a strategic standpoint, adaptive reuse of these facilities frequently involves less neighborhood opposition to planning and zoning approval requests than an attempt to get the same approvals on a vacant piece of land for a start-up development effort.

Some physical characteristics that make schools good candidates for conversion include:

1. Public spaces are adaptable:

    • Cafeteria converts into a dining room

    • Kitchen can be expanded/used as the commercial kitchen

FIGURE 11-1

| CONVERSION DREAMS ? | *OR* | PHYSICAL OR ECONOMIC NIGHTMARE ? |

The Right Approach

- The site <u>was</u> irreplaceable

- Approvals were obtained with relative ease

- You paid not more than 80% of alternative costs for:
  - Acquisition
      Plus
  - Renovation

- There were no major design trade-offs:
  - Suitable unit size and configuration
  - Appropriate building layout
  - Interior loaded hallways

The Wrong Approach

- The site was really <u>not</u> unique

- You paid too much for:
  - Acquisition
  - Renovation

- You rationalized away serious design flaws:
  - No showers
  - Bedrooms too small
  - Very narrow corridors
  - Long walk distances to insufficient common areas
  - Asbestos
  - Inadequate HVAC system
  - Etc.

Focus on the practical realization of a good end product and <u>don't</u> fall in love with your real estate !

2. The configuration of classrooms and hallways can generally be converted to corridors with living units:

    • Load-bearing walls and columns are usually easy to deal with in the adaptive reuse process.

3. Schools typically have a flexible "building shell." That means the basic exterior shell stays in place, while a number of changes can be made inside the building with relative ease.

4. In many cases, the auditorium can be left largely in place and be converted into a "senior village mall."

Hotels and Motels

A number of hotels and motels across the United States are facing depressed occupancy, and some markets may be permanently overbuilt. Many of these facilities can make excellent adaptive reuse candidates, while others should be subjected to the wrecking ball. Many older lodging facilities have now been bypassed by the interstate and new highway/arterial systems. Depending upon the neighborhoods in which they are located, some can become excellent conversion candidates. Many are located in traditional, well-established neighborhoods representing excellent in-fill locations in both suburban and urban areas.

In terms of design, a number of unsuccessful attempts have been made to convert austere budget motels that do not have interior hallways or suitably configured sleeping rooms. These attempts are clearly situation-driven, and miss the mark in the seniors marketplace. Conventional hotels with interior, double-loaded corridors and adequate sleeping rooms might make a good conversion to assisted living, but it is highly unlikely they could serve the independent living market that typically requires full-function kitchens (with complex plumbing requirements) and larger living areas. An exception would be a suite hotel, which we'll discuss later.

A frequent challenge in hotel/motel conversion is the relatively large number of rooms available for reuse. The resulting senior living unit count is often higher than the marketplace will probably absorb in a reasonable time frame.

Hospitals and Nursing Homes

Complete conversion of older hospitals and nursing homes sometimes appears to work well, but the perceptions of past (institutionalized) use can linger when you reintroduce facilities that suddenly offer upscale, high-ambiance retirement living.

The business base of hospitals – and, in some cases, nursing homes – is changing due to evolving trends in managed care and the impact of vertical integrated networks. Conversion of space within a hospital or reuse of a nursing home wing may provide good opportunities for adaptive reuse. But special caution must be exercised when converting existing health care facilities. There is frequently either the perception or reality of institutionalism. Some hospitals and nursing homes do have the potential for conversion to a residential/social model of assisted living, but most should probably focus on the medical model. The medical model conversion opportunities fall into two major business sectors:

- Conventional assisted living for seniors with complex medical needs

- Special care Alzheimer's/dementia units for seniors with both dementia and high acuity health needs

These medical market model concepts are discussed in detail in Chapters 31 and 32.

Apartments and Condominiums

Condominium and apartment developments can also offer the possibility of solid adaptive reuse considerations. As with hotels, these structures should have living units with interior loaded hallways. Their typical shortcoming is likely to be inadequate common/public spaces. These space requirements can represent 35 to 45 percent of the total area under roof for an assisted living community.

The portion of the total area devoted to common space in a typical apartment or condo is frequently 15 percent or less. However, there are some compensating strategies to consider:

- Sometimes an added building appropriately connected to the apartment complex can satisfy the new common space requirements.

- A "u-shaped" apartment or condominium complex footprint can feature a "commons building," including a dining room, commercial kitchen and space for other services in the center of the footprint, which connects the two ends of the building.

Apartments and condos can make good conversion candidates for <u>independent</u> living because they typically have the following characteristics:

- Separate sleeping rooms

- Full-function kitchens

- Adequate living areas

- Interior loaded hallways (in many geographical areas)

Condos and apartments of a more modest design (studios, alcoves, etc.) have the potential of being more readily adapted to assisted living where livable space requirements are less demanding than for independent living.

Specific Conversion Considerations

Living units that enter into the interior loaded hallways and projects that have adequate common space and public areas are key requirements when evaluating the overall suitability of an potential adaptive reuse structure. Obviously, the building's exterior elevations and "external look" are also very important.

Some characteristics to look for include:

- What is the exterior (first impression) look of the building?

- Are there patios and balconies?

- Are there aesthetically pleasing "breaks" in the contour of the vertical surfaces?

- Are there interesting building roof lines?

In other words, how appealing does the building look when one first observes it? Many facilities are functionally adequate, but appear to be far too institutional from a consumer perspective.

Design features such as the ability to meet current fire and safety codes and other licensing requirements must be carefully considered. It is amazing how often experienced operators overlook building codes and requirements that suddenly come into play when previous variances that were grandfathered no longer apply to the new owner.

What They See is What They Pay For

The paramount consideration is that the senior consumer marketplace only sees and gives credit to how *they* see the converted end product. Consumers really do not care what it took to get there, or why some of the obvious tradeoffs or compromises are still highly visible. If there is well-conceived competition nearby for comparison purposes, the converted product gets even less credit for the necessary conversion compromises.

Conversion Success Stories

In spite of all of these cautions, there are numerous success stories. Some examples include:

1. *A relatively new suite hotel* with full-function kitchens and separate living and sleeping areas became a troubled property in an overbuilt hospitality market. It was easily converted to independent retirement living because of its original configuration. The location was ideal, and the property offered the opportunity to convert one floor to assisted living. A new nursing section was added to one end of the property, and integrated with the original building.

2. *An aging hotel and convention center* was donated by the city to the local housing authority in order to serve modest gap-income seniors. The gap group typically has annual incomes between $12,000 to $25,000, and is extremely difficult to serve in a private-pay situation. This facility was able to avoid excessive capital costs and offer reasonable congregate services at modest fees.

3. *A large hospital campus* had its service delivery systems expanded into residentially-oriented assisted living and more medically-driven personal care. Through a combination of conversion of existing facilities and additional construction, both medical and residential-social models of assisted living were accomplished and integrated within the hospital campus.

4. *A demographically-obsolete elementary school* in an established mature neighborhood was successfully converted to freestanding assisted living. The neighborhood's residents had actively opposed previous new development efforts involving nearby vacant land. The adjoining neighbors were less concerned about approval of the school's adaptive reuse because the owner/operators assured them the "look and character" of the property would not change. It was a property to which the neighborhood had become accustomed over the past 30 years.

5. *A company in Paris has taken a different approach to adaptive reuse.* Paris is the epitome of urban density, yet this company finds urban sites of varying shapes and sizes and determines how many of their standard state-of-the-art living units can fit on the site. If this number is acceptable, they save the original building elevation/facades, demolish the existing structure and create a state-of-the-art structure with the original old European facades in place. The end result has the flavor of traditional Europe – with a state-of-the-art interior infrastructure – in a highly desirable location.

Each of these successful examples were the result of careful consideration of the ultimate end product design, its location and how the product would be perceived in the future by the senior consumer marketplace. Most importantly, none of the projects broke my four fundamental rules of adaptive reuse.

The successful approach to considering adaptive reuse is to consider what the marketplace needs and wants **first,** then determine whether the conversion candidate really meets those needs. While apparently simple, the reverse of this process is frequently undertaken. Remember that adaptive reuse works best if the site is irreplaceable and the ultimate turn-key cost is approximately 20 percent less than new replacement cost. This pricing advantage makes reasonable trade-offs easier to accept in the marketplace. This strategy can deliver a powerful product into the marketplace because it involves a unique location and excellent value at a surprisingly affordable cost for that particular market area. That is something that most consumers will notice. Absent of these advantages, adaptive reuse risk increases geometrically.

Adaptive reuse can play a significant role in delivering needed senior housing and health care while helping to balance an overbuilt real estate market. The strategy can also save classic structures from the wrecking ball.

ADAPTIVE REUSE – THE FOUR CRITICAL QUESTIONS TO ANSWER

1. Is the site truly irreplaceable in the primary market area?

2. Is the building really unique, with practical and cost-effective adaptive reuse potential?

3. Is the total turn-key acquisition and conversion cost moderately less (approximately 20 percent) than the replacement cost of a newly developed state-of-the-art assisted living facility?

4. Will the consumer understand and give appropriate credit for the inevitable tradeoffs and compromises in the end product that typically result from adaptive reuse process?

CHAPTER 12

INVESTING FOR IMPROVEMENTS
Physical Plants Also Age in Place

While most of us are aware that *residents* age in place, we frequently overlook or ignore another chronic aging trend - the gradual deterioration of *physical plants*. As the assisted living industry matures and we learn more about consumer preferences and needs, significant, innovative improvements are being made in the functional design and ambiance of newer state-of-the-art assisted living communities. This new trend is good, but it also represents a major challenge to the future viability of many older communities.

Your response to the inevitable facility aging process must focus on two important areas – the residents, and the community itself. The two are very complex, and inevitably interrelated.

Five Warning Signs

This aging process of physical plants is analogous to a senior's increasing chronic illness. Both represent a gradually deteriorating, but highly predictable, trend. People wear down; buildings do, too. Planning for appropriate physical plant capital investment is imperative, and must be executed in a pragmatic manner. There are five particular signs to look for which probably signal that at least some capital investment is necessary:

1. *Cosmetic wear and tear* – Examples are frayed or soiled upholstery, worn carpets, out of style drapes and faded wall coverings. It could also include cosmetic defects in the floor and wall surfaces and finishes in your public areas. Even if you provide outstanding care for your client/residents, small but obvious blemishes on furniture or other amenities may give the opposite impression. You certainly don't want that.

2. *Physical plant deterioration* – Leaky roofs or chronic failures of the heating, ventilating and air conditioning (HVAC) system usually are tell-tale signs of ignored or deferred maintenance. You can probably avoid higher repair costs later by tending to smaller, inexpensive problems as they occur. But if you've put off such repairs, they should be identified and handled immediately, before the situation becomes worse.

3. *Functional obsolescence* – The most obvious examples are kitchen and bathroom cabinets, plumbing fixtures and lighting in the individual living units. Also included would be dated furniture styles and electrical fixtures in the common areas. Outdated and drab interiors in public spaces inevitably create negative first impressions for potential residents and their families. Do you usually notice one or two new "little" problems every day? That probably means it's time to act before they're bigger – and more expensive.

4. *Increased operations costs* – Higher utility costs and hampered work flow are often signs that various types of capital improvement are necessary. Again, it may be a matter of tending to small challenges before they turn into major problems.

5. *Capital improvements by competitors* – It's one thing to keep your original physical plant functional, and another to remain competitive. If the "other guy" upgrades his facilities and you don't, you're handing him a marketing advantage. This doesn't mean abandoning common sense, of course; some facility operators become so obsessed with adding additional bells and whistles that they price themselves out of the market just to pay for all the extras. But it's wise to keep track of what your competitors are doing – and, when you can, to beat them to the punch.

Remember, you're trying to be in a position to respond to a dual threat – the inevitable aging process of your plant, and efforts by competitors to offer newer products with more attractive environments.

Five Specific Areas of Potential Capital Improvements

Just as there are five signals that it may be time to consider capital improvements, there are five specific areas to consider when planning these improvements (specific capital investment strategies are addressed in Chapter 18):

1. *Enhanced first impressions of the community* through improvements in the external site characteristics, including signs, paving repair, and lighting. In this way you establish a strong first visual impression. Don't forget it is possible to create interesting visual impressions through innovative, well-maintained landscaping. That old "first impression" adage is truer than ever in today's highly competitive business environment.

2. *Improved impressions of the building exterior,* including fresh paint, new color treatments and more interesting elevation facades and roof lines.

3. *Rejuvenation of interior public spaces* –This generally means using new materials and finishes to improve interior design accents, or adding new or renovated furniture.

4. *Back-of-the-house details*, including expanded and improved kitchen equipment, laundry facilities and energy-efficient heating, ventilating and air conditioning (HVAC) systems.

5. *Improvements to individual living units,* such as refinishing or replacing cabinetry, new carpeting, and refinishing vertical and horizontal surfaces. Individual living units are often improved on an attrition basis as they are vacated. These upgrade packages can also be offered to existing residents for a modest increase in monthly service fees.

The Unfunded Depreciation Dilemma

Faced with an aging physical plant, most operators can't help but wonder, *"How __did__ we get in this position in the first place?"* The answer may relate to the concept of depreciation as a generally accepted accounting practice – but is actually a non-cash (accrual) expense. That means you don't write someone a check for "depreciation" each month. Most buildings are depreciated annually over a 25 to 35 year period, using a conservative definition of the building's useful life. But "writing off" depreciation allows you to satisfy your CPA or auditor on paper, without actually investing any real cash in your aging community. This trap is called "unfunded depreciation," and it is creating major problems for many aging assisted living, and senior housing and health care communities. Most progressive new communities now deploy a Cap "x" strategy outlined in Chapter 18. Others have a pragmatic capital investment plan.

Capital Investment Planning – A Five-Step Process

To avoid the unfunded depreciation trap, answer this question: *"Now that we recognize the __problem__, how do we properly plan for the future?"* The answer is to deploy a pragmatic capital investment strategy. A good technique is to combine your actual facility experience with available industry standards and guidelines. Here is a suggested five-step approach (refer to Figure 12-1):

1. Create a revolving five-year plan, adding another 12 months with every year that passes.

2. Make a detailed list of potential capital investment needs – the components, subsystems, and materials that make up your community. The list should include the HVAC system, roofs, carpets, exterior and interior walls, caulking and sealing, etc.

3. Now, identify each item's life expectancy, determine its current age and project the expected life remaining. You're now in a position to estimate the likely cost, scope and timing for future repair or replacement.

4. Put all this information into a spreadsheet listing potential repair and maintenance details vertically, with five-year planning columns spread horizontally as outlined in Figure 12-1.

5. Insert budgetary cost estimates into this spreadsheet.

You now have the basis for a simple, effective, pragmatic and prioritized five-year revolving capital investment program.

Design Changes to Stay Competitive

Typical shortcomings in many older assisted living communities across the United States include:

FIGURE 12-1

SUMMARY OF A TYPICAL REVOLVING
5-YEAR CAPITAL IMPROVEMENT PLAN

Capital Investment Item/Category	Year/Capital Investment Required				
	2001	2002	2003	2004	2005
Mandatory Items					
1.	$	$	$	$	$
2.					
3.					
4.	*Complete this matrix and you'll be well on your*				
5.	*way towards developing a proactive capital*				
6.	*investment plan.*				
7.					
8.					
9.					
10.					
Total Dollars Required	$	$	$	$	$
Discretionary Items					
1.	$	$	$	$	$
2.					
3.					
4.					
5.					
6.					
7.					
8.					
9.					
10.					
Total Dollars Required	$	$	$	$	$

- Very small studio or alcove units

- No kitchenettes

- No showers in the individual living units.

- Shared bathrooms for semi-private occupancy of unrelated residents.

- Limited space in community/common areas in older buildings; space that is now desperately needed to serve the growing needs of both the aging resident's needs and the professional staff for offering expanded services.

- Insufficient size or ambience of dining areas. Some communities offer only self-service buffet lines, but with aging assisted living residents and competitive threats, full wait person table service is becoming an imperative.

The problems resulting from these typical functional deficiencies are exacerbated by areas of deferred maintenance, which in turn have significant impact on efficient operations.

Determining the Cost-Effectiveness of Capital Improvements

Some capital investments will require difficult value judgements to determine whether they are really worth the dollars you would have to commit. I like to use a quantitative approach that "reduces the decision to the lowest common denominator." This should be viewed in two perspectives:

1. What will be the incremental dollar impact (increase) in a resident's typical monthly service fees?

2. How – specifically – will the value of your community be enhanced?

Here's how to get started:

Individual Living Unit Improvements – One way to look at the cost recovery or value sensitivity of investing money in your individual living units is to determine how much *additional* monthly service fee Mrs. Barker will have to pay in order for you to break even on the additional debt service needed to fund those improvements. This involves the following common-sense process:

- Determine the amount to be invested in each individual living unit (let's say $10,000 per unit).

- Determine the interest rate to be paid on the new borrowed funds. This could be approximately 9 percent, if you're a for-profit entity, or as low as 6 percent for a not-for-profit organization.

- Use the debt constant concept described in Appendix B. This allows you to easily determine the annual increase in debt (both principal and interest payments) needed to pay for the improvements to that individual unit.

- Adjust for the vacancy factor. Since you can pay off your debt only through the revenue derived from occupied units, you must adjust your computations for vacancy; using a stabilized occupancy of 93 percent.

- Adjust for Debt Service Coverage Ratio (DSCR). This ratio simply states that your friendly lender wants about $1.25 in available cash for every dollar you owe in debt.

A Real World Example

Assuming a $10,000 investment per unit at 9 percent interest rate for 25 years with a 93 percent stabilized occupancy and a 1.25x debt service coverage ratio yields the following calculation:

$10,000 times a debt service constant of 10.07 percent (see Appendix B) = $1,007 per year

To adjust that figure for a 7 percent vacancy, we can divide the $1,007 by .93 to yield $1,083.

Now we need to increase that amount by 1.25x in order to satisfy our lender. That yields a total annual debt service obligation per unit of $1,354 per year.

Finally, let's determine what it will cost Mrs. Barker on a *monthly* basis. So, we will divide the $1,354 by 12 months, yielding approximately $113 per month.

Since Mrs. Barker would already be paying a base monthly service fee for assisted living of approximately $2,640, the $10,000 investment represents an increase of $113 or, about a 4 percent increase, in her monthly service fee. Note that $10,000 can purchase a substantial amount of improvements for one single living unit. Figure 12-2 provides a matrix of different levels of individual living unit capital improvement investments vs. borrowed money interest rates.

You can now judge whether or not the perceived value of those investments are worth a 4 percent – or $113 per month – increase in Mrs. Barker's monthly service fee.

FIGURE 12-2

COST RECOVERY/VALUE SENSITIVITY FOR CAPITAL INVESTMENT IMPROVEMENTS TO *INDIVIDUAL LIVING UNITS*

Individual Living Unit Capital Improvement	Break-Even Increase in Resident's Monthly Service Fee to Cover Incremental Increase in Debt Service on Borrowed/Invested Funds to Pay for Improvement[1]				
	6.0%	6.5%	7.0%	8.0%	9.0%
$ 3,000/unit	$25.98	$27.23	$28.50	$31.12	$33.84
5,000	43.30	45.38	47.50	51.87	56.40
7,500	64.95	68.07	71.25	77.80	84.60
10,000	86.60	90.75	95.00	103.74	112.80
15,000	129.90	136.13	142.50	155.61	169.19
20,000	173.20	181.51	189.99	207.48	225.59
25,000	216.50	226.88	237.49	259.35	281.99
30,000	259.80	272.26	284.99	311.22	338.39

[1]Indicated annual interest rate @ 25 years, 93% stabilized occupancy and a 1.25x debt service coverage ratio.

Common Area Improvements – In a similar manner, Figure 12-3 provides us with a summary of what the individual cost increases per resident's unit would be when substantial dollars are invested in *common areas* or the physical plant in general. The analysis is the same, except that, in this case, we are able to allocate or spread these new debt service costs across approximately 74 occupied assisted living units in our typical 80-unit community.

Figure 12-3 indicates that a $100,000 investment in improving the common spaces of an assisted living community will require each resident's monthly service fee to be increased by only approximately $14 per month. That's less than a 1 percent increase. The leverage of investing in common spaces is significant, because we are spreading the new debt service cost across *all* occupied units.

Don't Procrastinate

Many sponsors judge the severity of their physical plant problems by monitoring the relative degree of *existing* resident satisfaction. This approach can be dangerously misleading, because the mind-set of the existing residents in these aging facilities can represent a good news/bad news situation.

The good news is that many existing residents living in sub-par living units (by today's competitive standards) are generally quite content. Formal resident panels indicate a surprisingly high degree of existing resident satisfaction in these aging communities. While many are aware of and have visited the newer competitors, they still prefer their "home," and are either willing to accept or are not sensitive to their sub-par conditions. Some residents are even paying premium prices for their relatively low ambiance and impaired functional utility.

FIGURE 12-3

**COST RECOVERY/VALUE SENSITIVITY FOR CAPITAL
INVESTMENT IMPROVEMENTS TO
*COMMON AREA/PHYSICAL PLANT***

Typical Cost of Physical Plant Capital Improvement	Break-Even Increase in Resident's Monthly Service Fee to Cover Incremental Increase in Debt Service on Borrowed/Invested Funds to Pay for Improvement[1]				
	6.0%	6.5%	7.0%	8.0%	9.0%
$ 25,000	$2.71	$2.84	$2.97	$3.24	$3.52
50,000	5.41	5.67	5.94	6.48	7.05
75,000	8.12	8.51	8.91	9.73	10.57
100,000	10.82	11.34	11.87	12.97	14.10
125,000	13.53	14.18	14.84	16.21	17.62
150,000	16.24	17.02	17.81	19.45	21.15
175,000	18.94	19.85	20.78	22.69	24.67
200,000	21.65	22.69	23.75	25.93	28.20

[1]Indicated annual interest rate @ 25 years, 93% stabilized occupancy and a 1.25x debt service coverage ratio.

The bad news is that these positive attitudes of existing residents frequently mask the true reaction of the broader replacement market, which is the long-run lifeblood of any assisted living community. New prospects and their loved ones visiting these communities are generally much more critical in terms of their first impressions. They see an aging facility serving an older, frailer community of residents. This can represent an immediate turn-off. Sales and marketing trends indicate that new prospects tend to self-select themselves in a way that leads to an increasingly older and frailer profile of new residents who actually move into this type of community.

The professional staffs of these communities will usually start to recognize subtle changes in the viability of their community. Previously strong waiting lists start to soften resulting in a decreasing inventory of serious, qualified prospects. Stabilized occupancy begins to decline, and marketing momentum eventually stalls.

Many owner/operators and Boards of Directors may be reluctant to make relatively expensive, progressive capital improvement decisions, hoping that the downward spiral will level off to a plateau of acceptable performance. However, experience clearly indicates that such an operational, marketing and financial miracle is unlikely to occur in most of these aging communities. Capital improvement efforts should be implemented as a consolidated, proactive strategic initiative, rather than taking a fragmented, reactive band-aid approach.

Obsolete Locations

Many communities are now asking the strategic question, *"Will our current assisted living campus and community be an acceptable, appropriate and competitive option for seniors in five to ten years?"*

Some sponsors are relocating their campuses from changing, demographically obsolete and sometimes deteriorating neighborhoods to locations that will better serve their future needs. Others are studying the viability of adding an additional satellite campus to serve the expanding needs in their primary market area. This additional campus strategy can typically take two approaches: 1) a new campus including the full continuum of living arrangements or 2) a well-conceived satellite location usually specializing in one or more living arrangements or medical service delivery systems.

Financial Reserves for Future Capital Expenditures

Many sponsors ask, *"If I'm planning a new project, how many capital investment dollars should I reserve annually?"* Adequate capital replacement reserves must also be put aside for any new project. As discussed in Chapter 18, "adequate" generally means approximately $225 to $250 per unit or bed annually starting the second year of operation, or approximately 1.5 to 2.0 percent of operating revenues. Keep in mind that these factors are for new communities; older buildings could require considerably higher annual reserves. These assessments, which are usually treated as typical operating expense line items, should not be confused with your monthly maintenance department's operating budget for normal scheduled and preventive maintenance and routine minor repairs.

Win-Win Strategies

A number of specific strategies can be deployed when implementing a comprehensive improvement program for an aging community. Typically, a good place to start is with the enhancement of the overall site plan and campus landscape, with special emphasis on a strong sense of entrance to create a good first impression. Where practical, improving exterior elevations with creative treatments of roof lines and responding to deferred maintenance with new materials and colors have proven effective for many communities.

Special market niche applications should also be carefully considered during a comprehensive renovation and/or expansion effort. This would include purpose-built applications such as special Alzheimer's/dementia units, possible space for a home health agency and fresh approaches to rehabilitation and adult day care.

Retrofit by Attrition

Many communities find that, with these capital improvements, they must change their pricing and service delivery policies, but are concerned about existing resident reaction. To defer such changes indefinitely is not viable. Using a "new and improved" attrition upgrade strategy opens the gateway for reasonable changes in pricing and service delivery policies. The future viability of the community is gradually re-established. This approach involves a number of challenges. Still, it should prove very effective in the long run.

One of the most effective ways to gradually make changes on an existing campus is to have a master plan that addresses the *total concept,* but implements the necessary changes in a *phased* manner. The plan could include a unit-by-unit upgrade, or retrofit by attrition, as individual units become vacant. This approach minimizes the impact on existing residents, and even allows for a two-tiered pricing strategy as the newer, more state-of-the-art living units become available to future residents. You can even upgrade an existing resident's unit if they are willing to pay the increased monthly service fee.

It May be Time to Bite the Bullet

Must you constantly pony up for upgrades? No, but you'll probably pay an even higher price if you don't. A community with five to seven years of deferred maintenance in the five key areas noted in this chapter might have to ultimately invest at least $250,000. Economically, it may be the smart thing to do *now* – before your occupancy starts to sag.

The cost of borrowing for this $250,000 improvement would be about nine percent, totaling approximately $25,175 a year. In an 80-unit community, adjusting for vacancy and the required debt service coverage ratio, that would add about $425 per year to the cost of each occupied unit. To recover this return, you would have to increase monthly fees by about $35 per resident.

Approximately 10 to 15 percent of older communities across the United States may no longer be able to adequately serve future residents or be truly competitive in the marketplace. And the term "older, functionally obsolete community" may not necessarily mean one that has been operating for 15 to 20 years. Some five-year-old communities face serious obsolescence and deferred maintenance challenges. This is especially true in market areas that now have newer, state-of-the-art competition and only a finite number of available age and income qualified senior prospects to sustain the stabilized occupancy of all communities in the market area.

In an old TV commercial for the Fram automobile oil filter, a cagey auto mechanic stood by a smoking engine and held up a filthy oil filter as he said, ***"You can pay me now, or you can pay me later."*** Like skimping on an oil filter change, deferring needed repairs or replacements can be penny-wise and pound-foolish for senior housing sponsors. "Later" can be synonymous with "very, very expensive."

THE TOP FIVE AREAS OF
CAPITAL IMPROVEMENTS

1. Enhanced first impressions of the community:
   - Landscape
   - Signage
   - Roadways
2. Improved impressions of the building exterior:
   - Elevations
   - Roof lines
3. Rejuvenation of the interior public spaces:
   - Lounges
   - Dining room
   - Surfaces
   - Lighting fixtures
4. Back-of-the-house improvements:
   - Commercial kitchen
   - Laundry
5. Individual living unit enhancement:
   - Cabinets
   - Wall/floor coverings
   - Plumbing fixtures

Expected Outcome: Enhance value without runaway costs!

SECTION FOUR

Financial Considerations;

Capital Costs and Operating Expenses

CHAPTER 13

INITIAL CAPITAL BUDGETING
FOR A NEW COMMUNITY

Realistic Budgeting is the
Lifeblood of Successful Projects

Providing adequate capital for a new assisted living community is an obvious objective, yet one that frequently turns out to be troublesome. Many new owners and sponsors are in for a big financial wake-up call for two reasons: 1) erroneous initial capital cost projections and 2) unrealistic financial performance expectations for the future. If you want to attract favorable start-up financing and stay in business long term, you must start by taking a hard look at your basic numbers.

In order to demonstrate *sound* capital budgeting, this chapter contains specific dollar figures for a typical 80-unit project. Figures are expressed in 2003 dollars, representing national averages. Remember, industry financial guidelines are helpful, but relying solely on these *general* rules of thumb to *specifically* estimate your new assisted living project's financial performance can be dangerous. Each development is unique, with costs and overall financial performance varying from project to project and region to region. Projecting the financial performance of your new project means carefully evaluating two basic areas of cost: 1) the initial capital budget, and 2) ongoing operating expenses. This chapter deals with capital costs. Chapters 14 and 15 address ongoing operating expenses.

Top Twelve Elements of a Capital Budget

A complete, realistic capital budget includes more than just the bricks and mortar costs of your project. "Soft costs" play a critical role in the total development of your community.

A typical capital budget consists of at least twelve major cost elements shown in Figure 13-1.

The Cardinal Rule of Capital Budgeting:

Your capital budget should include all the significant expenditures necessary to bring your project to a stabilized occupancy of at least 93 percent in a reasonable time frame.

Typical Capital Costs

Figure 13-1 summarizes the top twelve elements of assisted living capital costs. A new, freestanding assisted living community typically has an all-inclusive project cost of $111,000 to $142,000 per unit. That is the total, all-in project cost divided by the number of units, stated in 2003 dollars. It includes a debt service reserve fund that may be required of not-for-profit tax-exempt bond financing.

FIGURE 13-1
SENIOR LIVING CAPITAL COST INDICES AND BENCHMARKS[1]

Element of Capital Cost	80 Units Assisted Living	150 Units Independent Living
1. Raw Land	$6,000 -$10,000 /Unit	$7,000 - $12,000 /Unit
2. Site Development	3,500 - 5,000	4,000 - 6,000
3. Hard Construction (Bricks & Mortar)	65,000 - 80,000	80,000 - 110,000
4. Furniture Fixtures & Equipment	4,000 - 5,500	4,500 - 6,000
5. Design & Engineering	3,000 - 4,000	4,000 - 5,500
6. Development Fee	3,500 - 4,000	3,500 - 6,500
7. Accrued Construction Interest	4,500 - 5,500	4,000 - 5,500
8. Working Capital/Fill-up Reserve Fund	4,000 - 5,000	5,000 - 6,500
9. Sales & Marketing	3,500 - 4,500	4,000 - 5,500
10. Debt Service Reserve Fund[2]	6,500 - 9,000	7,500 - 9,200
11. Financing/Underwriting	2,000 - 2,500	1,600 - 2,100
12. Project Contingency	5,500 - 6,500	9,400 - 21,900
Average Total (All-In) Cost Per Unit	$111,000 -$142,000	$134,500 -$197,200

Moore Diversified Services, Inc.
Moore Institute Data Base

---

[1]Indices and benchmarks reflect approximately 75% of current (2003) industry comparables; the remaining 25% can either be above or below ranges indicated herein.

[2]Typically required for tax-exempt bond financing.

To many, these per unit costs may seem relatively high – until you realistically consider *all* of the necessary hard, soft and intangible costs of bringing your project to 93 percent stabilized occupancy. Several key cost variables are often location-sensitive, such as developed land values and hard construction costs.

Land, site development and infrastructure costs can range from between $6,000 to $10,000 per unit for raw land and site development costs from $3,500 to $5,000 per unit. Land cost economics are sensitive to development density and your cost of capital (the interest rate of your long-term financing). Typical densities for senior housing facilities range from 15 to 20 units per acre for an *independent living* community to 18 to 22 units per acre for an *assisted living* facility. These densities generally include roadways, site infrastructure, building set-backs and parking. Factoring in spaces for employees, parking requirements are typically 0.75 spaces per unit, or slightly lower for assisted living.

At a 9 percent interest rate, your debt service per occupied unit per month for land and site development will be (approximately):

Raw Land	Site Development	Total Cost	Monthly Debt Service Per Unit[1]
$ 6,000/unit	$3,500/unit	$ 9,500/unit	$ 86.00
10,000	5,000	15,000	135.00

[1]Assumes 9%, 25-year mortgage for a community experiencing 93% occupancy.

Hard construction costs on a square foot basis can typically range from $90 to $115 per square foot, or approximately $65,000 to $80,000 per unit. This factors in both the resident's living area and necessary common spaces and circulation (hallways, stairwells, elevator shafts, etc.). It is important to put some of these broad categories of capital costs into proper perspective. Land and site development typically represents approximately 9 to 12 percent of the total project costs; hard construction costs 55 to 65 percent, and other soft costs 17 to 20 percent.

Design and engineering fees include your architect, civil engineer, structural engineer and other professionals necessary for the design process. Their fees are negotiable, and typically are about 5 percent of hard construction costs.

Furniture, fixtures & equipment (FF&E) usually includes all *movable* items, like dining room and public space furniture, office and other equipment, and artwork. Residents typically furnish their own living units with personal possessions. Commercial kitchen equipment is sometimes either double-counted or inadvertently omitted because it's a toss-up whether it should be in FF&E or the hard cost construction budget. One way or the other, make sure it's properly accounted for in your capital budget. On a per unit basis, overall FF&E costs typically range from $4,000 to $5,500.

Development fees are earned by those individuals who essentially make the project happen. They coordinate the process from inception to Certificate of Occupancy (COO).

These negotiable fees are typically in the range of 5 percent of hard construction costs.

Accrued construction interest is a pool of dollars that is needed to pay the interest on borrowed money during the construction period and prior to opening. Though it's easy to overlook, don't forget: You've got to pay your friendly lender even *before* your community is actually generating revenue.

Working capital/fill-up reserve funds are needed because assisted living has high fixed operating costs, leading to substantial operating losses during the fill-up period. The typical fill-up rate ranges between four to seven units per month *net.* The operative word is "net," because units turn over even in the initial stages of occupancy (see Chapter 35). An 80-unit assisted living community could have a cumulative negative cash flow (after debt service) of $4,500 to $6,000 per unit until the project reaches a break-even (cash flow) occupancy of approximately 80 to 85 percent. Break-even is defined as covering both operating expenses and debt service.

Initial sales and marketing budget covers the cost of the sales and marketing activities needed to bring your community to stabilized occupancy. This will probably add up to about $3,500 to $4,500 per unit. The budget should be supported by a detailed sales and marketing plan which includes all collaterals/brochures, program development, media costs, and sales office set-up and ongoing overhead expenses, plus base compensation and performance incentives for the sales and marketing staff.

TOP TWELVE CAPITAL BUDGET
COST ELEMENTS

1. Raw land
2. Site development
3. Hard construction ("bricks & mortar")
4. Furniture, fixtures and equipment
5. Design and engineering fees
6. Development fees
7. Interest accrued on construction debt
8. Working capital/fill-up reserve fund
9. Sales and marketing program
10. Debt service reserve fund
11. Financing and underwriting
12. Project contingency

Financing and underwriting includes the lender's financing fees and the cost of other professional services (legal, accounting, etc.) to properly formalize your borrowing plan/proposal.

Contingency funds should be provided in two areas of your capital budget:

- *Construction contingency* of at least 5 percent of the hard construction budget;

- *Overall project contingency* totaling at least 5 percent of your total, all-in (bottom line) capital budget for your project.

If there's bad news in the future, you're covered. The good news is, you may end up with surplus cash!

Debt service reserve fund is usually a requirement for not-for-profit organizations accessing tax-exempt bond financing. A typical fund requirement is to have a restricted reserve account totaling one year's maximum required debt service payments.

Remember: The basic strategy of sound assisted living capital budgeting is to identify and fund all costs associated with developing, financing, marketing and bringing your project to a stabilized occupancy of approximately 93 percent. At that point, your annual operating budget "kicks in" and funds ongoing operations expenses. This concept is depicted in Figure 13-2.

Putting it All Together

Accurately determining your total project cost is essential. Merely increasing your pricing to cover increasing costs could be a dangerous strategy. A project must not become totally cost-driven, pricing itself out of the market or offering consumers too little value for their money.

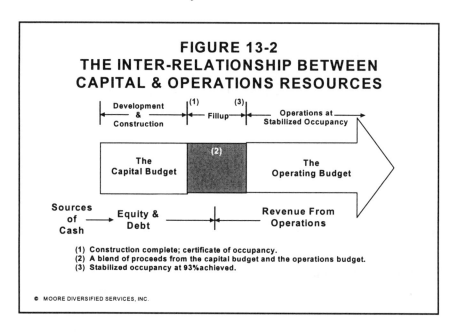

FIGURE 13-2
THE INTER-RELATIONSHIP BETWEEN
CAPITAL & OPERATIONS RESOURCES

(1) Construction complete; certificate of occupancy.
(2) A blend of proceeds from the capital budget and the operations budget.
(3) Stabilized occupancy at 93% achieved.

○ MOORE DIVERSIFIED SERVICES, INC.

In most instances, your goal should be to deliver comfortable yet affordable *Pontiacs* or *Buicks*, not extravagant *Cadillacs*. A concept called *value engineering* can help you decrease or control costs, while actually increasing consumer perceived value.

Value Engineering

Value engineering is the pragmatic reduction or control of capital costs without significantly changing the final "look" or operation of an assisted living community. The results of this effort should not negatively impact your competitive position, and should be largely invisible to the consumer marketplace. Value engineering starts with an exhaustive review of essentially every line item of capital cost. Through this process, it is not unusual to realize a reduction in total project costs of between three and seven percent. Sometimes the value engineering exercise actually *increases* costs – but only when the increase is reasonable and competitive, and there is a material and obvious value benefit to the future residents.

Value engineering of capital costs is best implemented using a two-tier process:

● *Tier 1 – Architect/Contractor Driven* – If you are still in the preliminary design phase, ask your development team what it would take to reduce overall costs by 10 percent. If your design and development process is further along, a cost reduction goal of 5 percent is probably more realistic. Your professional team may not reach your total value engineering goals but, more often than not, you'll be pleasantly surprised with the overall results.

● *Tier 2 – Owner/Sponsor Driven* – Now ask yourself, with the help of your professional design team and staff, what reasonable trade-offs are you willing to make in an effort to reduce costs. If an 80-unit project with a preliminary cost of

$9.6 million ($120,000/unit) could be value engineered by just 5 percent, the resultant savings would be $480,000. The savings impact on the reduction of individual monthly service fees would be approximately $55 per unit.

The simple calculations are as follows:

- Preliminary project cost of $9.6 million, or $120,000 per unit

- A five percent cost savings realized through the value engineering exercise, or $480,000

- Multiplying the $480,000 savings by a 10.1 percent *loan constant* results in a reduction in annual debt service of $48,480: $655 per *occupied* unit, or approximately $55 per unit per month.[1] Remember, debt service can only be paid by revenues from *occupied* units.

This may not seem like much, until you consider the possibility of investing some or all of that savings in other areas having a much higher impact on value. I call that "flash value." See Chapter 18 for details on this beneficial concept. You might also consider lowering the monthly service fee to be slightly more affordable and competitive.

---

[1]*Loan constant* – A convenient analysis factor which provides a single arithmetic factor for computing the combination of a specific interest (9%), and loan term (25 years). See Appendix B for additional loan constant details.

CHAPTER 14

ESTABLISHING REALISTIC OPERATING EXPENSE BUDGETS

Properly Evaluating All Costs is Critical When Projecting Expenses

In planning assisted living projects, sponsors and operators often underestimate resident acuity and the resulting turnover rates. They end up understating operating expenses, which causes them to set their prices too low. As a result, their projects suffer from unacceptable operating profit margins and inadequate cash flow. Eventually, residents receive an unpleasant surprise as monthly service fees reflect hefty, but necessary, increases. These problems can be avoided if the owner or sponsor starts with a realistic estimate of operating expenses.

Two Key Expense Ratios

Two important ratios can provide guidance when estimating and evaluating assisted living operating expenses. These ratios define the "envelope" of acceptable assisted living operations.

• *Operating Expense Ratio* – This ratio represents total *cash* operating expenses divided by net revenues. For a typical assisted living project, this ratio should range between 58 and 65 percent.

The inverse of the operating expense ratio is the **operating margin.** This is commonly referred to as either NOI, for net operating income, or EBITDA, earnings before interest, taxes, depreciation, and amortization. This operating margin typically ranges between 35 and 37 percent. And EBITDA, cash flow per share, and earnings per share have become the critical industry bottom line performance benchmarks for publicly traded assisted living companies.

● *Operating Expenses Per Resident-day* – You should also evaluate financials in terms of *dollars per resident day.* It's the most useful common denominator. Operating expenses per resident day in assisted living is defined as total annual operating expenses (or expenses by each major department) divided by the number of residents times 365 days. Resident-day expense ratios can provide an excellent, detailed evaluation of each line item of expense – especially when compared with reliable industry benchmarks.

Total operating expenses per resident-day should typically range from $50 to $55 in most market areas. These costs include basic shelter services and a *realistic* menu of direct, hands-on assistance with the Activities of Daily Living (ADLs). The rather broad range of this index reflects significant variables that can exist from project to project, market to market. These variables typically include labor costs, real estate taxes, utilities, supplies, etc.

Operating Expense Checks and Balances

As a helpful indicator, consider that the *operating expense ratio* shows the relationship between revenues and expenses, while the *expenses per resident-day index* is based <u>solely</u> on operating expenses. If your operating expense ratio appears high or out of line with industry guidelines (58 to 65 percent), the expenses per resident-day index can direct you to the source of your problem. There are two possibilities: Either your revenues are too low, or your expenses are too high. For example, if your operating expense ratio is 75 percent (high), but your operating expenses are $50 per resident-day (about normal), it is likely that your revenues are suppressed.

Estimating Operating Costs – An Overview

With assisted living acuity levels and resident turnover higher than many expected, most experienced operators consider themselves successful if they can hold direct and indirect operating expenses between $1,500 and $1,675 per unit per month. This translates into operating expenses of about $50 to $55 per resident-day. When sponsors conduct a detailed operating cost *sensitivity analysis,* they will discover another challenge – most assisted living operating costs are largely fixed when the doors open, and do not vary significantly as a function of occupancies between 80 and 93 percent. But there will be a huge swing in operating profit margins. That's because these margins vary as a direct function of revenues collected. This leads to what I call the "75/25 rule" for operating expenses.

The 75/25 Rule for Operating Expenses

Approximately 75 percent of your assisted living operating costs are fixed or only semi-variable, while just 25 percent are truly variable (raw food, etc.). There is very little variance in the total operating cost of an 80-unit community that has 60 units occupied (75 percent) vs. 74 units occupied (93 percent). But because revenues *are* directly variable, the lower occupancy could result in a significant cash flow reduction of over $175,000 annually.

"It's the Labor Costs That Are Killing Us"

Chapter 16 addresses assisted living staffing in detail. Overall labor costs represent at least 60 percent of total assisted living operating expenses. Typically, a community will have approximately .45 to .50 Full-Time Equivalent (FTEs) employees for every resident. An 80-unit community (at 93 percent occupancy) with approximately 36 FTEs in a market with average labor costs will have an annual direct labor payroll of approximately $720,000. Add up to 30 percent for fringe benefits (vacations, holidays, sick leave and insurance premiums) and payroll taxes, and the annual gross payroll is now about $936,000; or an average of $26,000 per employee. That's about $34.50 per resident-day, or 63 percent of the total costs for a community whose overall operating costs are $55.00 per resident-day.

Some Special Operating Expense Considerations

Operating expenses that may require special considerations include management fees, reserve for replacement and annual expense escalation.

Management fees – An important factor in assisted living. Typically, the management fee collected is approximately five percent of net revenues, but can range between four and eight percent. The management fee provides for the overall management and oversight of the community, but does not include many direct costs. Management fees are covered in detail in Chapter 36. As indicated in Chapter 21 on financing, your lender will probably want to see a 5 percent management fee included as a normal expense line item. Why? Because, as distasteful and unlikely as it may seem, your banker must always consider a foreclosure scenario where it is necessary to bring in third party asset management.

Reserve for replacement – Depreciation (as a non-cash expense) is usually not included in a typical operating statement. That's because the income statement is generally prepared and evaluated on a *cash basis,* less depreciation, amortization, interest and tax payments. However, a cash reserve for replacement fund must usually be created (as contrasted to technically *funding* depreciation) by assessing a specific dollar amount per unit each year. For a new project, a replacement reserve is created by directly expensing approximately $225 to $250 per unit per year. These funds are accumulated in a special reserve account, and are used for future capital investment or replacement needs. This allocation is in *addition* to the normal operations and maintenance department budget, which funds routine and scheduled maintenance of the community. This concept is commonly called the "Cap X" factor, an easy-to-remember abbreviation for *capital expenditures.*

Annual Expense Escalation – Assisted living financial pro formas typically assume an escalation of both revenue and expenses at approximately four percent per year. The actual inflation rate in the senior housing industry over the past ten years has been approximately 3.5 to 4 percent annually. That is essentially the same rate at which owner/operators have increased monthly service fees to their residents. Frequently, a positive one-point spread is used between *revenue increases* (five percent) and actual *expense inflation* (four percent). If successfully implemented, your out-year profits will grow at an even faster pace.

Putting it All Together – A Snapshot

Figure 14-1 depicts a summary of a typical *operating expense budget* in terms of both total dollars and per resident-day ratios. The operative word is "summary," because behind this one page of numbers might be 50 pro forma computer spreadsheets and voluminous work papers. Figure 17-1 in Chapter 17 shifts this operating expense budget into an overall *income statement;* showing how all the financial ratios and operating profit margins combine for a financially viable community.

FIGURE 14-1
80-UNIT ASSISTED LIVING COMMUNITY
OPERATING EXPENSE BENCHMARKS

Major Dept./ Cost Center	Annual Operating Expense Budget	Range of Expenses Per Resident-Day[1]	
1. Administration	$ 159,360	$ 5.45 to	6.35
2. Activities	47,540	1.70	1.85
3. Assisted Living (ADLs)	303,055	9.20	11.50
4. Plant Maintenance/ Security	124,515	4.05	5.20
5. Food/Dietary	338,435	10.70	14.40
6. Hsekping & Laundry	65,365	2.10	2.75
7. Transportation	24,850	.85	1.00
8. Property	155,575	4.60	6.90
9. Marketing & Sales	116,680	4.05	4.60
10. Management Fees	124,515	4.05	5.20
11. Reserve for Replacement	25,660	.85	1.05
TOTALS	$ 1,485,550	$ 47.60 to	60.80

CAUTIONS:
1. Each community and market area will have a unique operating expense profile.
2. Accounting systems and chart of account formats vary and could impact these benchmarks.

_____

[1]As an example, resident-days for an 80-unit assisted living community would be 80 x 365 days or 29,200 resident-days at 100% occupancy and 27,155 resident-days for 93% occupancy.

Moore Diversified Services, Inc.

<u>Caution</u>: **Don't force your operating expense budget into my sample numbers in Figure 14-1! Each community and market area will have a unique operating expense profile. In addition, accounting systems and chart of account formats vary and could impact these benchmarks.**

The Classic Financial Break-Even Model

Before you speculate on future returns, it is wise to completely evaluate the agony and the ecstasy of project *lift-off.* I've devoted all of Chapter 35 to this sobering perspective! Like our space program, the most critical phase of your mission is launching and initially manning your project – *without* any catastrophic events!

Figure 14-2 depicts the classic break-even chart applied to assisted living. You may have studied the concept in college, but this is how a pragmatic, practical application works in real life.

The break-even chart graphically depicts the following important points:

1. *Total fixed costs* – Certain operating expenses and debt service that represent fixed costs facing you every day after opening for business.

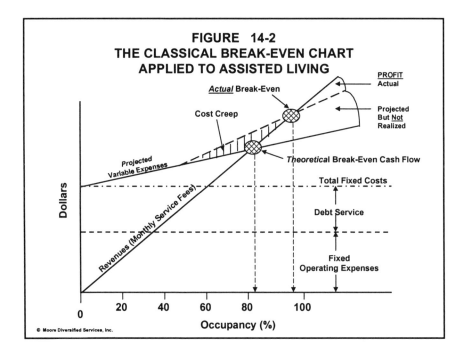

FIGURE 14-2
THE CLASSICAL BREAK-EVEN CHART
APPLIED TO ASSISTED LIVING

2. *Variable costs* – Expenses that "ride" on top of fixed costs to establish your total dollar outlay at various levels of occupancy.

3. *Revenues* – Gradually increase as a function of increasing occupancy (as do variable expenses).

4. *The break-even point* – The magic milestone (and moving target) that occurs when revenues equal the <u>sum</u> of both fixed and variable costs. This is the point where you make the happy transition from *loss* (<u>negative</u> cash flow) to *profit* (<u>positive</u> cash flow).

5. *Cost creep* – The culprit that *shifts* the actual break-even point, extending losses and requiring higher occupancy before you experience profits and positive cash flow. Some troubled communities *chase* this illusive break-even point – but never even come close to catching it!

Note: Cost creep is an <u>integral part</u> of your operating expense dynamics. It's covered in detail in Chapter 15.

The break-even concept is <u>not</u> just a dry academic theory. It is the essence of your assisted living financial dynamics!

An Expense Savings of $2.20 per Resident-Day Could Be Worth $569,000!

This is a pretty provocative statement, but it's true. Consider the following:

- An operating expense savings of $2.20 per resident-day represents a decrease of approximately four percent on total expenses of $55 per resident-day.

- Multiplying this savings by 27,155 resident-days (for an 80-unit community) equals reduction in expenses of $59,740 per year, and a corresponding increase in net operating income.

- The increased net operating income of $59,740 would be capitalized at 10.5 to 11.0 percent by an appraiser or potential buyer (see Appendix C). This results in an increase of $543,000 to $569,000 in the imputed value of your community.

● Alternatively, the typical monthly service fee for *each* resident could be reduced by about $65.

This example is a modern-day equivalent of Ben Franklin's old adage, *"A penny saved is a penny earned."* In the case of assisted living, *"A dollar saved annually is worth about $10 in imputed value."* It's obvious that the potential payoff is well worth the cost reduction effort.

Seven Ways to Keep Costs Under Control

How are astute operators keeping costs in check? There's no surefire solution, but here are seven strategies that have proven effective:

1. *Reduce both initial capital costs and ongoing operating expenses.* For example, a $5,000 per unit capital cost reduction will lower a resident's monthly service fee by about $40. This would represent about a 5 percent value engineering cost reduction on a community with an average total, all-in capital cost of $100,000 per unit. As mentioned earlier, a 4 percent, or $2.20 per resident-day, operating expense reduction could reduce monthly fees as much as $65.

2. *Build a project big enough to optimize operational efficiencies.* That allows you to *spread* your fixed and semi-variable costs across more revenue-producing units. But take care not to build more units than your marketplace can absorb. This involves a classic trade-off analysis between optimum operational efficiencies and excessive marketplace risk. The optimum size range in most markets is approximately 80 to 100 units.

3. *Where possible, avoid direct cost growth.* This involves cross-training your staff in key areas of assistance in daily living activities, food service, and housekeeping. This may lower the number of total employees needed. Reducing payroll by just three FTEs can lower labor costs by approximately $78,000 annually. Or this could reduce a resident's monthly service fee by about $85 per unit per month in an 80-unit community.

The $78,000 savings would also increase net operating income by the same amount which, when capitalized at 10.5 percent, would increase your project's imputed value by over $740,000.

4. *Make capital expenditure decisions that will stand the test of time.* "Low-balling" one-time capital costs in the wrong areas can raise operating expenses for the life of the project. This decision involves classic capital investment versus payback period analysis (see Chapter 18).

5. ***Make sure the project stands alone financially and is self-supportive.*** Then, and only then, factor in supplementary, non-operating income from private subsidies, charitable donations and other mission initiatives. Many not-for-profit board members assume their charitable mission of the past can automatically be projected into the future with their new assisted living community. Remember, assisted living is primarily a private-pay business with *very* limited reimbursement or entitlements at this time.

6. ***Consider a multi-tier pricing strategy.*** Charging a base rate for services needed by most residents, coupled with variable or tiered fees for everything else, allows each resident to pay for only as much actual assistance as he or she requires (covered in Chapters 15 and 23).

7. ***Develop a comprehensive, but flexible, initial financial pro forma.*** Make sure that your pro forma can quickly execute a sensitivity analysis and answer a number of "what if" questions: What if your actual expenses are two dollars higher than expected per resident-day? What if occupancy is three percent lower than the hoped-for stabilized rate of 93 percent? What if the project fills up more slowly than expected?

Begin your operating expense planning with a realistic estimation of the costs you are likely to encounter, and don't ever stop looking for ways to operate more efficiently. Facing the need for moderately increasing monthly service fees now may not be pleasant, but it's far better than procrastinating on inevitable decisions – resulting in steep increases to existing residents to adjust for early estimating errors or inevitable cost creep.

CHAPTER 15

ASSISTED LIVING COST CREEP
IS A FATAL BUSINESS DISEASE

Many Owner/Operators and Sponsors Are Experiencing a $1 Million-Plus Wake-Up Call

Keeping monthly fees reasonably affordable for seniors is a crucial part of survival, success and profitability for assisted living providers. But equally crucial is the other end of that economic balancing act, ensuring that increasing resident acuity and the resulting creeping costs do not infiltrate your profit margin, leaving your bottom line depressed and possibly bleeding red ink.

We now know that assisted living costs constantly shift. Containing these costs at acceptable levels has become one of the most significant challenges of the industry. It is generally recognized that initial fill-up and turnover rates are difficult to predict. Obviously, the typical assisted living resident suffers from chronic conditions that gradually – but predictably – deteriorate with time. This can result in significant cost creep and profit margin erosion *if* higher levels of care are provided *without* corresponding increases in pricing. In order to compensate for 35 to 40 percent annual resident turnover, many sponsors have modified their admission and discharge policies in an attempt to extend the average length of stay. Dealing with incontinence and dementia have become accepted operating policies for most sponsors.

Both public companies and private assisted living sponsors and operators are chasing the elusive optimum operating profit margin of 40 percent. Identified as Earnings Before Interest, Taxes, Depreciation and Amortization (EBITDA) by public companies, this critical ratio is defined as net operating income divided by net revenues.

The Real World of Cost Creep

The following scenario is being played out hundreds of times *daily* in assisted living communities all across the U.S.:

Resident aide or Housekeeper: *"Let me give you some additional help today, Mrs. Jones."*

Mrs. Jones: *"Oh, thank you – I just love living here at The Gardens of Westridge."*

Resident aide or Housekeeper: *"No problem, Mrs. Jones, I'm sure you'll feel better tomorrow."*

There are two big problems with this scenario:

1. Mrs. Jones *may* feel a little better tomorrow – but she has a chronic condition with gradually declining health that will require increasing assistance with the activities of daily living (ADLs). This will also increase the average direct care minutes (and cost) per 24-hour day for Mrs. Jones.

2. There are many residents like Mrs. Jones' in almost every assisted living community.

Consider this:

21st Century sound bite . . .
. . . RN to owner-operator
"80% of my total CNA time
is consumed by 20% of our residents!"

Cost creep is the most serious chronic business disease afflicting both for-profit and not-for-profit assisted living operators. But proper analysis, pragmatic cost accounting and sound pricing policies can be the miracle drugs that prevent a catastrophic epidemic.

Calculating the Financial Impacts of Cost Creep

Many new assisted living communities market themselves as offering a fixed monthly service fee of approximately $2,400 to $2,700. This pricing may appear feasible in some markets when you consider that *baseline* operating expenses are approximately $55 per resident-day, or $1,675 per month. But then there is debt service payments on a newly developed unit with an all-in cost of approximately $120,000. With 75 percent leverage, or $90,000 in debt at a 9 percent interest rate, debt payments will generally average about $965 per unit per month when assuming 93 percent stabilized occupancy and a debt service coverage factor of 1.3x. See Figure 17-1 in Chapter 17. These conservative estimates bring the total cost to be recovered involving a base rate of approximately $2,640 per resident per month plus miscellaneous revenues.

Let's now take a look at the arithmetic of cost creep. Figure 15-1 lays out this arithmetic in a simplified financial template format. You can use your own input assumptions to fit your specific community and market. Here are the assumptions that I've used for this realistic cost creep model:

- **Base Rate for CNA/Resident Aide** – The average hourly rate around the United States is approximately $8.50 per hour; you can insert your own prevailing wage rate for these type of workers.

FIGURE 15-1
COST CREEP ARITHMETIC

Input Assumptions:	
Base CNA/Resident-Aide Hrly $:	$8.50
Fringe Benefits @	25.0%
Indirect Time @	20.0%
Overhead Allocation:	15.0%
Desired Profit/EBITDA Margin:	40.0%

I. **Direct Care Cost:**
   * Base Salary CNA/Resident-Aide $ 8.50 /hr
   * Fringe Benefits @ 25.0% $ 2.13
           Subtotal - Direct Costs   **$10.63/hr**

II. **Other Cost Allocations:**
   * Indirect Time @ 20.0% $ 1.70
   * Overhead @ 15.0% $ 1.27
           TOTAL COST   **$13.60/hr**

   Profit / EBITDA Margin @ 40.0%[1] $ 9.07

Target Cost Recovery Per Hour	**$22.67/hr**

Or

MDS Database indicates that direct care averages 30 to 45 minutes per resident per 24-hour day →

$7.56	**$11.33**	**$17.00**
for a	*for a*	*for a*
20	**30**	**45**
minute segment	*minute segment*	*minute segment*
↓	↓	↓

Requires Additional Price Tier of:		
$230/mo	**$345/mo**	**$517/mo**
or	**or**	**or**
$2,758/yr	**$4,137/yr**	**$6,205/yr**

[1] Optional - depending upon individual operating strategies.

© **Moore Diversified Services, Inc.**

- **Fringe Benefits** – This includes your share of payroll taxes, health care benefits and other direct fringe benefit costs. This typically ranges between 20 to 30 percent of direct payroll costs.

- **Indirect Time** – Workers need coffee breaks and lunch breaks. This means that direct care personnel are unavailable to serve residents approximately 20 percent of the time in a typical 8-hour day. Because the residents' needs are frequently *very* time sensitive, this indirect (lost) time must usually be completely covered by someone else, and therefore must be factored into a pragmatic cost creep model.

- **Overhead Allocation** – Regardless of whether you're selling widgets or staff time by the hour, you should allocate a portion of your existing overhead to each element of additional "product" that you're selling.

- **Desired Profit/EBITDA Margin** – This can be a controversial issue, especially for not-for-profit organizations. I feel very strongly that each element of the "product" you offer should be assigned a target profit margin. The hard-to-reach profit margin goal for assisted living is approximately 40 percent.

Assuming that you have either accepted my input assumptions or inserted your own, we can now proceed with the cost creep arithmetic. In my example, the direct care cost is $10.63 per hour. When the cost allocations discussed above are added, this increases to almost $14.00 per hour. Assuming that you add a profit margin of 40 percent, the total *loaded* cost for a typical CNA or resident aide grows rapidly to almost $23.00 per hour!

Now, let's assume that one of your residents requires direct care over and above the industry average of 30 to 45 minutes per resident for a 24-hour day. This additional 30-minute segment (half an hour) results in an additional cost incurred by that resident of approximately $11.33 per hour, $345 per month, or $4,137 per year.

What you must decide is how many minutes of direct care per resident per 24-hour day is included in your *base monthly service fee*. The industry norm is approximately 45 minutes per resident per 24-hour day. Then, you must develop reasonably accurate measuring systems to determine which residents are consistently receiving higher levels of care each day. As Figure 15 -1 clearly demonstrates, the additional cost can range from approximately $2,800 per year to over $6,000 per year. Note that this is real cash; money that must either come out of your pocket *or* be fairly and equitably passed on to the resident and/or their families.

Why Cost Creep Can Easily Become a $1 Million Problem!

Figure 15-2 continues the analysis that was summarized in Figure 15-1. Note that the cost creep impact for an individual resident is now extended to approximately 30 percent of the total residents in a typical 80-unit assisted living community operating at 93 percent occupancy.

So if, eventually, 25 of your residents of your 80-unit community operating at 93 percent occupancy receive an average of 30 extra minutes per day of *uncompensated care,* the results will be financially devastating:

- *Total net income shortfall and lost cash flow* from those 25 units is $103,386 (Figure 15-2).

- *A decrease in the imputed economic value of your community.* While one can easily understand the lost cash flow monthly or annually in *operations,* it is sometimes difficult to realize this could only be the tip of the iceberg. When you look at an exit strategy (Chapter 38 tells you why *everyone* should have an exit strategy), you will note that a buyer or appraiser capitalizing the lost cash flow at a 10.5 percent capitalization rate used to determine value as discussed in Appendix C, results in losses in the economic value of your community ranging from approximately $650,000 to almost $1.5 million! This is certainly significant if you ever intend to sell your property, but it can also have a serious impact if you choose to refinance at approximately 75 percent of the *appraised value* of your community.

FIGURE 15-2
WHY COST CREEP CAN EASILY
BECOME A $1 MILLION PROBLEM!

Target Cost Recovery Per Hour		$22.67/hr	

Or

I. Per Resident	*$7.58*	*$11.33*	*$17.00*
Impact	*for a*	*for a*	*for a*
(Direct care in excess	*20*	*30*	*45*
of 45 minutes per resident/	*minute*	*minute*	*minute*
24 hour day)	*segment*	*segment*	*segment*

Requires Additional Price Tier of:		
$230/mo	*$345/mo*	*$517/mo*
or	*or*	*or*
$2,758/yr	*$4,137/yr*	*$6,205/yr*

II. Impact If Cost Creep Grows to 25 Residents:

25 Residents times =	$2,758/yr	*$4,137/yr*	$6,205/yr
Equals Lost Annual Cash Flow and	$68,955	*$103,386*	$155,125
Reduces Community Value (Impact @ 10.5% Cap Rate):	$656,710	*$984,631*	$1,477,381

Reduction in Value

As Figure 15-2 indicates, these loss figures continue to escalate rapidly as resident's direct care concentration increases.

Chapter 16 addresses staffing ratios. This includes pragmatic approaches for estimating the required staffing for a typical assisted living community for a *baseline level* of care for residents. Also included are computations for estimating increased direct care staff resulting from acuity creep that leads to cost creep. For example as Figure 16-4 indicates, the 25 residents receiving an additional 30 minutes of direct care per 24-hour day create the need for three additional direct care FTEs – the essence of the cost creep.

Cost Creep Financial Sensitivity for a Typical Project

Figure 15-3 depicts the significant financial sensitivity for a typical project experiencing cost creep. The input assumptions are typical for today's state-of-the-art assisted living community. Note that the cost creep input variables in this financial template reflect those conditions previously discussed in this chapter – using the basic financial model used in Chapter 17 which addresses the income statement. Figure 15-3 compares a baseline condition with the cost creep scenario:

1. **Debt Service** – Becomes unacceptable as it drops below 1.30x.

2. **Operating Profit/EBITDA** – Drops dramatically from 38.2 to 33.9 percent.

3. **Cash-on-Cash Return on Invested Equity** – Drops from over 9 percent to 5 percent.

4. **Imputed Market Value at 10.5 percent Cap Rate** – A reduction of approximately $1.0 million!

5. **Internal Rate of Return (IRR)**[1] - Significant drop; would no longer meet typical lender/investor criteria.

Using the templates in Figures 15-1, 15-2 and 15-3 as a guideline, you can run your own numbers.   But if you're experiencing conditions at all similar to the examples in this chapter, your bottom line expected (or unexpected?) outcomes could be almost the same.

So far, we've isolated key, complex issues so that they can be addressed individually. However, there are two other chapters that *must* become an integral part of your cost creep considerations; Staffing Patterns (Chapter 16) and Tiered Pricing Strategies (Chapter 23). All three of these chapters must be evaluated simultaneously in order to develop seamless, appropriate strategies. Clearly the appropriate strategic response and prescription for the cost creep business disease is accurate staff and cost projections and cost recovery through tiered pricing.

---

[1]IRR is a measure of a project's annual financial return giving consideration to the time value of money.

FIGURE 15-3
COST CREEP SENSITIVITY FOR A
TYPICAL ASSISTED LIVING PROJECT

Input Assumptions

Number of Units:	80	Total Cost:	$9,600,000
Assumed Occupancy:	93.0%	Equity @ 25% =	$2,400,000
Cost Per Unit:	$120,000	Debt @ 75% =	$7,200,000
Base Monthly Service Fee:	$2,640	Loan Interest Rate:	9.0%
Operating Expenses PRD:	$55.00	Amortization (Yrs):	30
Baseline Direct Care Level:	45 minutes per resident day/24 hour day		
Net Annual Resident Days:		27,156	

Additional Cost Creep

Average # of residents requiring additional care:	25 residents
Average additional care time/resident (minutes/day):	30 minutes/day
Estimated cost/additional 30 minute interval:	$11.33 /resident/day

	With-out Cost Creep	With Cost Creep
INCOME STATEMENT:		
Gross Annual Income	$2,534,400/yr	$2,534,400/yr
Vacancy Factor @ 7.00%	(177,408)	(177,408)
Net Rental Revenues	$2,356,992	$2,356,992
Other Revenues	$ 46,886	$ 46,886
Net Revenues	$2,403,878	$2,403,878
Operating Expenses	(1,485,550)	(1,485,550)
Additional Care (Cost Creep)	0	*(103,386)*
NET OPERATING INCOME	$918,328/yr	$814,942/yr
Debt Service	(695,520)	(695,520)
CASH FLOW	$222,808/yr	$119,422/yr
PER UNIT SUMMARY:		
Operating Expenses	*$18,569/unit*	*$18,569/unit*
Net Operating Income	*$11,479/unit*	*$10,186/unit*
Cash Flow	*$2,785/unit*	*$1,493/unit*

KEY FINANCIAL RATIOS		
Debt Service Coverage (DSCR):	1.32	1.17
EBITDA	38.2%	33.9%
Operating Expense Ratio:	61.8%	66.1%
Cash-on-Cash Return on Equity:	9.3%	5.0%
Imputed Market Value @ 10.5%	$8,745,981	$7,760,400

© Moore Diversified Services, Inc.

CHAPTER 16

STAFFING PATTERNS

To Realistically Control Labor Costs,
Focus on Direct Care Staffing

Assisted living operators frequently ask me, *"How do I know if my labor costs are really in line?"* Good question, deserving a detailed answer. Most sponsors and owner/operators have quickly realized that in order to remain financially viable, they must have a *thorough* understanding of the true costs of operating their assisted living communities; with *special focus* on direct labor costs. Assisted living is *very* labor-intensive, and this is the most critical operational issue for both for-profit owner/operators and not-for-profit sponsors in the new millennium.

Consider this: Staffing represents 65 to 70 percent of operating expenses for most assisted living communities. For a community with typical operating expenses of $55 per resident-day, staffing adds up to about $35 per resident-day. Approximately 70 percent of a community's full-time equivalent employees (FTEs) are paid at the lower end of the wage scale, from $7.00 to $10.00 per hour. There isn't much room for a downward adjustment in hourly rates. Yet the overall average cost per employee for *all* positions – loaded for payroll taxes and fringe benefits at 22 to 25 percent – is approximately $26,000 a year, or $11.50 per hour.

Many factors push labor costs upward. The need to provide increased assistance with the activities of daily living can result in operating cost creep. See Chapter 15 for details. Periods of low unemployment, resulting in tight labor markets, also make it hard to keep labor costs down. Meanwhile, labor unions are eyeing senior housing and long-term care as one of their few remaining possibilities for membership growth. Increases in the minimum wage certainly impact operating costs, and employee turnover among direct care workers has become an enormous problem.

Effectively controlling costs and responding to these labor challenges requires a detailed understanding of your staffing patterns. Now, more than ever, you should initially focus on three key departments that have the most impact on your operating costs. Your three most costly and labor-intensive departments are: 1) dietary, with typical operating expenses of approximately $10.70 to $14.40 per resident day; 2) direct resident care, at $9.20 to $11.50 a day; and 3) administration, at $5.45 to $6.35 a day. Except for direct care and dietary, you can expect your core staff positions (typically administration, security, activities, marketing, maintenance and transportation) to remain relatively stable in number with moderate employee turnover rates.

The Challenge of Direct Care Staffing

Direct resident care staffing represents perhaps the greatest operations challenge in the assisted living industry. Direct care involves those staff members who provide hands-on assistance with the resident's daily living activities. Resident assistants and certified nurses' aides are frequently paid salaries equivalent to the fast food industry or other entry-level job sectors. But their responsibilities in assisted living care are frequently more demanding, often stressful, and, therefore, less desirable, notwithstanding how much compassion they may feel for the seniors in their care. In a nutshell, you are dealing with potential for high turnover among these employees, who spend most of their time one-on-one with the residents. Yet to the residents and their families, these employees – for the most part – are considered the most trusted, beloved staff members.

Direct Care Staffing Patterns

Direct resident care staffing patterns vary with each community. However, there are some helpful guidelines that can be used for general planning and benchmarking purposes. These are summarized in Figure 16-1. For an 80-unit community, a typical direct care aide-to-resident ratio might be one aide for every 17 residents (1:17) on first shift, 1:20 for second shift and 1:40 for third shift.

Special care Alzheimer's/dementia units require more intense staffing ratios, typically 1:7 for first shift, 1:9 for second and 1:15 for third. Note, again, that these staffing ratios can vary by community, resident profile, relative acuity level and state and local regulations. Using these general staffing patterns while serving residents in an 80-unit community at 93 percent occupancy would require about 12 total direct care FTEs.

FIGURE 16-1
TYPICAL ASSISTED LIVING
DIRECT CARE STAFFING RATIOS

	Direct Care Work Shift			Total *Baseline* Direct Care FTEs
	First	Second	Third	
				80-Unit AL^2
• Assisted Living	1:17 -^{1}	1:20 -	1:40 -	13.9 -
	1:20	1:25	1:50	11.5
				24-Unit ALZ^2
• Special Care	1:7 -	1:9 -	1:15 -	10.8 -
Alzheimer's/	1:9	1:11	1:20	8.6
Dementia				

Caution:
Staffing patterns must be customized for each community's unique situation, resident profile and specific acuity/ADL levels.

Basic Assumptions:
1. Industry average of 45 minutes of direct care per resident in 24-hour period. Does not include increases necessary for acuity creep.
2. Direct care staff productivity @ 80%
   - Breaks   • Meal Time   • Vacations   • Etc.

See Chapter 15 for more details on these assumptions.

^{1}1:17 = one FTE for every 17 residents to provide ADL assistance
^{2}93% occupancy; 7-day week

Moore Diversified Services, Inc.

This level of staffing would provide an average of 45 minutes of basic "hands-on" direct care or assistance per resident in a 24-hour period. But many communities are realizing the need to provide at least an *additional* 20 minutes of direct care for a number of their frailer residents. This increased ADL care intensity translates to increased direct care FTEs and an additional operating cost of approximately $250 to $350 per resident/month. This is demonstrated in Chapter 15.

To control labor costs, concentrate on your direct care staff. Bearing in mind that staffing patterns must be customized to fit a community's unique situation and resident profile, you'll probably need about .45 to .50 *total* FTEs for every occupied unit. That works out to approximately 40 FTEs for an 80-unit assisted living community operating at 93 percent occupancy. Approximately 12 to 13 of these 40 FTEs are direct care workers. Special care units for residents with Alzheimer's and related dementia require even more direct care time per resident (see Figure 16-1).

The Universal Worker Concept

A popular assisted living staffing concept, the "universal worker," was developed several years ago. In theory, the universal worker concept breaks down the barriers and inefficiencies of "departmentalization" within a community, theoretically resulting in fewer FTEs required for direct care, housekeeping, and meal service. Lower level employees would be cross-trained to assist residents with the activities of daily living, do housekeeping chores in both the resident units and common areas, and also provide assistance with meal service and various other resident activities. Advocates of the universal worker anticipated increased employee job satisfaction and enhanced morale. The resident would benefit by interfacing in a seamless manner with primarily one staff person per shift rather than several. Expected results included increased resident bonding and less confusion, two critical factors in resident satisfaction.

Well, some indirect and intangible benefits have been realized, but the jury is still out on the true operational efficiency of the universal worker. Hard evidence of actual staff reductions and tangible cost savings is scarce. Cross-training employees at or near the entry level for multiple tasks has presented some challenges. One innovative owner/operator is offering small hourly incremental pay increases as employees gain additional skills.

The "Arithmetic" of Direct Care Staffing Ratios

I have frequently been asked about the "magic" of computing assisted living direct care staffing ratios. It's not *magic,* just simple *arithmetic.* Figure 16-2 summarizes the approach.

```
┌─────────────────────────────────────────────────────────────┐
│                         FIGURE 16-2                           │
│                                                               │
│                       THE "ARITHMETIC"                        │
│                  OF DIRECT CARE STAFF RATIOS                   │
│                                                               │
│  1.  Demand - For Direct Care                                 │
│                                                               │
│        ●  80 units @ 93% occupancy:  75 residents             │
│                                                               │
│        ●  75 residents @ 45 minutes/24 hour day x 7 days =    │
│           23,625 minutes/week                                 │
│                                                               │
│  2.  Supply - Staff Loading                                   │
│                                                               │
│        ●  Direct care staff @ 8 hours/day x 5 days x 60       │
│           minutes/hour x 80% efficiency = 1,920 minutes/      │
│           productive work week                                │
│                                                               │
│  3.  Total Care Demand  = 23,625 minutes/week = 12.3 FTEs     │
│      Supply (1.0 FTE)         1,920  minutes/week             │
│                                                        ▼       │
│                                                               │
│                                               For 3 shift,    │
│                                               7 day week      │
│                                                               │
│  Moore Diversified Services, Inc.                             │
└─────────────────────────────────────────────────────────────┘
```

It is basically a three-step process:

1. Compute the <u>demand</u> for direct care using a baseline assumption of approximately 45 minutes of direct care per resident per 24-hour day.

2. Compute the <u>supply</u> in terms of the net productivity of one direct care staff member using a normal 40-hour week, factoring in employee downtime for meals, other work breaks, vacations, etc.

3. Now, simply compare the demand versus supply to compute the total number of required FTEs.

The example shown in Figure 16-2 is for an 80-unit community operating at 93 percent occupancy, with residents receiving an average level of direct care of 45 minutes per 24-hour day. Considering the relative productivity of a typical direct care worker, an 80-unit community would require slightly more than 12 FTEs to cover a three-shift, seven-day week. Note that this compares quite consistently with the direct care staffing ratios that were presented earlier in Figure 16-1.

Figure 16-3 shows a staffing snapshot for an 80-unit assisted living community. Note that the FTE per resident staffing ratio (for every occupied unit) is approximately .50, as indicated earlier in this chapter. The loaded cost per employee is approximately $26,000. This is a composite cost which includes the best-compensated individual (the Executive Director) down to the entry-level workers (meal service workers, housekeepers, direct care aides, etc.).

FIGURE 16-3

STAFFING SNAPSHOT FOR AN 80-UNIT COMMUNITY[1]

Staffing

Total Staff Positions:	**32**
Total Full Time Equivalents (FTEs):[2]	**40**
FTE/Resident Ratio: 0.50	
Average Base Hourly Rate/FTE:	**$10.10**
Average Annual Salary Cost/FTE:	**$21,000**
Taxes/Benefits Factor: 25.0%	
Average Annual Benefits Cost/FTE:	**$5,250**
Total Annual Cost/FTE:	**$26,250**

_____

[1]All employees – not just direct care
[2]Includes weekend impact – beyond 40 hours/employee

Moore Diversified Services, Inc.

Financial Optimization Vs. Quality of Care Trade-Offs

In developing a win-win, cost-effective staffing strategy, it is extremely important to strike a delicate balance between the *financial-driven* objectives of your organization and the *realistic* implementation of resident quality of care and life satisfaction in the trenches. It's one thing to strategize the staffing dilemma in the board room – but an entirely different challenge to successfully execute on the front lines. The wisest employers have tremendous respect for those front-line professionals who provide endless love, care and patience to their residents. Employees who feel valued do better work, and we must never forget that those working in assisted living communities often have to do their jobs in a time-sensitive, stressful environment.

Incremental Impact of Direct Care Staffing
Resulting From Acuity Creep

Figure 16-4 uses the simplified arithmetic outlined in Figure 16-2 to compute the *incremental* direct care staffing impact for an 80-unit community where 25 residents receive an additional 30 minutes per 24-hour day of direct care due to higher acuity. In this example, the staffing must be increased (through either overtime or new employees) by an additional 2.7 FTEs. This will add approximately $71,000 in annual operating expenses. Unless you recover this cost with innovative pricing strategies, the value of your community has decreased, using a 10.5 percent capitalization rate, by about $675,000. Chapter 15 provides complete details on the critical cost creep issue.

FIGURE 16-4

DIRECT CARE STAFFING
INCREMENTAL IMPACT: 25 RESIDENTS RECEIVING
AN ADDITIONAL 30 MINUTES PER 24 HOUR DAY[1]

1. **Demand**

   - **25 residents @ 30 extra minutes/24 hour day x 7 days = 5,250 minutes/week**

2. **Supply**

   - **Direct care staff @ 8 hours/day x 5 days x 60 minutes/hour X 80% efficiency = 1,920 minutes/productive work week**

3. **Total New Demand** = **5,250** **minutes/week**
   Supply **1,920** **minutes/week**

   = 2.7 *additional* FTEs ➤ *For 3 shift,*
   7 day week

---

[1]*Over and above* industry direct care average of 45 minutes per resident per 24 hour day.

Moore Diversified Services, Inc.

Cost Sensitivity of One Additional Employee

It is useful to consider the marginal cost sensitivity of just one additional direct care employee. Using $8.50 per hour, a 25 percent fringe benefit factor, overhead recovery and profit leads to a loaded cost of about $23.00 per hour. This, in turn, results in the need for an *added* cost recovery of about $55.00 per month per resident for an 80-unit community operating at 93 percent occupancy. This factors in fringe benefits, indirect downtime, overhead and profit. See Figure 15-1 in Chapter 15. So each additional direct care employee who is not covered appropriately in your pricing can erode your profit margin by approximately 1 percent.

Financial success in the future rests very heavily on five major strategies: 1) solid cost accounting; 2) pragmatic cost controls; 3) practical, ongoing value engineering; 4) establishing tangible budgets and cost/profit centers (departments); and 5) making department heads fully accountable.

Here are five strategic initiatives to consider:

1. Zero-Base Your Core Staffing – Start by writing a realistic job description for every position, including specific goals, objectives and – most importantly – tangible *expected outcomes* from each staff member. Remember, there's a big difference between non-productive *activities* versus real *results*. In each case, ask, *"How can this person help to absorb other necessary tasks?"*

2. Monitor and Respond to Cost Creep – Many sponsors report that frailer residents need more direct care than the industry baseline average of 45 minutes per 24-hour day. This results in the need to increase either compensated or uncompensated care due to increasing resident ADL needs.

3. Attempt to Minimize Employee Turnover – While obviously trying to minimize labor costs, you must strike a delicate balance between current labor costs, plus the *added* costs of new initiatives that may reduce costly employee turnover. This could include a modest increase in hourly rates, or changes to your fringe benefit package to remain competitive in your local labor market. Hiring and training new employees is a very expensive process.

4. Consider Using the Fractional Employee Concept – Some operators are using a combination of part-time employees and regular employee overtime to reduce the total number of full-time employees who expect costly fringe benefits. This is the essence of the Full Time Equivalent (FTE) employee concept. For example, some sponsors are carefully sequencing dining operations to optimize labor productivity and minimize downtime. One sponsor picks up students at a local high school to assist with the evening meal, and then takes them home.

5. Exploit Available Economies of Scale – If you are a large, multi-facility operator, using a regional office/cluster management concept, try to realize economies of scale by shifting some of your non-direct care core staff expenses, such as a portion of marketing function and activities planning, from the individual community to the "central office level." While not easy, you might be able to spread some of these fixed costs across more than one community and a larger number of revenue-producing units. If you are a small, regional operator, you can consider implementing some of the same strategies with more modest success. If you are a single facility operator, you obviously face significant challenges in competing with bigger industry players who are enjoying increased economies of scale.

This staffing situation will continue to present challenges as industry consolidation continues. But with consistent attention to detail and a laser sharp focus on your operations, you can continue to be viable, although you may have to accept the reality of slightly lower operating profit margins.

Balancing Care Quality and Costs

Bringing staffing ratios and operational costs back into line is a very difficult and traumatic experience for many existing assisted living operators. Many of their problems stem from the fact that they have not implemented any zero-based budgeting initiatives for years. This year's budget was merely built on last year's actual expenses while adding apparently justifiable inflationary increases.

Department heads certainly have a responsibility to protect the integrity of their department, treating their employees fairly and delivering consistent quality of care to the residents. But sponsors, owners, and operators also have a responsibility to remain competitive and deliver the highest value and quality of care at the lowest cost for their residents. Striking this delicate balance appears to fly in the face of logic on the part of many existing operators. They rationalize that any significant reduction in cost would cause them to become a "greedy uncaring operator" with deteriorating quality of care and declining inspection scores. While these are certainly unacceptable outcomes, serious inefficient operations are frequently masked because of the legitimate concern for quality of care.

It's true that there have been horror stories regarding unacceptable quality of care standards because of unrealistic cost-cutting by some assisted living operators. However, other serious problems that have not received significant publicity and disclosure are the inefficient operations resulting in unnecessary increased costs. These unnecessary costs go uncorrected by many assisted living sponsors and are being passed on to the senior. In the past, these high cost pass-throughs have worked in the marketplace because the intensity of competition was much lower than it will be in the future.

There is a middle ground of optimum operations which assisted living operators must achieve as a 21st century organization (see Figure 16-5). Operators must walk a thin line and strike a delicate balance between unrealistic, inappropriate cost-cutting at one end and inefficient operations and inflated costs at the other. Don't let broad mission objectives and your legitimate concern for delivering high quality of care prevent you from addressing serious operations problems.

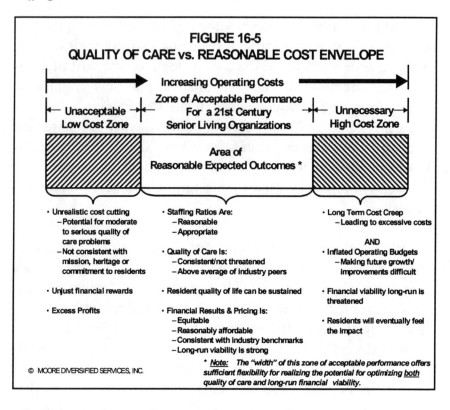

FIGURE 16-5
QUALITY OF CARE vs. REASONABLE COST ENVELOPE

Increasing Operating Costs

Unacceptable Low Cost Zone	Zone of Acceptable Performance For a 21st Century Senior Living Organizations	Unnecessary High Cost Zone
	Area of Reasonable Expected Outcomes *	

- Unrealistic cost cutting
  - Potential for moderate to serious quality of care problems
  - Not consistent with mission, heritage or commitment to residents

- Unjust financial rewards

- Excess Profits

- Staffing Ratios Are:
  - Reasonable
  - Appropriate

- Quality of Care Is:
  - Consistent/not threatened
  - Above average of industry peers

- Resident quality of life can be sustained

- Financial Results & Pricing Is:
  - Equitable
  - Reasonably affordable
  - Consistent with industry benchmarks
  - Long-run viability is strong

- Long Term Cost Creep
  - Leading to excessive costs

  AND
- Inflated Operating Budgets
  - Making future growth/ improvements difficult

- Financial viability long-run is threatened

- Residents will eventually feel the impact

© MOORE DIVERSIFIED SERVICES, INC.

* Note: The "width" of this zone of acceptable performance offers sufficient flexibility for realizing the potential for optimizing both quality of care and long-run financial viability.

CHAPTER 17

THE INCOME STATEMENT

It's the Financial Engine of Your Community

An assisted living community's income statement is frequently viewed by operators, investors and lenders as a cash-producing black box. But since the "black box" term has fallen out of favor with most Wall Street analysts, let's say that very sensitive revenues and expenses make up the high performance *financial engine* of your assisted living community. Accountants call this engine your income statement.

Assume for the moment that your assisted living financial engine is much like those that power a high performance aircraft. With you as the pilot, you'd like to experience at least three favorable outcomes: 1) operating your machine in an efficient manner, 2) not constantly flying at the edge of the envelope and 3) always having a soft landing!

Operating in an efficient manner means striking a delicate balance between the revenues you collect and the expenses you must pay – resulting in a reasonable profit margin. What is reasonable? Well, many industry experts can't seem to agree on a consistent set of benchmarks. But the key financial ratios that many are shooting for in assisted living is a direct operating expense ratio of 60 percent with a corresponding operating profit margin of 40 percent. This margin is defined by dividing operating profits by net revenues collected. It is commonly expressed as *Net Operating Income (NOI)* or for public companies, the fancy term of *Earnings Before Interest, Taxes, Depreciation and Amortization (EBITDA)*. Many industry analysts now feel that there's no way to consistently achieve an operating profit margin *in excess* of 35 to 37 percent. The 40 percent margin is seen as an elusive, moving target – primarily due to resident acuity creep leading to operating cost creep. But whether you're a for-profit or not-for-profit operation, you must come close to at least a 35 percent plus operating profit margin. If you don't, you'll find yourself flying at the edge of the envelope with an unstable aircraft – and you will <u>not</u> have a soft landing!

Six Components That Drive the Income Statement

Check to see if you have all of these necessary components in your financial plan:

1. A cost-effective **Design Concept** – Chapter 10

2. A realistic **Capital Budget** – Chapter 13

3. An accurate estimate of **Operating Expenses** – Chapter 14

4. A detailed **Cost Creep Projection** model – Chapter 15

5. A detailed **Pricing Strategy;** *Baseline Pricing* covering normal operating expenses (Chapter 22) and a *Tiered Pricing Strategy* to respond to cost creep (Chapter 23)

6. A mutually acceptable (borrower/lender) **Project Financing Plan** – Chapter 21

Also, review your exit strategy potential outlined in Chapter 38.

The Typical Income Statement

Figure 17-1 presents an income statement for a typical 80-unit assisted living community. I've shown a possible scenario . . . if you're really value engineering and "scrubbing" all of your costs from day one.

Note: The income statement has three major sections: I) key input variables, II) financial performance and III) key financial ratios. The itemized numbers in the text sub-sections are cross-referenced to those in Figure 17-1. The typical scenario is presented in Figure 17-1 and summarizes the financial performance **in the first full year of stabilized operations.**

FIGURE 17-1
ASSISTED LIVING'S FINANCIAL ENGINE
Income Statement For An 80-Unit Community

I. INPUT VARIABLES

1.	Average Monthly Service Fee:	$2,640	Total Cost:		$9.6 Mil
2.	Operating Expenses PRD:	$55.00	*Equity @ 25%*	=	$2.4 Mil
3.	Cost Per Unit:	$120,000	*Debt @ 75%*	=	$7.2 Mil
	Number of Units:	80	Loan Interest Rate:		9.0%
			Amortization (Yrs):		30

II. FINANCIAL PERFORMANCE

4.	Gross Annual Income	$2,534,400/yr
5.	Vacancy Factor @ 7.0%	(177,408)
6.	Net Rental Revenues	$2,356,992
7.	Other Revenues	46,886
8.	Net Revenues	$2,403,878
9.	Operating Expenses	(1,485,550)
10.	NET OPERATING INCOME	$918,328 /yr
11.	Debt Service	(695,520)
12.	CASH FLOW	$222,808 /yr

III. KEY FINANCIAL RATIOS

13.	**Debt Service Coverage (DSCR):**	**1.32**
14.	*EBITDA*	*38.2%*
15.	*Operating Expense Ratio:*	*61.8%*
16.	*Cash Flow/Unit (unleveraged)*	*$11,480*
17.	*Cash Flow/Unit (leveraged)*	*$ 2,785*
18.	*Cash Return on Total Investment (unleveraged)*	*9.6%*
19.	*Cash-on-Cash Return on Equity (1st year):*	*9.3%*
20.	*Internal Rate of Return*	*17.9%*

© Moore Diversified Services, Inc.

I.   Key Input Variables – When developing an income statement for a typical assisted living community, there are three critical input variables:

(1) ***Base monthly service fees*** are the fees charged for a particular unit type for a "base level" of services. This would include all shelter components (living unit, food, housekeeping, utilities, etc.) and a base level of assistance with the activities of daily living. This base level is typically defined as approximately 45 to 60 minutes per resident per 24-hour day for *direct, hands-on* care. Residents needing increased assistance with ADLs above the base level are typically charged incrementally higher fees, using the tiered pricing concepts outlined in Chapter 23.

(2) ***Operating expenses per resident day*** typically range from $50 to $55. You should always evaluate your financials in terms of *dollars per resident day*. It's the most useful common denominator. Operating expenses per resident day in assisted living are defined as total annual operating expenses (or expenses by each major department) divided by the number of residents times 365 days. Total operating expenses per resident-day should typically range from $50 to $55 in most market areas. These costs include basic shelter services and a *realistic* menu of assistance with the Activities of Daily Living (ADLs) – as described above under base monthly service fee. This input variable represents the highest risk of eroding profit margins. For more details, see Figure 14-1 in Chapter 14.

(3) ***Total cost per unit*** is the total all-in cost, which is your *total* project cost divided by the number of units. Don't confuse this with just hard construction cost per unit.

II. Financial Performance – This is the heart of the income statement, and contains the following key elements:

(4) ***Gross annual income*** is the total number of units multiplied by their average base monthly service fees. In the Figure 17-1 example, we are using an average monthly service fee of $2,640/month multiplied by 80 total units x 12 months.

(5) ***Vacancy factor at 7 percent*** is typically the industry standard for assisted living. Most operators find that consistently operating assisted living above 93 percent occupancy becomes difficult due to the relatively high turnover of residents.

(6) ***Net revenues*** is the gross annual income reduced by the vacancy factor.

(7) ***Other revenues*** include various ancillary charges such as toiletries, medicines, incontinence products, guest meals and other additional a la carte services.

(8) ***Net revenues*** represent the end result of the factors listed above.

(9) ***Operating expenses*** are shown as an average of $55 per resident day (PRD).

Resident days are computed as follows:

> 80 units x 93 percent occupancy
> x 365 days/year:
>
> = 74 units x 365 days = 27,010 resident-days/year

Total Operating Expenses @ $55 PRD = $1,485,550

(10) ***Net Operating Income (NOI) before debt service*** is frequently expressed as "EBITDA" – earnings before interest, taxes, depreciation and amortization. In this example, the NOI is $918,328. Sometimes this NOI or EBITDA is viewed as the average *unleveraged* (before debt payments) cash flow <u>per unit or bed</u>. In this case, unleveraged average cash flow per unit is $11,480 (before debt service).

(11) ***Debt service*** (in this example) consists of a financing plan that is 75 percent debt and 25 percent invested equity, with a 9 percent interest rate and a 25-year loan amortization period. The amount financed depends on the all-in cost per unit. The debt component is 75 percent of the total project cost of $9.6 million or $7.2 million.   Note that a not-for-profit could probably execute 100 percent financing with approximately a 7 percent interest rate, using tax-exempt bonds.

(12) ***Total annual cash flow <u>after</u> debt service*** is cash left over after paying all the operating expenses and the mortgage. In this example, annual cash flow at stabilized occupancy is $222,808 or $2,785 per unit.

III. Key Financial Ratios – These are the vital signs indicating either a healthy, marginally performing or troubled community.

(13) *Debt service coverage ratio* is the key lender safety margin. Lenders typically require $1.25 to $1.30 of uncommitted available cash for every dollar of maximum annual mortgage payment. The ratio is defined as net operating income (available cash) divided by annual debt service (mortgage payment).

(14) *Operating margin* is sometimes called "EBITDA margin" and is the net operating income (operating profit) divided by net revenues. Assisted living operating margins should come in somewhere between 32 and 40 percent.

(15) *Operating expense ratio* is the inverse of the operating margin, and is defined as operating expenses divided by net revenues. The operating expense ratio should be in a range from 60 to 68 percent.

(16) *Cash flow per unit <u>unleveraged</u>* is the average amount of annual cash produced by each unit. It's defined as net operating income divided by the <u>total</u> number of units <u>before</u> debt service.

(17) *Cash flow per unit <u>leveraged</u>* is the cash that's available <u>after</u> all expenses are covered *and* debt payments are made.

(18) ***Cash return on total investment unleveraged*** (*before* debt service) typically ranges from 9 to 11 percent in the early years and is heavily influenced by the *total cost per unit*. (In this case, $120,000).

(19) ***Cash-on-cash return on invested equity*** (*after* debt service) typically ranges from approximately 8 to 11 percent.

(20) ***Internal rate of return (IRR)*** is a fancy financial term which takes into consideration the *time value* of your invested (not borrowed) cash. This financial ratio answers the question, **"What is my average annual (percent) return on my invested cash – from the *first day* I invested it until some defined point in the future when I expect to get it back?"** It also considers all dividends or profits distributed and assumes the proceeds of a future sale.

Planning for a "Soft Landing"

A "soft landing" can also be described as a graceful exit strategy. Happiness is not just positive cash flow – it means *sufficient* positive cash flow. Let's say you want to either sell or refinance your assisted living community. A potential buyer or lender will evaluate the performance of your financial engine by focusing on your income-producing black box; paying you about 9.5 times your net operating income (a capitalization rate of 10.5 percent). That, of course, assumes that you have properly allocated all of the appropriate expenses. The buyer or lender will likely be looking for three things you might have omitted from your income statement. They are 1) management fees at approximately five percent of net revenues, 2) a cash reserve fund for replacement is a typical allocation required by lenders (as contrasted to technically funding *depreciation*) by directly expensing approximately $225 to $250 per unit per year, 3) a 5 percent operating expense contingency. These safety margins will keep your lender comfortable, a potential buyer motivated and help you avoid flying at the dangerous edge of your performance envelope.

Sensitivity of Financial Returns

A review of assisted living financial returns often evokes strong reactions! Some industry analysts say there's no way to achieve an EBITDA operating margin *in excess* of 37 percent. The 40 percent margin is clearly a moving target, and it will probably take several years of market maturity before these numbers really stabilize. Despite these anomalies, it's always useful to evaluate the potential *sensitivity* of your community's financial performance.

For example, higher returns could be realized as indicated in the example depicted in Figure 17-2 with a modest *increase* in leverage – setting debt at 80 percent (vs. 75 percent) of the project cost. The critical debt service coverage ratio would be approximately 1.23x, possibly still acceptable to most lenders.

Other key financial variables include driving down the total cost per unit (where practical) and/or modestly increasing pricing – assuming that you will remain competitive in your market area.

Cost/Unit and Debt Ratio Sensitivity

Let's experiment with the $120,000/unit, $2,640/month service fee, the operating expenses of $55 per resident day and the 75% / 25% debt-to-equity ratio illustrated in Figure 17-1. If it were possible to change the total cost/unit and/or modestly increase the average monthly service fee and/or increase our leverage, we would experience dramatic improvement in cash flow and cash return on invested equity – *after* debt service.

In the example in Figure 17-1, the unit cost of $120,000 delivered a 9.3 percent *cash return on invested equity* – assuming a debt-to-equity ratio of 75%/25% and a monthly service fee of $2,640/month. But as Figure 17-2 indicates, you can achieve a substantial improvement in your returns if some key financial factors can be changed.

Caution: You obviously can't make arbitrary changes to your pro forma in isolation; your lender, construction contractor and the marketplace may represent significant barriers.

FIGURE 17-2

FINANCIAL RETURN ON INVESTED EQUITY SENSITIVITY ANALYSIS

	Cash Return on Invested Equity[1]					
Debt/Equity	75%/25%			80%/20%		
Monthly Service Fee	$2,375	$2,640	$2,900	$2,375	$2,640	$2,900
Total (All-In) Cost/Unit:						
• $ 85,000	18.4%	24.6%	33.7%	20.6%	28.3%	39.7%
• $ 95,000	13.4	19.0	27.1	14.3	21.3	31.5
• $115,000	6.0	10.6	17.4	5.1	10.9	19.3
• $120,000	4.6	9.0	15.4	3.3	8.8	16.9
Operating Expenses PRD	$50.00	$55.00	$58.00	$50.00	$55.00	$58.00

---

[1]80 units, 93% occupancy, 9% interest, 30-year mortgage
© Moore Diversified Services, Inc.

In the example in Figure 17-1, annual cash flow per unit (leveraged) was $2,785. Figure 17-3 demonstrates how this performance can change dramatically by being able to adjust the previously-mentioned financial variables. Note that the cash returns in Figure 17-2 and the cash flow per unit in Figure 17-3 are computed before "other revenues" which are reflected as item seven in Figure 17-1.

FIGURE 17-3

CASH FLOW PER UNIT SENSITIVITY ANALYSIS

	Cash Flow Per Unit[1]					
Debt/Equity	75%/25%			80%/20%		
Monthly Service Fee	$2,375	$2,640	$2,900	$2,375	$2,640	$2,900
Total (All-In) Cost/Unit:						
• $ 85,000	$3,907	$5,227	$7,168	$3,497	$4,816	$6,757
• $ 95,000	3,183	4,502	6,444	2,724	4,044	5,985
• $115,000	1,735	3,054	4,995	1,180	2,499	4,440
• $120,000	1,373	2,692	4,633	793	2,113	4,054
Operating Expenses PRD	$50.00	$55.00	$58.00	$50.00	$55.00	$58.00

[1] 80 units, 93% occupancy, 9% interest, 30-year mortgage
© Moore Diversified Services, Inc.

The Holding Period "Harvesting" Effect

Your financial ratios will also improve with time – assuming you continually compensate for cost creep, and pay attention to operations details. The financial performance in Figure 17-1 reflects the *first full year of stabilized occupancy.* If you increase your fees by five percent annually and your expenses escalate at four percent, your operating profit margin (NOI) in the second year will increase from 38.2 to 38.5 percent, thanks to fixed debt and the power of prudent leverage.

Your income statement *outputs* are dependent upon many variables (your costs, the effectiveness of your operations, the competitive marketplace, etc.). And these outputs obviously determine the relative success of your entire project.

Sponsors are frequently criticized for catering primarily to the upscale market. But just as a high performance engine burns a lot of fuel, your assisted living community burns cash and is very sensitive to monthly service fee revenue and operating expenses. Assisted living has a high performance financial engine that can deliver excellent financial results. But as the examples in this chapter show, and as many are now painfully aware, there is little margin for performance error.

CHAPTER 18

GETTING CREATIVE WITH CAPITAL INVESTMENT

Five Simple Strategies That Can Produce Dramatic Results

Chapter 13 addressed the development of an initial assisted living capital budget for a new 80-unit community. This chapter deals with some subtle, but still important, strategies, and how investing in ongoing capital improvements is a crucial part of keeping your senior living community in competitive condition. In planning a capital investment strategy, many owners and sponsors frequently commit three tactical errors: 1) they spend money on the wrong things; 2) they lose sight of their overall strategic objectives; or 3) they pay too much for less-than-optimum value.

Two Important Time Frames

In developing a new assisted living project or improving an existing one, there are situations wherein capital expenditure decisions must consider two distinct time frames. These two time frames are:

- *Short Run* – The Initial (One Time) Capital Cost Investment Impact

● ***Long Run*** – The Ongoing (Perpetual) Operating Cost of Ownership

Cost of Ownership Considerations

To plan effectively, you must carefully weigh the short run capital cost expenditures (immediate capital costs, such as new heating, ventilation and air conditioning systems) against the long run costs of ownership (ongoing operating costs such as maintenance, utilities and insurance). Investing less in capital improvements in the short run can sometimes be very expensive over your total ownership period. These cost considerations become very important if you plan to hold your property for more than five years. Even if you plan to be a short term property owner, realize that your ultimate sale value can be adversely impacted by your earlier "short run" capital investment mentality. The buyer's due diligence efforts will likely detect flaws in your original capital investment planning.

These simple steps should help you make important cost of ownership trade-off decisions:

1. ***When considering two alternative capital investments, evaluate the payback period and calculate the impact on total project value.*** How many years of operation are required for the operational savings/benefits to result in financial break-even or recovery of each of your alternative initial investment options? This can be a simple arithmetic calculation (dividing the initial cost of the capital investment by the estimated annual financial

benefit or savings) or a more sophisticated discounted cash flow analysis. Ideally, your payback period should be somewhere between three and five years. From that point forward, there should be an ongoing positive financial impact.

For example, let's assume that a combination of capital expenditure decisions costing a total of $50,000 could save $1,000 a month in total operating expenses. Using the simplified approach, that additional $12,000 per year in additional net operating income would pay back your initial investment in about four years. Keep in mind that these annual operating expense savings will likely be realized far beyond the initial payback period, and possibly over the entire useful life of the community.

2. Estimate the total impact on project value. To determine the increased intrinsic value of your project, you should *capitalize* the incremental increase in net operating income resulting from the capital investment[1]. The *capitalization rate* is the cash return (percentage) that reasonable buyers or investors would expect to realize on their cash investment. This would obviously be influenced by their perception of relative risk. Appendix C briefly describes the capitalization rate concept.

---

[1]Net operating income equals revenue minus operating expenses (before depreciation, amortization, interest payments and applicable taxes).

Continuing with the example from Item 1, that same $12,000 annual savings would also increase the economic value of your community. An investor expecting a 10.5 percent return on cash investment should, therefore, be willing to pay or invest about an additional $114,000 for your community. So with that $50,000 investment, the value of your community is likely to be increased by approximately $114,000.

3. *Value engineer your capital investments.* This means lowering or controlling capital costs without significantly detracting from the look, operational efficiency or marketplace acceptance of your community. The results of this effort should be largely invisible to the consumer marketplace. This concept is addressed in Chapter 13.

4. *Let the "flash value" concept influence capital investment.* Flash value is a fairly obscure, but surprisingly simple, way of quantifying, and thereby maximizing, perceived value in the eyes of the consumer. This concept is defined as follows:

$$\textbf{Flash Value Index} = \frac{\textbf{What Consumer Thinks an Item Costs}}{\textbf{Your Actual Cost}}$$

Through consumer testing (focus groups, etc.), you can identify a menu of design features and amenities that exhibit a "flash value index" of greater than two to one. This means that the consumer thinks the item is worth at least twice as much as your actual cost. You should incorporate a number of highly favorable flash value items into your project. Typical high flash value items in seniors housing include high-quality wood molding or millwork, walk-in closets, unusual (but attractive) public spaces, recessed solid-core living unit entry doors, incandescent vs. fluorescent lighting, wall coverings, interesting roof lines, and "breaks" in exterior elevations. The list could go on, but the ideal outcome is for senior prospects and their family to comment, *"This place sure seems to offer a lot for the money!"*

5. The "Cap X" Concept. Owner/operators and lenders are also using a capital investment concept called "Cap X" (for Capital Expenditure) or "reserve for replacement." This is an imputed operations expense line item of approximately $225 to $250 per unit per year, which is allocated and reserved for future capital needs of a routine, generally predictable nature (cosmetic refurbishment, etc.). Some organizations establish the Cap X requirement as 1.5 to 2.0 percent of revenues. This concept is also discussed in Chapter 14 on operating expenses.

Note that the above figures are for relatively new projects with essentially no deferred maintenance. These factors must be increased for older properties with existing capital improvement needs.

You can view the "Cap X" concept as an alternative for funding depreciation. From an accounting perspective, depreciation is considered a non-cash expense. This means that, in any one year, you may not actually spend cash for that line item. But totally unfunded depreciation is a recipe for trouble. Cap X is the solution. Buyers and appraisers will usually impute a Cap X factor that will reduce their opinion of your community's value. This can suddenly become a troublesome issue for the owner-operator because "Cap X" is an expense line item, and every dollar is subject to the previously discussed capitalization rate of approximately 10.5 to 11.0 percent.

Capital investment is not just spending money for obvious needs. It involves spending the *right amount of money* for the *right items* at the *right time*. This requires prudent capital investment planning, optimizing financial returns to the owner/operator while delivering positive impacts and tangible benefits to current and future residents.

Both of these lofty goals can be accomplished with the help of the basic capital investment principles that were outlined in this chapter.

CREATIVE ASSISTED LIVING CAPITAL INVESTMENT
FIVE SIMPLE STEPS

1. **Evaluate the investment payback period.**

2. **Estimate the total impact on project value.**

3. **Value engineer for cost savings.**

4. **Invest in *flash value* to enhance perceived value.**

5. **Consistently deploy the "Cap X" Concept.**

CHAPTER 19

ASSISTED LIVING AS A *FULL* MEDICAL TAX DEDUCTION

Everyone Has the Right to Legally Avoid Taxes

Caution: The information and observations contained in this chapter may be subject to varied interpretations by senior care professionals. Each sponsor and owner/operator should seek independent advice and counsel from their own professionals. Sponsors should always advise Senior consumers to obtain independent second opinions on this important matter.

How would you like to offer your assisted living prospects and existing residents a 13 to 20 percent discount on their year 2001 and future monthly service fees – without costing you anything? Sounds too good to be true? It's possible.

First, ask your accountants and financial advisors if they think your residents can deduct the *complete* assisted living monthly service fee costs – including all of the shelter, services and care components. Second, do some homework on your own. IRS Publication 502, *"Medical and Dental Expenses"*, (Year 2000 version), states "you can include in medical expenses the cost of medical care in a nursing home or *home for the aged* for yourself, your spouse or your dependents. *This includes the cost of meals and lodging in the home if the main reason for being there is to get medical care.* Do not include the cost of meals and lodging if the reason for being in the home is *personal*." (Emphasis added by the author.) But a reasonable rationale would be that the main purpose for being in nursing or assisted living *is* primarily to "get (consistent) medical care" – not for "personal" or discretionary reasons.

IRS Publication 502 further defines the typical situation as involving a *chronically ill individual.* (Again, emphasis has been added by the author.)

"You are chronically ill if you have been certified by a licensed health care practitioner within the previous 12 months as one of the following:

1. *You are unable, for at least 90 days, to perform at least two activities of daily living without substantial assistance from another individual,* due to loss of functional capacity. Activities of daily living are eating, toileting, transferring, bathing, dressing and continence

or

2. You require substantial supervision to be protected from threats to health and safety due to severe cognitive impairment."

Doesn't that sound like your typical high-acuity assisted living resident?

Adult Children Can Also Take Deductions

In some cases, adult children may also benefit from the tax deduction if their parent qualifies as a dependent. That means the adult children are providing at least 50 percent of the parent's financial support, <u>including</u> the assisted living monthly service fee. Check later in this chapter and with your accountant for specific details.

The 7.5 Percent Exclusion

The publication also advises the taxpayer how the deductions work.

"You can deduct only the amount of your medical and dental expenses that is ***more than 7.5%*** of your adjusted gross income (line 34, Form 1040). In this publication, the term '7.5% limit' is used to refer to 7.5% of your adjusted gross income. The phrase 'subject to the 7.5% limit' is also used. This phrase means that you must subtract 7.5% (0.075) of your adjusted gross income from your medical expenses to figure your medical expense deduction."

But most income-qualified Seniors are already at that threshold deduction level due to their current medical expense deductions (prescription drugs, medical co-payments, etc.).

The Big Picture

Figure 19-1 provides a big picture summary of the assisted living medical deduction concept. Here is a typical example of how this might work in your community:

1. Your prospect or resident has a Social Security income of $800 per month, or $9,600 per year. Added to that is $30,400 representing her existing savings portfolio annual returns or pension. Combined, that's a total gross income of $40,000.

2. Before considering the assisted living medical tax deduction, her accountant tells her that only $5,520 of her $9,600 Social Security income is considered taxable – resulting in an *adjusted gross income* (for tax purposes) of $35,920 (see Figures 19-1 and 19-2 for details).

3. If she chooses not to itemize her deductions, she can also claim a *standard deduction* of $5,500 and a *personal exemption* of $2,800. These deductions total $8,300 (Figure 19-1).

4. Her existing medical deductions for prescription drugs and miscellaneous medical co-payments average $210 per month, or about $2,500 per year.

5. But she cannot normally deduct these medical expenses because 7.5 percent of adjusted gross income (exclusion) is $2,695 (Figure 19-2). So, her taxes on her adjusted gross income, less $8,300 in deductions, are computed to be $4,325 or an *average* tax rate of approximately 16 percent (Figure 19-1).

That leaves her with an after-tax disposable income of $8,075 *after* paying her modest assisted living monthly service fee of $2,300 per month, or $27,600 per year ($40,000 minus $27,600 minus $4,325 equals $8,075).

But now she produces an opinion memorandum from her assisted living owner/operator suggesting that she seek *independent* advice regarding the deduction of the full monthly service fee of $2,300 per month or $27,600 per year. Her accountant now figures that her taxable income has dropped from $27,620 to $5,715, and her tax bill is reduced from $4,325 to $860 (Figure 19-1). Her annual after-tax disposable income after paying $27,600 in annual assisted living fees *increases* 43 percent, from $8,075 to $11,540.

In summary, she gets a $3,465 cash bonus or a 13 percent after-tax dollar *discount* on her monthly service fees. She has significantly increased her discretionary spending power. These savings are even more dramatic for seniors with gross incomes of $60,000+ as indicated in Figure 19-5. This analysis shows that a higher income senior – with an income of $61,500 – can realize an after-tax reduction in monthly service fees of *20 percent*.

Note that some medical deductions cannot be claimed if they have been reimbursed by either private insurance or the Medicare and Medicaid programs. And, unfortunately, low-to-moderate income seniors, who currently pay little or no taxes, will realize little benefit from this concept.

FIGURE 19-1

ASSISTED LIVING MEDICAL TAX DEDUCTION - THE BIG PICTURE

I. **Basic Premise**

The full monthly service fee (shelter, services and care) should be a tax deductible medical expense above the exclusion of 7.5% of a Senior's adjusted gross income.

II. **Impact**

An effective after-tax cost savings of 13% ($3,465) to 20% ($5,630) for Seniors in the $40,000 and $61,500 income categories, respectively. The deduction effectively lowers a typical *base* monthly service fee from $2,300 to $2,011 (for $40,000 income) and down to $1,830 for $61,500 income (see Figure 19-5).

III. **Simplified Example for Senior With $40,000 Income**

	Without AL Medical Tax Deduction	*With* AL Medical Tax Deduction	Reference Exhibit
• Gross Income	$40,000	$40,000	19-2, 19-3
• Adjusted Gross Income (AGI) for Tax Purposes	35,920	35,920	19-3
• *Standard* Tax Deductions & Personal Exemption	(8,300)	(2,800)[1]	19-3
• Total Deductions – Including *Medical* Tax Deduction *Net* of 7.5% AGI Exclusion	- 0 -	(27,405)	19-3
• Adjusted Taxable Income	$27,620	$ 5,715	(Item IV)
• Taxes Paid	4,325	860	
• After-Tax Disposable Income – *After* Paying Taxes & Assisted Living MSF	8,075[2]	11,540	19-4
• Effective After-Tax MSF Cost	$2,300 /mo.	$2,011 /mo.	19-4
• Annual Savings ($ or %)	0/0	$3,465 or 13%	19-4

Moore Diversified Services, Inc.

[1]When itemizing deductions, the $5,500 standard deduction is not allowed.
[2]$40,000 minus $27,600 minus $4,325 equals $8,075.

A Big Break for the Senior Consumer

Figures 19-2 through 19-4 provide more step-by-step details on the important computations leading to the assessment of the impact of the medical tax deduction.

Think of it this way. The after-tax benefit to a senior with a gross annual pre-tax income of $40,000 is equivalent to *rolling back* your *base* monthly service fee prices 3 years to 1998, 1999 levels. That's assuming you normally escalate your pricing 4 percent annually. For a senior with a gross annual pre-tax income of $61,500, the effective price roll back is about 5 years – to 1996/1997 levels.

Deduction Can Also Apply to CCRCs

This potential medical cost deduction is not limited to assisted living. IRS publication 502 states, "You can include in medical expenses a part of a lifecare fee or 'founder's fee' you pay either monthly or as a lump sum under an agreement with a retirement home. ***The part of the payment you include is the amount properly allocable to medical care.*** The agreement must require that you pay a specific fee as a condition for the home's promise to provide lifetime care that includes medical care."

There are other important requirements and restrictions, so applicable IRS publications must be reviewed in detail. Always check everything you can before assuming such deductions are permissible under tax law.

Recap of a Complex, but Beneficial, Situation

Figure 19-6 recaps a complex, but very beneficial, situation. An obvious question might be, ***"If this is a legitimate tax benefit, why is it just becoming common knowledge in the assisted living arena?"*** In fact, several major assisted living companies have been quietly implementing this concept. They see it as their "competitive advantage" – so why spread the word to competitors? Though some professionals feel the IRS may challenge such deductions, they also believe the regulations are clear and the deductions will prevail.

Medical Tax Deductions for Adult Children

Similar tax rules apply if any adult child provides more than 50 percent of the financial support for their parent. There are many other details to consider but simply stated, the son or daughter can add the assisted living medical tax deduction to *their* tax return – using *their* effective tax rates.

A final reminder: Both owner/operators and senior consumers should seek independent counsel on this very important matter.

Also keep an eye on the current administration's initiatives on tax law changes.

FIGURE 19-2

ASSISTED LIVING MEDICAL TAX DEDUCTION
IMPACT ANALYSIS

<u>**Situation Summary**</u>

- Total assisted living monthly service fee: $2,300/month, $27,600/year

- Medical tax allowable deduction threshold:

  - Deductions must be greater than 7.5% of adjusted gross income

- Average (widow) Social Security income: $800/month, $9,600/year

- Other income comes from savings portfolio interest, dividends and (in some cases) employer pension fund

<u>**Adjusted Gross Income**</u>

Gross Income:

	Gross	Taxable
• Interest and Dividend Income	$30,400	$30,400
• Income from Social Security	9,600	5,520[1]
Total Gross Income	$40,000	
Adjusted Gross Income (AGI)		***$35,920***

- Medical expense deduction
  exclusion @ 7.5% of (AGI) $35,920 x .075
                                     = $2,695/year

Source: Moore Diversified Services, Inc.

_____

[1]$4,080 of Social Security income is not taxable income.

FIGURE 19-3
TYPICAL TAX DEDUCTION EXAMPLE - WITH/WITHOUT
DEDUCTING ASSISTED LIVING MONTHLY SERVICE FEE (MSF)

	Assisted Living MSF Deduction			
	No Assisted Living Deduction		With 7.5% Medical Exclusion ($2,695 Exclusion)	
	Gross	Taxable	Gross	Taxable
I. Gross Income				
• Interest & Dividend Income	$30,400	$30,400	$30,400	$30,400
• Income from Social Security	9,600	5,520	9,600	5,520
Total Gross Income	**$40,000**		**$40,000**	
Adjusted Gross Income (AGI)[1]		**$35,920**		**$35,920**
II. Conventional Tax Deductions				
• Standard		($5,500)		- 0 -[1]
• Personal Exemption (Including 65+)		(2,800)		(2,800)
Subtotal Taxable Income ➡		$27,630		$33,120
III. Medical Tax Deduction				
• Allowable Expenses Greater than 7.5% times Adjusted Gross Income (7.5% x $35,920) = ➡				$2,695
• Actual Medical Deductions (Other Than AL)				(2,500)
• Assisted Living Deductions		- 0 -		(27,600)
IV. Total Deductions				
• **Net Allowable Medical Tax Deduction - After Exclusion of 7.5% of AGI:**		**($8,300)**		**($27,405)**

Source: Moore Diversified Services, Inc.

---

[1]We're now *itemizing* deductions; cannot take *standard* deductions.

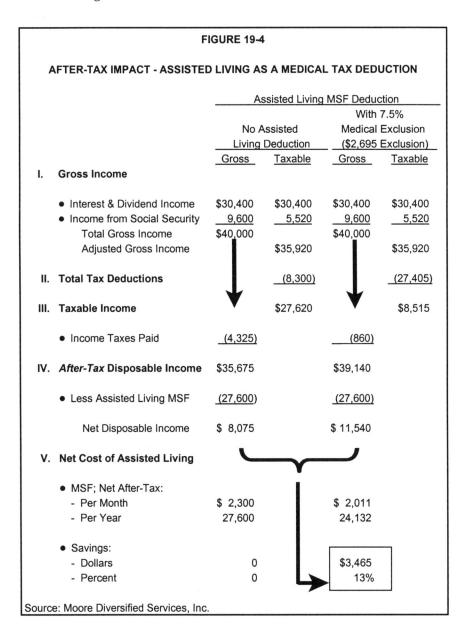

FIGURE 19-4

AFTER-TAX IMPACT - ASSISTED LIVING AS A MEDICAL TAX DEDUCTION

	Assisted Living MSF Deduction			
	No Assisted Living Deduction		With 7.5% Medical Exclusion ($2,695 Exclusion)	
	Gross	Taxable	Gross	Taxable
I. Gross Income				
• Interest & Dividend Income	$30,400	$30,400	$30,400	$30,400
• Income from Social Security	9,600	5,520	9,600	5,520
Total Gross Income	$40,000		$40,000	
Adjusted Gross Income		$35,920		$35,920
II. Total Tax Deductions		(8,300)		(27,405)
III. Taxable Income		$27,620		$8,515
• Income Taxes Paid	(4,325)		(860)	
IV. *After-Tax* Disposable Income	$35,675		$39,140	
• Less Assisted Living MSF	(27,600)		(27,600)	
Net Disposable Income	$ 8,075		$ 11,540	
V. Net Cost of Assisted Living				
• MSF; Net After-Tax:				
- Per Month	$ 2,300		$ 2,011	
- Per Year	27,600		24,132	
• Savings:				
- Dollars	0		$3,465	
- Percent	0		13%	

Source: Moore Diversified Services, Inc.

FIGURE 19-5
ASSISTED LIVING MEDICAL TAX DEDUCTION SUMMARY

	Comparison for Senior With $40,000 Annual Income		Impact for Higher Income Senior Consumer ($61,500 Income)
	Without Deduction	With Deduction	With Deduction
I. Total Gross Income			
• Interest and Dividends	$30,400	$30,400	$50,000
• Gross S.S.	9,600	9,600	11,500
Total	$40,000	$40,000	$61,500
• Less Portion of S.S. Not Taxable ($9,600-$5,520)	(4,080)	(4,080)	(1,725)
II. Adjusted Gross Income (AGI) (for Tax Purposes)	$35,920	$35,920	$59,775
Deductions:			
• Standard	(5,500)	- 0 -	- 0 -
• Exemptions	(2,800)	(2,800)	(2,800)
Subtotal	($8,300)	($2,800)	($2,800)
III. Taxable Income	$27,620	$33,120	$56,975
IV. Medical Tax Deduction			
• Other Than AL		$ 2,500	$ 2,500
• AL Monthly Service Fee		27,600	27,600
Subtotal		$30,100	$30,100
• Deduction Exclusion @ 7.5% of AGI		(2,695)	(4,485)
• Allowable Medical Deduction	- 0 -	27,405	25,615
V. Adjusted Taxable Income	$27,620	$ 5,715	$31,360
VI. Income Taxes Paid	4,325	860	5,375
VII. Recap			
• Total Gross Income	$40,000	$40,000	$61,500
Income Taxes Paid	(4,325)	(860)	(5,375)
Net After-Tax Disposable Income	$35,675	$39,140	$56,125
• Less AL MSF	(27,600)	(27,600)	(27,600)
After-Tax Discretionary Income	$ 8,075	$11,540	$28,525
VIII. Effective MSF	$2,300 /mo.	$2,011 /mo.	$1,830 /mo.
IX. Effective Annual Savings on AL MSF			
• Dollars	- 0 -	$3,465	$5,630
• Percent	- 0 -	13%	20%
@ Gross Income of		$40,000	$61,500

Source: Moore Diversified Services, Inc.

FIGURE 19-6
MEDICAL TAX DEDUCTION SUMMARY
RECAP OF A COMPLEX, BUT BENEFICIAL SITUATION

Basic Premise

The <u>full</u> monthly service fee (shelter, services and care) may be a tax deductible medical expense above the exclusion of 7.5% of a Senior's adjusted gross income.

	After-Tax Monthly Service Fee Saving Senior's Gross Income	
The Bottom Line [1]	$40,000	$61,500
● Monthly	$ 289 /Mo.	$ 470 /Mo.
● Annual	$3,465 /Yr.	$5,630 /Yr.
● Percent Savings	13%	20%

Impact

An effective after-tax cost savings of 13% ($3,465) to 20% ($5,630) for Seniors in the $40,000 and $61,500 income categories, respectively. The deduction lowers a typical modest *base* monthly service fee from $2,300 to $2,011 for $40,000 income Seniors and down to $1,830 for those reporting $61,500 income.

Source: Moore Diversified Services, Inc.

_____

[1]Assumes a modest *base* monthly service fee of $2,300/mo.

CHAPTER 20

TAPPING A $1.1 TRILLION RESOURCE

Senior's Home Equity Impact on Seniors Housing

The pent-up equity in a senior's home is playing a dual but conflicting role in our industry today. For a typical senior, the home represents a difficult emotional and economic decision hurdle, sometimes even a sales and marketing deal-killer. But, properly positioned, this valuable asset can also be converted into a significant selling opportunity for seniors housing. As seniors contemplate moving into retirement communities, most must address the sale of their home. On one hand, most recognize their changing personal needs and the growing hassles and expense of home ownership. But seniors also have strong emotional and almost unbreakable ties to the home that most have lived in for perhaps 40 to 50 years.

A Huge Financial Asset

Home equity represents a huge asset for many age 75+ seniors. Consider these startling statistics:

1. *The home ownership rate* is approximately 77 percent for seniors 75 and older; most with mortgages paid off free and clear.

2. ***The median value of their pent-up home equity*** in 2002 is approximately \$110,000. In aggregate, we're talking about total pent-up assets worth more than \$1.1 trillion!

Figure 20-1 summarizes these statistics.

FIGURE 20-1

TAPPING A \$1.1 TRILLION RESOURCE
HELD BY SENIORS 75 AND OLDER

Median Home Value	**\$110,000**
Ownership Rate	**77%**
Pent-Up Home Equity Asset Value	**\$1.1 Trillion**
Average Annual Growth of Home Equity	**\$66 Billion**

Moore Diversified Services, Inc.

Senior housing in the form of independent and assisted living primarily serves single or widowed seniors over age 75. And single-person homeowner characteristics vary as a function of age. For the 75+ age group:

- 70 percent are either widowed (60 percent), divorced (5 percent) or never married (5 percent).

These statistics apply to 11.6 million senior households. When combined, these households have a significant potential impact on our industry. In addition, the $1.1 trillion in gross potential pent-up home equity is probably growing by at least $66 billion per year (approximately 6 percent) because of moderate annual home value appreciation coupled with the modest growth in the 75+ age cohort. This means that a large percentage of age 75+ seniors who have a seniors housing and health care affordability gap of about $1,000 per month could sell their home, thereby, increasing their savings portfolio and their affordability. Many would now be able to afford to pay the market rate monthly service fee without spend-down! Others could adopt a very prudent spend-down strategy that would be financially responsible. Of equal importance, the strategy could optimize their quality of life.

Need Versus Want

In helping seniors put this asset to work, we must address two important and sometimes apparently conflicting issues; what seniors really *want* and what they actually *need*. Seniors want to stay at home – pure and simple. They are very attracted to their cherished home full of love and memories. Sure, it's now bigger than they really need and maintenance has become a bigger challenge as the years go by. But every nook and cranny of that home reminds them of a lifetime of experiences.

The Opportunity to Serve Needs

There is a significant opportunity to creatively and prudently unleash the tremendous economic clout of the senior's home equity asset while helping them to live their remaining life with dignity and optimum independence, and with physical and financial security. We can also assist them in leaving a financial legacy to their children; an important financial goal that for many may well have started as far back as the Great Depression era or World War II.

We have the service delivery systems to help many seniors avoid the steep nursing home cost spend-down ramp that has devastated many of their hopes and dreams of the past 20 years. Today, 70 percent of all nursing census days are associated with Medicaid residents. Many seniors did not enter the nursing home as a low income Medicaid qualified patient, many had their financial legacy slip away as they had to spend down their lifetime of savings.

Sure, asset shifting is still prevalent in many areas of the United States, but so is unnecessary and accelerated spend-down of assets. "Preservation of assets" and "leaving a legacy" are going to be the key sound bites and market positioning platforms for successful senior living and health care sponsors in the 21st century.

Seniors and their families really need practical, credible guidance to satisfy five critical objectives and situations that they face in their later stages of life: 1) expanded living and health care options; 2) increased affordability; 3) security and peace of mind; 4) preservation of assets (leaving that legacy); and 5) a practical, time-phased plan to accomplish all of the above. For many, this can be accomplished by helping seniors put their biggest asset to work in innovative and prudent ways. Recent changes to capital gains tax laws allow seniors to sell their current home while not purchasing (owning) another one, yet paying essentially zero capital gains tax.

With properly executed financial strategies, seniors can enjoy an expanded income stream (increased affordability), tax avoidance, preservation of assets (leaving a legacy), and estate liquidity as they face the inevitable challenges of later life.

Increased Challenges When Tapping Home Equity

We've been tapping this $1.1 trillion resource for over 25 years, but prudent financial investment and planning is becoming a major priority for Seniors and their families. It can also become a major marketing obstacle. So it's time to take a new look at an old concept. Let's start with some basics. Seniors directly or indirectly use their liquidated home equity to help pay for assisted living, independent living or entry fees into CCRCs.

There are two basic strategies that can be deployed when helping seniors and their families make these very difficult decisions.

1. *Liquidating home equity to increase affordability* –
Here's a typical real world scenario:

- Mrs. Barker has a current income of $35,000 and she and
  her family make the difficult but necessary assisted
  living decision. The monthly service fee is $2,500.

- She sells a $110,000 home and nets $100,000 after
  sales/closing costs:

    - There is no capital gains tax impact

- The $100,000 is added to Mrs. Barker's existing savings
  portfolio netting 5 percent or a $5,000 annual return
  after-tax.

- Her annual income is increased from $35,000 to $40,000.

- She is now income qualified for the monthly service fee
  of $2,500 or $30,000. If she qualifies for and takes the
  full medical tax deduction (Chapter 19; Figure 19-1), she
  will have an annual after-tax disposable income of over
  $11,000.

From a strategic standpoint, with the aggregate home equity
impact, you've probably increased the age and income qualified
depth of your market by about 200 to 400 senior households.
An 80-unit project absorption would represent approximately 20
to 40 percent of that range.

2. *Develop prudent spend-down strategies* – Many seniors may not economically qualify for your community – even after the added income from their expanded savings portfolio. Some seniors may also experience financial distress after moving into assisted living. That's where the prudent and financially responsible spend-down strategies outlined in Chapter 30 come into play.

More and more Seniors are seeking financial advice from families and third party professionals. So sponsors trying to tap the $1.1 trillion resource will find their pricing strategies spending more time under the microscope in the future.

CHAPTER 21

FINANCING SENIOR LIVING PROJECTS

Things Get Complicated as You Approach the Loan Closing Table

In the late 1990s, lenders introduced a new industry sound bite. They informed the senior housing and health care professionals that they were "embarking on a flight to quality". Properly decoded, this meant lenders were going to focus more on safe, high-quality loan transactions. They would be less inclined to be partners in projects involving greater risk. This "flight to quality" really represented a dramatic change. Most lenders had aggressively pursued assisted living opportunities in the early-to-mid 1990s.

Back then, most *refinancing* was almost a slam dunk. Assisted living was considered a hot development opportunity. There were significant debt and equity dollars chasing the senior housing and health care sectors. Financing *new* projects was always more complex, and frequently more difficult.

There are, of course, exceptions, but now lenders focus almost exclusively on experienced sponsors and owner-operators who have assembled impressive professional teams and, ideally, operate a *portfolio* of properties. As a potential borrower, you must also have a sound market feasibility study and a comprehensive financial plan. There are several other important issues to consider.

Have a well-conceived, pragmatic strategic business plan – That's the central theme of this entire book! But pay particular attention to the first 20 chapters. Figure 21-1 also provides some helpful benchmarks.

Assemble an impressive, experienced professional team – Don't hire the naive "never-say-no feasibility consultant," or the inexperienced architect who wants to learn this business at your expense. Most importantly, decide how you can most cost-effectively develop and operate your community. Review Chapter 36, which deals with developing an internal resource versus a third party management contract.

Detailed market feasibility studies and comprehensive financial pro formas must be closely integrated. The market feasibility study's findings – (*outputs*) – must drive the financial pro forma *inputs*. In addition, your pro forma must accurately reflect your projected development costs, estimated operating expenses, and expected revenues. As your project progresses, any cost increases or other significant financial changes must be programmed into the pro forma. If the revised pro forma indicates that increased revenues are needed, then, obviously, service fees must be increased. But first the market feasibility study must be reworked to determine whether the necessary service fee increases are, in fact, acceptable in the competitive marketplace. Refer to Appendix A for more details on market and financial feasibility.

FIGURE 21-1
ASSISTED LIVING INDICES & RULES OF THUMB

	Range Covering Approx. 75% of the Market	
	Low	High
I. Lender Criteria		
1. Debt Service Coverage Ratio	1.25	1.35
2. Loan to Value	75%	85%
3. Implied Equity	25%	15%
4. Capital Reserve for Replacement (per unit)	$225	$250
II. Operations/Pricing Criteria		
1. Operating Expense Ratio	58%	63%
2. Operating Expenses PRD	$50-$55	$55-$60
3. Average FTE's per Unit		
• Assisted Living	.45	.55
• Dementia	.50	.60
4. Management Fee as a Percent of Revenues	4.5%	5.5%
5. Percent of Cash Flow Disposable Income Used for Monthly Service Fees	75%	80%
6. Assisted Living Fees as a Percent of Prevailing Private Pay Nursing Rates	75%	80%
7. Operating Margin (EBITDA)	42%	37%
III. Capital Budget Criteria		
1. Total Cost/Unit	$110,000	$140,000
2. Land Cost/Unit	6,000	10,000
3. Marketing Cost/Unit	3,500	4,500

Industry Benchmarks Can Be Both Helpful And Dangerous - Use With Caution

Moore Diversified Services, Inc.

How Much Can I Borrow? Lenders are tightening loan criteria on borrowers' terms sheets. The important ratios of "loan to value" and "loan to cost" have taken on new definitions. In today's market, you can probably borrow about 70 to 75 percent of your new project's total estimated cost or indicated value. The other 25 to 30 percent must be provided by you in hard cash (for a new project), or very strong collateral (for the refinancing of an existing Senior living community). Chapter 13 provides more details on determining a realistic cost for your existing or planned project. Your borrowing power will also be affected by your debt service coverage ratio, which we'll discuss later in this chapter. If you are a not-for-profit organization, it is possible to obtain 100 percent financing using tax-exempt bonds.

You Must Prepare a Comprehensive and Realistic Capital Budget. Lenders particularly want to see several capital budget items frequently overlooked by the borrower. One of these is a comprehensive working capital reserve fund. For example, there will be significant negative cash flow in the early months of initial fill-up for your new project, as most of your operating costs are fixed or, at best, only semi-variable. In fact, only about 20 to 25 percent of your operating expenses are truly variable (raw food, some utilities, housekeeping, etc.). A typical assisted or independent living community takes 12 to 18 months after opening to reach break-even cash flow (after debt service). During that critical fill-up period, your project may experience cumulative negative cash flows of at least $300,000 to $400,000. This shortfall must be funded by the working capital reserve fund.

Another area frequently overlooked by borrowers is the cost of early sales and marketing activities needed to initially bring your community to stabilized occupancy. These costs will probably add up to about $3,500 to $4,500 per unit for assisted living, and frequently in excess of $5,000 per unit for independent living. This budget allocation includes all collateral/brochure design and production, marketing, program development and sales office overhead expenses. The budget also includes base compensation and performance incentives for the sales and marketing staff.

Obviously, the ultimate accuracy of your hard construction cost estimate is very critical, and will undergo significant scrutiny by lenders. Currently, hard construction costs average approximately $90 to $115 per square foot in most areas of the United States. But depending upon how tight your local labor market is, padded contractor and subcontractor bids may give you financial heartburn! **Always** factor in local market costs rather than relying on generic regional or national figures. The fact that you took this extra step should help impress potential lenders.

From a lender's perspective, the basic strategy of capital budgeting for a new assisted living community is to identify and fund all costs associated with designing, developing, financing, marketing and bringing the project to a stabilized occupancy of approximately 93 percent. At that point, the annual operating budget kicks in, and there should be sufficient operating revenues to cover both ongoing operating expenses and debt service. See Chapter 13 for the development of a detailed capital budget.

Develop a Solid, Comprehensive Financial Pro Forma –
A detailed pro forma outline is contained in Appendix A.
Simply stated, the pro forma should detail both initial capital
needs and realistic projections of how your community will
perform over the long run.

***Lenders Want a Sound Income Statement and an Exit
Strategy*** – Lenders must always consider the distasteful prospect
of foreclosure, so they require a sensible borrower exit strategy
well before approving your loan.   Along with a carefully
conceived, comprehensive capital budget, you must develop an
income statement with at least two important financial
safeguards.   Lenders want to see a management fee of
approximately five percent of revenues, along with a reserve for
repair and replacement of approximately $225 to $250 per unit
annually.   The concept is called "Cap X" (for future Capital
Expenditures).   The management fee allows the lender to hire
another asset manager (if necessary) and the "Cap X" allowance
is intended to keep the property in a "like new" condition.
Chapters 14 and 36 address the details of management fees and
"Cap X," respectively.   Lenders will probably also want an
additional safety margin in the form of an overall operating
expense contingency factor of about five percent

Factoring in the "Cap X" allocation and the five percent
management fee presents a good news/bad news situation. The
good news is that these safeguards certainly help insure the
success of your project. The bad news is, these factors are
considered normal operating expense line items, which lower
your project's net operating income and indicated value. That,
in turn, reduces how much money you can borrow.

The Debt Service Coverage Ratio Is the Lender's Acid Test. This critical lender ratio is defined as available annual Net Operating Income (Revenue minus Operating Expenses) divided by the peak annual debt service (principal and interest) you will have to pay. Simply stated, lenders want $1.25 to $1.35 in available cash (Net Operating Income) for every $1.00 you owe in annual debt payments. This is the cash available after deducting *all* operating expenses, including the previously discussed management fee and "Cap X" factor. Tax-exempt bond financing for a not-for-profit organization usually has an additional requirement. Underwriters routinely require you to reserve an amount of cash equal to one year's total debt service payments; this is allocated as a debt payment reserve fund. This cash must usually be placed in a restricted reserve account.

How much will my loan cost? Not-for-profit organizations enjoy the lowest interest rates being charged. These involve variable-rate tax-exempt bonds, which currently average 5 to 6 percent. Creditworthy for-profit borrowers closing on *construction loans* typically receive interest rates from .5 to 1.5 percent over the prime rate. Conventional *long-term financing* rates are likely to be 1.5 to 2.5 percent over the yield on similar term treasury bonds; or currently in the 8 to 9 percent range. **Caution: These rates are constantly changing. Always be certain you have the most current rate information available!**

Unique Opportunity for Not-For-Profits – There is a favorable window of opportunity for not-for-profits considering the funding of a new project or refinancing of existing assets.

As indicated earlier, not-for-profits can typically obtain 100 percent financing at a relatively low cost of capital (attractive interest rates). But, many not-for-profits also have significant cash on their balance sheets, and, being appropriately conservative, many are reluctant to consider taking on debt.

But the current cost of borrowing opportunity involves a benefit called positive arbitrage. That's a fancy Wall Street term meaning the likely annual return on *investing* your existing funds is higher than the annual cost you would pay for *borrowed* money.

Let's say you need to fund a new 120 assisted and independent living unit addition to your campus. The total, all-in cost is $120,000 per unit, or $14.4 million for the entire project. Tax-exempt bond interest rates could be as low as 6 percent, but you've been averaging at least 10 percent on your investments over the past 5 years. That is a 4 percent positive arbitrage involving over $575,000 annually! You might consider a blended risk strategy by borrowing approximately 70 percent of the needed funds ($10 million) and investing $4.4 million in equity. Your positive arbitrage benefit on the $10 million is $400,000 per year. If you invest your organization's funds in a senior living project, you should normally structure your financial plan so that a cash return on these invested funds is at least 10 percent annually.

Six Pitfalls Facing the Borrower

Securing a loan means more than just meeting your lender's requirements. The lender-borrower relationship must be balanced and equitable. In drafting the final loan agreement or "terms sheet," you should take care to avoid, or at least be aware of, six potential problem areas:

1. *Excessive loan cross-collaterization* – Lenders may ask you to pledge other existing assets on your campus for a long period of time as additional security for your new or refinanced assisted living project. As an alternative, request that this cross-collateralization (if initially necessary) be eliminated after a relatively short period of demonstrated success with the newly-financed project.

2. *Requiring too much cash equity* – Prudent borrowing or leveraging will optimize your financial returns. Currently, the acceptable debt-to-equity ratios range from 65 percent debt and 35 percent equity to a higher ratio of 75%/25%.

3. *Excessive loan pre-payment penalties* – Many lenders charge a penalty if you attempt to pay your debt off sooner than the agreed-upon term. This concept is identified by a fancy term called "yield maintenance". Try to negotiate a declining scale prepayment penalty clause, in which the penalty decreases or "burns off" with time, allowing you to pay off or refinance your loan without significant penalty before the end of the original contractual loan term.

4. *Personal liability* – Some loans are "nonrecourse," meaning lenders look only to the property being financed for security, while others attempt to secure other collateral, including your personal financial assets. Avoid personal liability, or pledging other unrelated assets, if at all possible.

5. *Loans that mature or come due before the end of the amortization period* – Some lenders will provide a loan with a <u>10-year term</u> but structure payments with a <u>25-year amortization</u>. This means the loan *looks like* a 25-year pay-off, but actually becomes due in ten years. While this can be a good financial arrangement, make sure you plan for the 10-year "bullet loan" balloon payment.

6. *Upfront financing costs versus fixed interest rates* – Lower permanent interest rates frequently require higher one-time upfront financing costs, frequently called "points." A point is a one-time charge that equals one percent of the total loan amount. This tradeoff consideration between lower rates vs. higher financing fees is usually more sensitive for loans of less than $10 million.

Other things being equal, if a loan with lower interest rates (and higher initial points) would cost you the same as one with higher rates but a lower upfront cost *within five years,* it's generally better to go with the lower interest rate loan.

The days of simply assuring your lender, ***"If we build it, they will surely come,"*** are over. Lenders want to see a definitive plan that identifies and funds all costs associated with developing, financing and marketing your Senior living community. That means bringing your project to a stabilized occupancy of approximately 93 to 95 percent in a reasonable time frame. At that point of stabilization, your operating budget will kick in, and there should be sufficient revenues to cover ongoing operating expenses, debt service and entrepreneurial profit.

Regardless of the type of financing you're after, remember that things <u>always</u> get more complex as you approach the loan closing. Knowing ahead of time what your lender is likely to ask can make the process much easier.

And remember this: Lenders are in the business of making loans. If you present them with a proposal that is obviously well-thought out, you assure them that you are a pragmatic professional who is obviously a much better risk than a disorganized dreamer with big plans and limited strategy. Lenders realize it is to their benefit to associate with borrowers who have realistic goals and sensible ways to achieve them. Additional planning **before** you approach lenders will pay off!

SECTION FIVE

Pricing

CHAPTER 22

CREATING AN OPTIMUM
PRICING STRUCTURE
Win-Win Pricing Strategies
for Financial Success

"Let's forget all this warm and fuzzy talk. What does this place really cost?" That's what your potential residents and their loved ones really want to know. Often, that's the last thing we want to tell them! We are in a service-enriched, benefit-driven business, yet we have to sell easy-to-understand, honest value. Easier said than done!

Effective assisted living pricing involves striking a delicate balance between:

- Covering your total costs, while delivering acceptable financial ratios,

    and

- Being affordable, competitive and consumer-driven for your market area

These objectives are at opposite ends of the pricing spectrum, which frequently presents significant challenges. Serious, *yet avoidable,* mistakes are being made by many sponsors at both ends of the pricing trade-off spectrum.

Owner/Operator Perspectives

Sponsors must develop sufficient operating revenues to adequately cover:

- Operating Expenses
- Debt Service

But just covering these obligations is not enough; you must also realize acceptable operating profit margins, debt service coverage ratios, and net cash flow to satisfy investors and/or to fund mission objectives.

Sounds simple, but as we observed in Chapter 15, cost creep makes operating expenses a constantly-moving target, which, obviously, increases the difficulty in establishing fair, consistent pricing.

The Consumer Marketplace Perspective

The optimum assisted living pricing structure for Senior consumers must demonstrate at least five market-driven attributes. It should be:

- Easy to Understand
- Equitable
- Perceived as Good Value
- Affordable
- Seamless (shelter vs. care costs)

The last two attributes represent the biggest pricing challenges for assisted living sponsors. Many senior prospects and their families will have serious initial concerns about the affordability of your community. These concerns must be creatively and tactfully addressed during the sales and marketing process. Many assisted living pricing structures are not seamless. An example is when senior residents get two uncoordinated bills at the end of the month. One comes from the owner/operator for basic shelter services (living unit, meals, housekeeping, etc.) and another from a third-party home health agency for care. (See Chapter 2 for more details.)

The Service-Enriched, Value-Added Concept

Regardless of your ultimate pricing structure, remember you're in a *value-added, premium price service delivery business*. Look at it as if it were similar to an entree listing on the dinner menu of a fine restaurant. If you were to unbundle *everything*, your resulting base (reduced) pricing would probably drive most consumers into sticker shock! You stand a much better chance of marketplace success by creating a value package through the effective combination of an array of *benefits* (not *features*).

PRICING MUST STRIKE A DELICATE BALANCE

Market-Driven

1. Affordable
2. High perceived value
3. Competitive in the marketplace
4. Provide hedge against inflation
5. Credible and rational

Project-Driven

1. Covering operating expenses
2. Servicing underlying debt
3. Provide lender safety margins
4. Cash for other missions
5. Entrepreneurial profit

Covering Capital Costs and Operating Expenses

Pricing is a two-step process. These are: 1) cover all your current basic capital costs (debt service and investor return) and operating expenses; and 2) provide a hedge against normal inflation and future cost creep (defined in Chapter 15).

Figure 17-1 in Chapter 17 presented an assisted living operating scenario that is likely to exist in many markets in 2001 to 2002. This operating scenario drives the development of a pricing strategy outlined in Figure 22-1.

FIGURE 22-1

**KEY ELEMENTS OF
ASSISTED LIVING PRICING**

Cost to be Covered	Monthly Cost	Percent of Total Cost
• Operating Expenses @ \$55 PRD[1]	\$1,675/mo	63%
• Debt Service Payment[2]	785	30
• Cash Flow/ Entrepreneurial Profit[3]	180	7
Total Monthly Service Fee	\$2,640/mo	100%

[1]Per Resident Day
[2]\$120,000/unit @ 75% debt, 25% equity, 9% interest, 30 years
[3]Also provides acceptable and required debt service coverage ratio of 1.3x.

It should be noted that the pricing outlined above is for "base level" assisted living services. That means all shelter services (living unit, housekeeping, food, etc. and a reasonable array of assistance with the activities of daily living). The term "reasonable" can best be defined by citing the national average, which indicates that residents in assisted living are typically receiving "base level" assistance with the activities of daily living that involves approximately 45 to 60 minutes per resident per 24-hour day of direct, hands-on care. Those residents requiring assistance with ADLs above that level are typically subject to tiered pricing and add-on fees of approximately $240 to $360 (or higher) per month for additional level of care. (See Chapter 23 for more details.)

If you think you'd like to offer a "more affordable" price in your market area, you first must face the reality of this financial summary. Where can you cut costs? And by how much?

Capital Cost Sensitivity Versus "Affordable Assisted Living"

Note in Figure 22-1 that operating expenses represent more than 60 percent of the required monthly service fee. Further, debt service costs for land and "bricks and mortar", etc. require approximately 30 percent of the monthly service fee. This subtle point is often overlooked when well intended organizations chase the moving target of *"affordable assisted living"*. Operating expenses are very difficult to reduce, so most sponsors focus on capital costs. But, if you could reduce debt service payments by as much as *50 percent,* you would only reduce the required monthly service fees by approximately $390 per month, or 15 percent. That means monthly bills would be reduced from, possibly, $2,640 to $2,250. That's a start, but it surely doesn't meet the affordability objectives of most sponsors, or the needs of hundreds of thousands of seniors.

The sensitivity of capital costs cuts both ways. These capital costs are relatively insensitive when trying to create true *affordability* at the low end of the pricing spectrum. But modest changes in capital costs become much more sensitive in avoiding *premium pricing,* while attempting to deliver *acceptable operating margins* at the upper end of the pricing envelope. Remember, at this point in the pricing strategy development, we've covered vacancy factor (seven percent), reasonable profit/positive cash flow, debt service and operating expenses for basic shelter and an array of services offering *reasonable* assistance with the Activities of Daily Living (ADLs). But as Chapter 15 points out, additional cost creep in the early life of a project can increase operating expenses and cause significant erosion of operating margins. I know I mention cost creep a lot. That's because it should always be part of your ongoing planning. To pretend otherwise would be misleading.

Mitigating the Impact of Cost Creep

Due to increased resident acuity levels resulting from aging in place, you will inevitably experience *operating cost creep.* Simply stated, the cost for providing assistance with ADLs will grow as all of your residents age in place. Implementing a proactive resident discharge policy will likely cause your annual turnover ratio to soar above the industry norm of approximately 40 percent. Most owner-operators come to the realization that responding to legitimate cost creep is largely a pricing issue.

Four Basic Pricing Structures

Some industry leaders initially believed that tiered or a la carte pricing was confusing, and not market-responsive. But realities of cost creep have changed their minds. Four different types of pricing structure are now common in our business. These include: **1) flat monthly rate; 2) a la carte charges; 3) tiered rate; and 4) point/time index.** Tiered pricing strategies are detailed in Chapter 23.

Final Checks and Balances on Pricing

Three additional guidelines can provide a final check and balance on your overall pricing effectiveness:

- *Assisted Living Pricing versus Prevailing Nursing Rates* – Assisted living pricing should be approximately 70 to 80 percent of prevailing semi-private nursing rates in your market area. For example, when nursing bed rates are $120/day or $3,600/month, assisted living monthly service fees should average not more than $2,500 to $2,900. You can use this comparison to your advantage in sales and marketing, as you ask potential residents and their families to objectively compare your community's capabilities with the nursing alternatives.

- *Consumer Affordability Thresholds* – Seniors can typically spend approximately 75 to 80 percent of their *disposable after-tax income* for assisted living monthly service fees. This means that their annual after-tax, disposable income must range from approximately $38,000 to $44,000 in order to pay monthly service fees of $2,500 to $2,900. If these qualifying incomes seem shockingly high, review Chapters 25 to 29 on affordability, Chapter 20 on home equity impact and Chapter 30 on prudent spend-down strategies. Also consider this – assisted living is a cost-effective response and alternative to growing home health care costs, especially when the senior needs continuous assistance. Some home health costs as much as $80 for less than a one hour in-home visit. For that same $80, assisted living can essentially provide 24 hours of care *plus* complete housing and shelter services. Home health care is a very viable service delivery system for short-term needs. But the concept becomes far less efficient as needs increase.

● *Price-Value Index* – A helpful check and balance is to divide the individual base monthly service fees of each of your assisted living units by their individual living unit floor areas, coming up with a dollar-per-square-foot value index. Do the same thing for your competitors to see how you stack up. I'm not suggesting that consumers typically make assisted living decisions on a dollars-per-square-foot basis, but our focus groups and other research clearly indicate that consumers draw at least subliminal impressions that signal something like, *"This sure looks like a lot for the money."* In any event, it's good to see how you stack up with your competitors.

There are other important issues that affect pricing. For the most part, they are addressed in major chapters within this book. So to develop a more complete frame of reference on pricing, you need to also address these other issues:

1. **Flash Value** – Chapter 18

2. **Pricing for Improvements** – Chapter 12

3. **Affordability** – Chapters 25 through 29

4. **Spend-down** – Chapter 30

5. **Home Equity Impacts** – Chapter 20

The ultimate pricing challenge that spans the life of your community is to provide the services residents need while covering all of your costs, and making a fair and reasonable profit while developing an effective counter-attack for inevitable assisted living cost creep.

CHAPTER 23

TIERED PRICING - THE CATCH - 22
OF ASSISTED LIVING

*How to Stay Flexible, Fair – and
Financially Viable*

*"I really like the Gardens at Westridge, but how do we
know what the cost will be if my needs change in the future?"*

*"Mother, you're right. I'm concerned about their 'one
price fits all' policy."*

Every now and then, we must deal with some serious *Catch-22* business dilemmas. For those who haven't read that novel by Joseph Heller, a *Catch-22* is an unwinnable situation, where no matter what decision is made, or how well-meaning or necessary, the outcome somehow turns out wrong. That certainly is the case with deciding how to solve the serious cost creep dilemma.

Resident acuity levels in assisted living are rising well beyond what many industry observers expected. That leaves not-for-profit sponsors and for-profit owners and operators scrambling to maintain acceptable operating margins while providing a relatively high level of assistance with Activities of Daily Living (ADLs). Responding to residents' needs can minimize the problem of resident turnover rates, which may exceed 40 percent a year. But it also creates a whole new financial challenge. If you don't track your costs and price your services appropriately – and that isn't easy to do – you can lose hundreds of thousands a year in unbilled labor. If, on the other hand, you charge more for added services, you open yourself to criticism that you pretend to offer one price while secretly planning to inflate patient bills. Hence, the catch-22.

When increased resident acuity levels result from aging in place, you inevitably experience *operating cost creep.* Simply stated, the cost for providing assistance with ADLs will grow as your residents get older and require more hands-on care from staff. Yet, if you implement a proactive resident discharge policy, this will almost certainly cause your annual turnover ratio to soar above the industry norm of about 40 percent.

To really bring this issue into focus, let's summarize the very common cost creep scenario detailed in Chapter 15:

1. Resident aides and other staff, out of compassionate professionalism, provide increasing help to residents; most will rationalize that a few extra minutes here and there are no big deal. Besides, it's just the right thing to do.

2. The residents and their families perceive this additional help to be temporary. Most likely, it isn't. Instead, the seniors are experiencing long-term physical, mental, and/or emotional deterioration. That's simply one of the hard truths of nature, which many family members may not want to accept, but which professional caregivers must deal with daily.

3. In most assisted living communities, at any given time as many as 30 percent of all residents are involved in this inexorable process.

4. Industry benchmarks indicate that the typical baseline direct care per resident for a 24-hour day averages about 45 to 60 minutes. Many frail residents needing extra help can consume an *additional* 20 to 30 minutes a day.

5. These additional half hours of help can cause a community to incur additional real costs of approximately $360 per month per resident, or over $4,300 per year.

6. When that impact is multiplied by some 25 residents in the community, the total cash impact approaches $108,000 annually. That's significant in ways residents and their families simply don't realize.

7. Potential buyers or real estate appraisers will likely use a 10.5 to 11 percent capitalization rate to establish your community's value. In cases such as we have just described, the value of your community has been reduced by approximately $1 million simply because of cost creep.

A more detailed analysis of this crucial cost creep issue is contained in Chapter 15. (Refer specifically to Figures 15-1 through 15-3 for detailed financial calculations.)

The answer to this dilemma – tiered pricing – was initially resisted by the industry, but now is commonly accepted as a necessary pricing strategy. Several industry leaders had initially taken the position that tiered, or a la carte, pricing was confusing to residents and their families. No one, of course, wants to appear to be gouging clients when they are most vulnerable. But the stark realities of cost creep are unarguable, as is the reality of significant operating profit margin erosion. You are in the health care business, but it is still a **business**.

Four Basic Pricing Structures

The four pricing structures are:

1. **Flat Monthly Rate**
2. **A La Carte Charges**   ⎫ **Usually added to a**
3. **Time Increment System**   ⎬ **base monthly rate**
4. **Tiered Rates**   ⎭

Obviously, it's time to rethink our pricing strategies. Each of the four basic assisted living pricing options have unique characteristics:

● *Flat monthly rate.* You charge a basic monthly service fee that varies only as a function of the living unit *type* (studio, alcove, one-bedroom). There are no provisions for cost creep except across-the-board rate increases for residents living in that particular unit type. These pricing strategies can be implemented, but, essentially, you are asking lower acuity, better-functioning residents to subsidize other residents' higher care needs and costs.

• *A La Carte ADL packages.* You add charges for specific help with certain individual ADLs. This doesn't require one resident to subsidize another's care – that's the advantage. But *A La Carte* requires you to estimate various ADL assistance costs, then administer just the right amount of care to fit specific ADL's. That isn't always easy. This approach often lends itself to the perception – frankly, the reality – that consumers are being "nickeled and dimed." Inevitably, resident dissatisfaction is going to result.

• *The time increment system.* This involves the classic "time and motion" philosophy originally developed early in the twentieth century for the manufacturing industry. You provide a common level of services to all residents for a base monthly fee, while offering additional services and assistance with ADLs above that level, but for an extra charge. These additional services are typically provided and measured in 15- to 20-minute increments daily, with pricing based on your cost of labor and your profit margin, as illustrated in Chapter 15. For residents and their families, though, it's still like being charged a base price for a baked potato and extra for butter, sour cream, and chives. People are simply more comfortable being told that they'll pay a certain price for something. If they know the limits of a specific service level, then they will more likely understand when they must pay more for additional services.

• *Tiered pricing.* This combines the best features of the first three pricing options, creating a series of definitive service tiers or levels of direct care that reflect the real costs of providing unique and increasing assistance with a *combination* of ADLs.

I call this an ADL value-added package. The appropriate service and pricing tiers are established for each resident using an initial comprehensive assessment approach that is monitored on a regular basis. Moving from one tier to the next typically costs the resident approximately $240 to $360 more per month for each tier. Many sponsors have three tiers; some have as many as four or five.

This concept basically packages or groups the flat rate plus a la carte charges into *definable pricing levels or value packages.* Now everyone involved knows exactly what a package of necessary ADL services is going to cost, period. With less possibility of misunderstanding, your relationships with your residents and their families can only be strengthened.

Tiered Pricing Levels Defined

These levels might be defined as follows for a particular assisted living community:

Level I:
Included in Base Rate:
- Three meals daily
- Daily snacks
- Therapeutic diets
- Weekly housekeeping
- Social, cultural and educational programs
- On-call *occasional* assistance with ADLs
- Scheduled transportation

- Emergency call system
- Health and wellness assessments
- Medication *reminders*

Industry benchmarks indicate that Level I reflects approximately 30 to 45 minutes of *direct care* per resident per 24-hour day.

Level II:
Additional $300 per Month:[1]

- All Level I services
- *Regular* assistance with ADLs
- Assistance with self-managed incontinence
- *Supervision* of medication
- Occasional reality orientation
- Occasional escort service to meals/activities

Notice how stronger *adjectives* are used to reflect increasing intensity of care. This is important; they reflect a sense of controlled urgency. The message ought to be clear – you're simply doing extra things that need to be done for the resident's comfort and safety.

Level III:
Additional $300 per Month (From Level II):

- All Level I and II services
- *Frequent* assistance with ADLs
- Assistance with manageable incontinence
- Daily housekeeping

---

[1]Each incremental level of care is an additional $300 per month.

- Medication *administration*
- Escort service to meals/community activities
- Frequent reality orientation

Levels IV, V:
There are typically Levels IV and V for residents with additional, more intensive special care needs. These levels are determined for each resident via a professional assessment and would typically include special care dementia residents.

The key to making this system work is a detailed time measurement system, one that will let you know when you have crossed the 45-minute per 24-hour day baseline for assistance that is included in the monthly fee, and that later helps monitor resident adjustments from one tier to the next. Be careful not to price yourself out of the market. To cover an additional $360/month for an additional 30 minutes of daily care, Mrs. Jones would need another $6,000 in qualifying after-tax annual income – unless she uses some of her discretionary income, spends-down some of her savings or receives help from her children.

Once you've decided on a tiered pricing plan, you must present it in a positive way to your residents and their families. Many will resist, rationalizing that their loved one's need for increasing help is only temporary. They may suspect your staff is making arbitrary judgments. You must provide very strong evidence that price changes are justified, always remembering this is a difficult time for residents and their loved ones.

Consider this approach: *"Mr. and Mrs. Jones, we feel that your mother should pay only for services she needs and uses. Therefore, we charge a base rate for services typically required by her and all of our residents, such as a flexible meal program, housekeeping, a private living unit, scheduled transportation and some basic assistance with the activities of daily living. We also have an equitable pricing policy for providing additional services that your mother might need in the future – either temporarily or on a continuing basis. You can be certain that you will always pay only for services of direct need, value and benefit to your mother."*

This sends a clear message to residents and their families that you are flexible, fair – *and* financially responsible. It also tells your lenders and investors that you plan to remain financially viable and sustain projected operating margins.

Face it – cost creep is an industry constant. It must be met with appropriate increases in revenues. Tiered pricing is the answer.

Putting It All Together – Rethinking Your Pricing

To be sure your price is right, you must first estimate the true cost of operating your community, which typically includes two major cost components – *debt service payments* and *operating expenses*. These cost elements are discussed in Chapters 13 and 14, respectively. Next, you must develop an equitable pricing policy that communicates both the value of your community and responsible charges to the consumer, while remaining competitive in your local market and delivering consistently favorable financial results. Clearly identifying all costs beyond basic shelter, meals and housekeeping, and requiring residents to pay for them as needed is the fairest strategy for everyone involved.

Five Steps to Developing Effective Tiered Pricing

1. *Determine your direct baseline costs.* These include the expenses that will essentially be incurred by *all* your assisted living residents: food, housekeeping, utilities, maintenance, management and administration, plus approximately 45 minutes per resident per 24-hour day of direct care. It also includes the payment of the underlying debt, a charge that will vary as a function of unit type (studio, alcove, one-bedroom, etc.). Spread these direct costs, along with an allocation of other appropriate overhead expenses, across the number of units that represents stabilized occupancy – typically 93 percent.

2. *Now, develop procedures to periodically measure the actual assistance required by each resident in performing their activities of daily living (ADLs).* This detailed assessment should be an integral part of the initial admissions process. It should also be updated periodically, both on a regularly-scheduled basis and at any time a major change in the resident's condition is observed. Do not put off reassessing the additional demands changed patient conditions may place on your staff. The process is analogous to the detailed case work-up and patient monitoring used in nursing.

3. *Translate unique resident ADL care needs into required skill levels and staff loading.* Determine the costs involved in delivering the required care for each resident. Identify the job descriptions, skill levels and additional time per day needed to deliver care for each individual resident. (See Chapter 16 on staffing for guidance in this area.)

4. *Develop pragmatic and consistent scoring criteria.* Each ADL need above baseline costs must be assigned a weight, or score, based on the degree of additional effort required by the staff member and the resulting additional cost incurred.

5. *Translate the scoring criteria into three to five discrete, tiered pricing levels.* Group the scoring results into three to five definitive categories, and assign a cost to each as suggested earlier in this chapter. Then *load* this direct cost to take into consideration not only the caregiver's direct hourly wage rate, but also fringe benefits and a reasonable overhead allocation and profit. Refer to Figures 23-1 and 23-2 and additional details in Figure 15-1 in Chapter 15.

As assisted living evolves, pricing will become more complex. This is partly because resident acuity levels are much higher than many operators expected, and also because more consumers are comparing costs and value of their many senior living options. This makes it even more vital that pricing policies are flexible enough to address future costs, while retaining competitive attraction to potential clients.

COVERING COST CREEP IS
A FIVE STEP PROCESS

1. **Determine your baseline costs.**

2. **Develop policies and procedures to measure the specific assistance in daily living required by individual residents.**

3. **Translate unique resident care needs into required skill levels, and estimate reasonable additional charges to deliver this care.**

4. **Develop pragmatic, consistent scoring criteria**

5. **Translate the scoring criteria into three to five discrete, tiered pricing levels**

FIGURE 23-1

THE FINANCIAL SYNERGY OF TIERED PRICING[1]

Direct Care Cost
- Base Salary CNA/Resident-Aide $ 8.50/Hour
- Fringe Benefits @ 25%   2.13
                    Subtotal - Direct Costs $10.63/Hour

Other Cost Allocations
- Indirect Time @ 20%[2]   1.70
- Overhead Allocation @ 15%   1.27
   Total Cost $13.60/Hour
   Profit/EBITDA Margin @ 40%[3]   9.07
   Target Recovery Per Hour $22.67/Hour
             Or
   $11.33 Per 30 Minute Segment Per Day
             Or an Additional
   Price Tier of $345 Per Month, $4,135/Year

---

[1]See Figures 15-1 and 15-2 for more details.
[2]Lunch, coffee breaks, downtime, etc.
[3]EBITDA = Earnings Before Interest, Taxes, Depreciation and Amortization

Moore Diversified Services, Inc.

FIGURE 23-2

TIERED PRICING RATES

Using the figures from Figure 15-2 in Chapter 15, you might set up the following price tiers:

Additional Daily Care Needs	Additional Charge		
	Per Day	Per Month	Per Year
20 Minutes	$ 8.00	$240	$2,880
30 Minutes	$12.00	$360	$4,320
45 Minutes	$17.00	$515	$6,180

Source: Moore Diversified Services, Inc.

CHAPTER 24

SHARED OCCUPANCY DELIVERS MODEST AFFORDABILITY

Semi-Private Accommodations Require Lifestyle Trade-Offs

It is generally recognized that assisted living is a very viable *private pay* shelter and service delivery system. But the search for a truly affordable market model is eluding many Seniors and most sponsors. That's because only about one-third of today's 80+ Seniors can truly afford to private pay for assisted living <u>without</u> sponsor subsidies, spend-down of their savings portfolio or financial help from their children. Even when these alternative payment options are considered, there is still a tremendous unmet need and potential market for more affordable assisted living.

Medicaid waivers and other government subsidy programs could help subsidize assisted living for moderate- and low-income residents, but the near-term expansion of such programs appears unlikely. What's more, many industry professionals do not favor third-party payor programs because they fear that regulations are sure to follow – and that the reimbursement rates may be too low to result in both good care and reasonable operating margins.

Affordability is a Tough Nut to Crack

The old adage that life is full of both opportunities and trade-offs which are heavily influenced by one's economic status is certainly true with assisted living. Like it or not, we all have our economic stations in life. Sponsors and owner/operators have generally done a good job addressing that sector of the market dealing with age 80+ Seniors who have minimum after-tax incomes of $35,000 to $40,000 or more. But many sponsors find it almost impossible to consistently deliver truly affordable assisted living by significantly reducing monthly service fees. That's because about 70 percent of a typical assisted living community's base monthly service fee of $2,500 for a modest sized unit is needed just to cover vacancy factor, profit and operating expenses of approximately $55 per resident-day. The remaining 30 percent is needed to cover the "real estate" costs, debt service and debt service coverage margins.

Achieving affordable assisted living is tough, but possible. As Figure 24 -1 indicates, for every $200 per month reduction in *private occupancy* monthly service fees, over 160,000 additional age 80+ Seniors nationally would qualify for private pay assisted living. Assuming approximately 30 percent have an actual need (incidence level) for assisted living, the adjusted potential would be 48,000 seniors. Further, assuming that only 10 percent would actually opt for assisted living results in an increase in current demand for 4,800 units, or the equivalent of approximately 60 80-unit communities. This potential grows to approximately 300 equivalent 80-unit communities if the base monthly service fee can be reduced further; from approximately $2,500 per month to $1,650 per month through *shared occupancy* as indicated in Figure 24-2.

FIGURE 24-1

**REDUCTION IN MONTHLY SERVICE FEES
CREATES SIGNIFICANT DEMAND**

	Reduction in Monthly Service Fee	
	Private Occupancy	Shared Occupancy
• Base Monthly Service Fee	$2,500/Mo.	$1,650/Mo.
• Potential Reduction in Monthly Service Fee	(200)	(850)
• Additional Age 80+ Seniors Who Become Income Qualified	160,000	810,650
• Assume 30% *Need* Assisted Living	48,000	243,200
• Assume 10% Would Actually *Opt* for Assisted Living	4,800	24,320
• Number of Equivalent New 80-Unit Communities Demanded	60	300

Moore Diversified Services, Inc.

```
┌─────────────────────────────────────────────────────────────────┐
│                          FIGURE 24-2                              │
│                                                                   │
│                  SHARED OCCUPANCY DELIVERS                        │
│                  AFFORDABLE SERVICE FEES                          │
│                                                                   │
│  *Private* Single Occupancy Fee                                   │
│                                                                   │
│    ●  Studio/Alcove Unit                     $ 2,500 /Month       │
│                                                                   │
│  *Shared* Occupancy Economies:                                    │
│                                                                   │
│    ●  *Shared* Debt Service Per Unit *          (550)             │
│                                                                   │
│    ●  *Shared* Property Expenses                                  │
│       Saving $5.00 Per Resident Day            (155)              │
│                                                                   │
│    ●  *Reduced* Operating Expenses                                │
│       @ $2.50 Per Resident Day                  (75)              │
│                                                                   │
│    ●  *Decrease* in Operating Margin           (65)               │
│                                                                   │
│       Monthly Service Per Resident          $ 1,650 /Month        │
│                                                                   │
│  * $120,000/Unit, 75% Debt, 25% Equity, 9%, 25 Years, 11% Cash Return │
│                                                                   │
│  Moore Diversified Services, Inc.                                 │
└─────────────────────────────────────────────────────────────────┘
```

The time has come to seriously consider the difficult but beneficial strategy of providing for shared living arrangements of unrelated individuals in an assisted living setting. Since "semi-private" is an oxymoron, I suggest that 21st century market positioning for this concept be called "shared occupancy", "companion suites" or "friendship suites."

The Nursing Home Comparison

Assisted living is frequently compared to the traditional nursing home, with most of these comparisons being unfavorable for the nursing home (relative cost, ambience, independence, etc.). Yet, the shared occupancy assisted living concept actually builds upon the commonly-accepted semi-private nursing bed occupancy option. Nursing homes have consistently demonstrated that private pay, semi-private occupancy is an acceptable service delivery system. While shared occupancy in assisted living is certainly not optimum, it offers more ambience, less institutionalism than nursing. And it will probably be necessary in order to accommodate the needs of a very large economic sector of the Senior living market in the future.

Market Positioning

Achieving appropriate shared occupancy market positioning is an integral part of an affordable assisted living product strategy. Properly responding to one's economic status in life has always been a major marketing strategy. Airlines, for instance, have dropped their earlier "second class" economy tickets for terms like "coach" or "main cabin." Ocean liners have dropped the *Titanic*'s "steerage" class for friendlier terms such as "Promenade Deck." But the fact remains that many consumers are knowingly making practical, affordable, value-driven economic trade-off decisions almost daily.

A 1998 survey conducted by the National Center for Assisted Living (NCAL) indicates that approximately 78 percent of today's assisted living communities offer at least *some* type of shared living options. In most cases, these options typically represent limited and fragmented efforts which lack a purpose-built design, effective market positioning or detailed operating strategies. Shared occupancy accommodates both the traditional and the non-traditional situations.

The traditional situation involves married couples when one of the spouses (most frequently, the husband) needs to be close to reasonably consistent and structured assistance with the activities of daily living. The other spouse is usually relatively healthy, but willing to live in an assisted living environment with reasonable ambience in order to sustain companionship and to access the necessary support for the spouse that he/she can no longer consistently provide. Many also make this difficult decision because they can't afford to maintain two households.

The non-traditional situation is one with huge market potential. It typically exists when two *unrelated* individuals choose to share assisted living accommodations. While certainly a lifestyle trade-off, seniors accept this living option for any of three basic reasons: 1) because of a prior shared living experience; 2) because of the desire (or need) of each to share accommodations for purposes of companionship; or 3) to

solve a difficult affordability challenge. Economic considerations are usually the major factor when Senior consumers and
their families consider the difficult decision of shared occupancy
of unrelated individuals. Sometimes, shared occupancy is
associated with a live-in caregiver.

The "Equal Turf" Strategy

Reasonable privacy, dignity and affordability are the key
attributes for implementing a truly market-responsive shared
occupancy strategy. There is one more very important element
to the strategy. I call it "equal turf." That means, wherever
possible, each resident should have privacy and dignity in an
equal turf environment, which means each has *equal* private
space within the living unit.

Developing a Shared Occupancy Strategy

Let's look at the practical process of developing a shared
occupancy strategy involving design and financial
considerations. First, we must recognize that it won't be easy.
At age 80+, unrelated individuals living in shared
accommodations require a certain degree of "compatibility
matching." This matching must be repeated if one of the
Seniors dies, moves out or is transferred to nursing. Shared
bathrooms have always been a particular challenge, but certainly
it is easier if the two individuals involved are reasonably
compatible.

There are basically three shared occupancy living unit designs that can likely deliver favorable economics for your community: 1) The typical assisted living studio unit of approximately 350 s.f., wherein the layout is very similar to a (relatively austere) semi-private nursing room; 2) A modified one-bedroom design/space plan of about 400 to 450 s.f., where each resident has "equal turf" in their individual/private sleeping areas with a modest shared sitting area; and 3) A larger two-bedroom configuration of approximately 600 s.f., which encompasses private, equal turf sleeping areas and a larger shared living area. All three models have a shared bathroom. Regardless of the model type, you must attempt to offer reasonable privacy, dignity and affordability – and, wherever possible, equal turf; both residents should have equal opportunity for dignified privacy.

The Economics of Shared Occupancy

There are two ways to evaluate the economics of shared occupancy: The *marginal* financial impacts of considering a single private unit vs. a shared occupancy unit in isolation, and a more comprehensive strategy wherein a majority of assisted living units are planned to be offered as shared occupancy. Beware of the marginal analysis trap. The marginal analysis considers only the incremental (new) increase in expenses, the added *direct* cost of the second occupant. The more comprehensive approach considers the full allocation of all necessary fixed costs (overhead) and profit objectives for each resident. The marginal analysis is helpful, but remember you must fully allocate all of your relatively heavy fixed costs (and profit objectives).

Shared occupancy can reduce a typical private base monthly service fee from about $2,500/month to approximately $1,650/month (as demonstrated in Figure 24-2). These reductions include cost sharing by each occupant of the debt service/return on equity ($550), the property-related expenses ($155), other operating expenses ($75) and a modest decease in operating profit margin ($65). These numbers are based on a community with total costs of $120,000 per unit with 75 percent debt, 9 percent interest, a 25-year term, and 25 percent equity with a 11 percent cash return.

A simple, pragmatic rule in initiating your pricing analysis should be to consider that your shared occupancy monthly service fee for each resident will likely be approximately 60 to 70 percent of your private occupancy service fee for a particular existing unit. It's always best to build your cost estimates and pricing from a fresh look at your existing operations.

A word of caution: The numbers reflected in this shared occupancy analysis are typical – but they will vary by geographic region, your individual cost structure and the unique characteristics of your community.

If this reduced monthly service fee can be realized, a community with appropriate, purpose-built unit designs and effective market positioning could expand the national market by as much as 415 equivalent 80-unit assisted living communities – as indicated in Figure 24-3. Figures 24-4 through 24-6 provide additional information to help you with your shared occupancy strategy.

Today, not many operators are entering the market with an exclusive shared occupancy product. A more conservative approach would be to consider offering selected and diversified offerings of *both* private and shared occupancy. The concept may also play a meaningful role in troubled property workouts – responding to a market correction.

We can certainly design or modify living units that provide effective sheltered living in a shared occupancy *setting*. We can run the numbers to establish affordable and profitable shared occupancy *pricing*. But the real challenge is consistently achieving compatibility between two unrelated older individuals who are naturally very set in their ways and sometimes forgetful. What works reasonably well in semi-private nursing may or may not be directly and consistently transferrable to shared occupancy assisted living. But as we operate in the 21st century, we must expand our strategic approaches to affordability; building upon tried and true approaches while also pushing the creative envelope.

<u>Caution</u>: Shared occupancy is still relatively rare in new, market rate, private pay assisted living. While the concept does attempt to address the complex affordability issue, anecdotal evidence of broad-based marketplace acceptance is still quite limited.

FIGURE 24-3

EXPANDING THE MARKET . . .
. . . PRIVATE VS. SHARED OCCUPANCY IN ASSISTED LIVING

	Monthly Service Fee	Qualifying Income Needed[1]	Additional 80+ Income Qualified Households	80-Unit Assisted Living Communities Affordable [2]
Private Studio	$2,500	$44,000	0	0
vs . . .				
Shared Occupancy Units:				
● Studio	$1,500	$26,500	1,102,150	415
● "Equal Turf"	$1,650	$29,150	810,650	300

---

[1]Pre-tax qualifying income, allowing 20% to be set aside for discretionary spending, with no help from children.

[2]Assuming 30% of the income qualified seniors qualify for assisted living and 10% opt for it.

Moore Diversified Services, Inc.

FIGURE 24-4

RUNNING THE NUMBERS . . .
. . . PRIVATE VS. SHARED OCCUPANCY IN ASSISTED LIVING
(80 Units-Beds)

	Private Studio	Vs.	80 *Units* - 160 *Beds* Shared Occupancy Options	
			Studio	"Equal Turf"[1]
• **Living Area S.F.**	350		350	450
• **Apprx. All-In Cost/Unit**	$110,000		$112,000	$120,000
• **Base MSF**	$2,500		$1,500	$1,650
• **Operating Expenses Per Resident Day**	$55		$41	$45
• **Resident's Qualifying Income**	$45,000		$26,450	$29,150

---

[1]Private, equal sleeping areas

Moore Diversified Services, Inc.

FIGURE 24-5

DEBT SERVICE PER SHARED OCCUPANCY UNIT

	Single Occupancy	Shared Occupancy
Unit Size	350 s.f.	450 s.f.[1]
Total Livable Area	28,000 s.f.	36,000 s.f.
Public/Common Space @ .45	23,000	29,455
Total Area Under Roof	51,000 s.f.	65,455 s.f.
All-In Cost per Unit	$95,000	$120,000
Debt Service and Investor Return – Debt Constant = 10.08 75% Debt; 25% Equity	$7,175/Year or $600/Month	$9,072/Year or $756/Month
Adjust for 93% Occupancy	$645/Month	$815/Month
Shared Debt Service	No	$407/Resident
Return on 25% Equity @ Approximately 11% TOTAL	215 $860/Month	143 $550/Month

[1]Could possibly deliver 450 to 475 s.f. unit for $120,000 all-in cost.

FIGURE 24-6
SHARED OCCUPANCY OPERATING EXPENSE RATIONALE
(93% Stabilized Occupancy)

Single Occupancy "Achievable" Operating Expenses (80 Units, 74 Residents)		Shared Occupancy Operating Expenses (80 Units, 149 Residents)	Rationale Shared Cost	Plus Premium
Administration	$ 5.46 PRD	$ 2.73 PRD	x	0
Activities	1.62	1.00	x	25%
Assisted Living	9.59	8.91	x	93
Plant Mainten./ Security	4.26	2.56	x	20
Food/Dietary	11.58	10.0	x	86
Hskpgy./Lndry.	2.24	1.25	x	10
Transportation	0.85	.50	x	18
Property	5.33	3.20	x	20
Marketing/Sales	3.99	2.50	x	25
Managemnt. Fees	4.26	3.15	5% of Revenues	
Reserve for Replacement	0.88	.53	x	20
	$50.06 PRD	$36.33 PRD		

PRD = Per Resident-Day

SECTION SIX

Affordability

CHAPTER 25

AFFORDABILITY IS A GREAT IDEA, BUT IT'S MORE TALK THAN ACTION

How Low Can We Really Go?

Sometimes I feel like CBS 60 Minutes commentator Andy Rooney, fussing at a world that overlooks the obvious realities of life. Recently, my pet peeve has been all the rhetoric about affordable assisted living. I often ask myself the question, **"Is truly affordable assisted living going to be a reality in the future, or is it only another classic oxymoron?"**

Don't misunderstand me. I am by no means an opponent of affordable assisted living. If we could solve this huge financial dilemma, *everyone* would win. We would be able to meet the enormous social and financial needs of our older population, and our companies would grow exponentially. But, sadly, life is not that simple.

Frequently, I hear well-intentioned people making statements about affordability that are the equivalent of political sound bites from inside the Washington Beltway. They're meant to sound great, and they do. But most of them fail to pass the reality test. And that's because we conveniently avoid answering these six defining questions:

1. What is your *financial* definition of "affordable"? (See Chapter 26)

2. What pricing do you *really* need to cover your operating expenses and debt service costs? (See Chapter 27)

3. What can millions of seniors with modest incomes really afford to pay? (See Chapter 28)

4. What is the financial impact or additional financial augmentation (subsidies) that must be provided by either not-for-profit sponsors or for-profit owner/operators?

5. In many instances, aren't we actually just cost-shifting to some seniors, utilizing their abilities to pay to cover a number of subsidized units - and then calling the end result "affordable assisted living"?

6. Will Medicaid waivers and other state and local initiatives remain universal, multi-year, predictable entitlements, or are they just limited experimental programs?

**Finally, after all the well-intended rhetoric, the
bottom line question is,
*"What's the required monthly service fee – and
how many seniors can afford to pay it?"***

Affordability is such a complex, important issue that I've devoted four chapters to it here:

1. Affordability Defined   Chapter 26

2. What Sponsors and Owner-
   Operators Need   Chapter 27

3. What Seniors Can Afford to
   Pay for in Assisted Living   Chapter 28

4. Nine Pathways to Affordable
   Assisted Living   Chapter 29

Strap yourself in – this can't help but prove an interesting ride!

CHAPTER 26

AFFORDABILITY DEFINED

We Face Huge Social
and Economic Challenges

Attempts to deliver legitimately affordable assisted living must factor in three economic classes of seniors.

I.   The "Entitlement Group" – Incomes Under $12,000

Seniors with reported incomes under $12,000 per year typically qualify for various government entitlement programs, such as the HUD 202 and Section 8 seniors housing, which offer low monthly rent initiatives. But keep in mind that the original concept of the HUD 202 or Section 8 programs assumed seniors would live *independently* (preparing their own meals, etc.). It was initially presumed seniors would not need assistance with typical activities of daily living. But many of these programs started 25 years ago – thanks to improved health care, among other advances, the number of low income seniors who have aged in place and need assisted living has skyrocketed beyond the initial projections of a quarter-century ago. Sadly, but predictably, there are no consistently-funded entitlement programs to pay for these additional services.

II.   The "Gap Income Group" – $12,000 to $25,000

The greatest unmet need in senior housing today is the obvious lack of affordable services and living options aimed at serving seniors with incomes that are moderate, but not low enough to qualify for subsidies or government entitlements. Nor can they afford to fully private pay for assisted living. Labeled the *"Gap Income Group,"* this sector of the senior market has annual incomes between $12,000 and $25,000. In 2003, these seniors will represent about 28 percent of all the households over age 75 in the United States.

III.   The "Market Rate (Private Pay) Group" – $25,000+

Many seniors with incomes in excess of $25,000 qualify for *"market rate"* assisted living. That means they can afford to pay prevailing rates beginning at the lower end of today's assisted living private pay pricing spectrum.

The Gap Group Economic Squeeze

Figure 26-1 illustrates how the Gap Group is caught in an economic squeeze between the other two economic classes of seniors – the very low income group who qualify for significant entitlements, and the income-qualified market rate group who can afford to "private pay" for a wide variety of senior living options. Trapped between these two economic classes, the Gap Group is significantly underserved and represents *very* large numbers. Figure 26-2 depicts this economic conundrum. Note these are 2003 demographic projections.

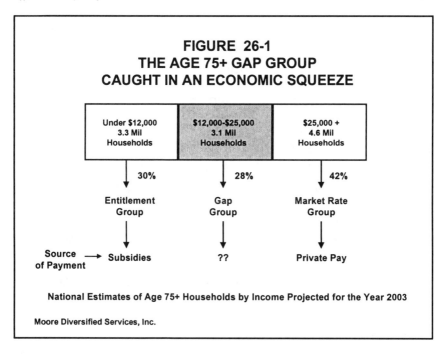

**FIGURE 26-1
THE AGE 75+ GAP GROUP
CAUGHT IN AN ECONOMIC SQUEEZE**

Under $12,000 3.3 Mil Households	$12,000-$25,000 3.1 Mil Households	$25,000 + 4.6 Mil Households
30%	28%	42%
Entitlement Group	Gap Group	Market Rate Group

Source of Payment → Subsidies   ??   Private Pay

National Estimates of Age 75+ Households by Income Projected for the Year 2003

Moore Diversified Services, Inc.

Nationally, approximately 30 percent of the age 75+ households report annual incomes of $12,000 or less. The "market rate" group reporting incomes of $25,000 or more represents about 42 percent. That leaves 28 percent, or approximately 3.1 million, aged 75+ households that are largely underserved.

Affordability Gap

As Figure 26-3 dramatically demonstrates, the Gap Group's affordability limits fall far short of adequately covering today's required independent or assisted living monthly service fees.

These monthly fees typically range from $1,000 to $2,000 for independent living, and approximately $1,900 to $3,600 for various levels of assisted living.

FIGURE 26-2

THE GAP INCOME GROUP
BY THE NUMBERS (Age 75+)
(Number of Households in Typical Markets)

	Under $12,000		$12,000 - $25,000		$25,000 - $40,000		$40,000 +	
	No.	%	No.	%	No.	%	No.	%
• Total U.S.	3,301,984	30%	3,085,233	28%	1,813,929	17%	2,733,708	25%
• Atlanta	31,122	32	24,086	25	14,979	16	26,504	27
• Boston	43,962	31	41,584	29	22,170	15	35,916	25
• Dallas	24,804	30	19,023	23	12,816	16	26,249	31
• Denver	16,119	26	15,134	25	10,418	17	19,980	32
• Phoenix	30,765	25	31,894	26	23,510	19	37,005	30

Figures for typical metropolitan areas in the year 2003

Source: Claritas
        MDS Analysis

FIGURE 26-3

AFFORDABILITY OF THE GAP GROUP
Typical Primary Market Area

Gross Pre-tax Income	Ability to Pay/ Affordable Service Fee[1] Independent Living	Assisted Living	Number of Households in a Typical Market Area
$12,000-$14,999	$ 585-$ 730	$ 720-$ 900	2,800
15,000- 19,999	730- 975	900- 1,200	3,200
20,000- 24,999	975- 1,220	1,200- 1,500	3,400
Typical Required MSF	$1,000-$2,000	$1,900-$3,600	

Actual pre-spend-down affordability levels of the age 75+ *gap group* fall well below typical senior living *private pay* pricing requirements.

_____

[1]Assumes a 10% *average* tax bracket and a senior's spending criteria of 65% and 80% of disposable income (after-tax) for independent living and assisted living monthly service fees, respectively – with no spend-down or help from family members.

Moore Diversified Services, Inc.

Without considerable spend-down or help from children, a senior's qualifying annual income would likely have to exceed $25,000 – and that's in after-tax dollars! Figure 26-4 presents the big picture of assisted living affordability. Chapter 30 deals with spend-down, and Chapter 27 provides more details on what seniors can afford to private pay for assisted living.

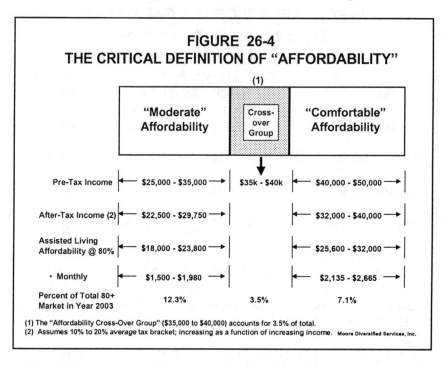

FIGURE 26-4
THE CRITICAL DEFINITION OF "AFFORDABILITY"

(1) The "Affordability Cross-Over Group" ($35,000 to $40,000) accounts for 3.5% of total.
(2) Assumes 10% to 20% *average* tax bracket; increasing as a function of increasing income. Moore Diversified Services, Inc.

The Entitlement Group will be dependent upon just that – public or private sector entitlements. The Gap Group represents a total national potential of over 75 projects, assuming an average senior housing project size of 80 units and a modest 10 percent total market share for senior housing. Figure 26-2 depicts Gap Group gross potential within a community's primary market area in typical major metropolitan areas; while Figure 26-3 shows typical potential for an individual project's primary market area.

When the impacts of aging-in-place intensify and reach crisis levels, the Gap Income Group will finally be widely recognized as a huge economic and social challenge. Breaking down the existing economic barriers with creative solutions that stand the test of time and financial viability will be difficult to achieve. But if this lofty goal is accomplished, the result will perhaps be the biggest breakthrough in effectively serving seniors in the 21st century.

CHAPTER 27

AFFORDABILITY PARAMETERS
FOR TODAY'S ASSISTED LIVING
What Sponsors and Operators Need

As we've seen in Chapter 26, a realistic definition of "affordable" is elusive. In determining how much a senior can spend for assisted living, we must first make two important qualifying income adjustments. Available demographics on seniors provide *pre-tax income,* but seniors must pay for assisted living in *after-tax dollars.* Ideally, they should not spend more than 80 percent of their *after-tax disposable income* for monthly service fees. Spend-down of assets is certainly a reality; I've addressed this important concept in Chapter 30.

The Price Sensitivity of Assisted Living

Assisted living pricing sensitivity is driven by the need to cover both capital costs and operating expenses. The sensitivity of these costs cuts both ways. At the low end of the pricing spectrum, it is difficult to significantly reduce capital costs enough to create true affordability. That's because a $1,000 per unit decrease in capital costs – using borrowed money at 9 percent interest rate – provides only a $100 per year, or $8.40 per month cost savings for the resident. At the high end of the pricing spectrum, both capital costs and operating expenses come into play when trying to strike a balance between avoiding premium pricing, while still delivering acceptable operating margins.

Using a fancy term favored by economists, assisted living pricing is very *inelastic.* This means that monthly service fees can't realistically <u>drop</u> below a specific economic floor in attempting to achieve true affordability. But moderate market price <u>increases</u> at the high end can lead to premium pricing, and possibly wide swings in critical operating ratios and financial returns.

The Operator's Pricing Needs Quantified

Let's look at a typical 80-unit "market rate" assisted living community with operating expenses of $55 per resident day (in 2003 dollars), or $1,675 per resident month, and a total, all-in development cost of $120,000 per unit, financed at 9 percent with 75 percent debt and 25 percent equity. Note that all-in cost includes land, site development, bricks and mortar, and soft costs – everything to bring the project on-line and achieve stabilized occupancy of 93 percent. Figure 13-1 in Chapter 13 summarizes the typical all-in costs for an 80-unit assisted living project, while Figure 17-1 in Chapter 17 shows a complete income statement.

These figures, which represent average costs in 2003, require residents to pay monthly service fees of about $2,640. This fee covers operating expenses of $1,675 (63 percent of the fee), a debt service payment of $785 (30 percent), and cash flow/ entrepreneurial profit of $180 (7 percent), and vacancy factor of $200 (7 percent). Figure 22-1 in Chapter 22 depicts this typical 80-unit assisted living pricing model.

Cracking the Affordability Nut By Reducing Pricing

So, if you'd like to offer a more affordable assisted living community in your market area, you must first answer this critical question: *Where can you realistically cut costs? And by how much?*

Capital Costs – Operating expenses are difficult to reduce, so most sponsors initially focus on capital costs. But if, in the previous example, you could reduce capital costs and resulting debt service payments by as much as *50 percent,* you would reduce the required monthly service fees by only $390 per month, or 15 percent - from $2,640 per month to $2,250 per month. That's because debt service costs are only about 26 percent of your monthly service fee requirements. So, it's not easy to achieve significant affordability by tightening the reins on just capital costs or interest rates. In fact, someone could *give* you the land and building, and you might still have a significant affordability challenge!

Operating Costs – Seniors in assisted living, regardless of their economic station in life, need three meals daily, comprehensive shelter services, high quality of care, and significant assistance with their activities of daily living. If they didn't, they would be living happily in their own homes. Whether for-profit or not-for-profit, sponsors and owners find it difficult to deliver these services for less than $50 to $55 per resident day, or $1,520 to $1,670 per month. Some are actually experiencing operating costs in excess of $60 per resident day because of the acuity/cost creep business challenge addressed in Chapter 15. *Operating costs are the economic affordability nut that <u>must</u> be cracked.*

Some sponsors are making progress in reducing operating costs through property tax abatement or elimination, the selected use of volunteerism, deploying the universal worker concept, and providing in-kind service contributions. Others pin their hopes on revenue enhancements, trying initiatives such as shared occupancy by unrelated individuals, spend-down of senior's liquidated home equity, and endowments. (Chapters 20, 24 and 30 address these important issues.)

The Unbundled Service Trap

Still others have tried unbundling their services and, in effect, looking the other way. They do this by offering shelter and living services only, assuming the seniors will otherwise fend for themselves. This appears to reduce cost, but it frequently merely shifts costs, creating major problems for low-income seniors who have escalating needs for assistance with their activities of daily living (those unbundled services), but no additional funds to pay for such help.

Solving the affordability challenge will require the execution of realistic, hard-nosed strategies, not just politically correct rhetoric. Chapter 29 addresses nine ways to fight – and eventually win – the affordability battle for the gap income group addressed in Chapter 26.

CHAPTER 28

WHAT SENIORS CAN
AFFORD TO PAY

Is "Affordable Assisted Living" an Oxymoron?

Some sponsors and owner/operators consider assisted living service fees of $1,500 to $1,800 per month affordable. Well, at $1,500 per month, or $18,000 per year, a senior in the *average* 10 percent tax bracket paying 80 percent of her after-tax income for assisted living would need a gross annual pre-tax income of approximately $25,000 (see Figure 28-1). In 2003, approximately 42 percent of those 75 or older will have this much. (See Figure 26-2 in Chapter 26.)

Even at a monthly service fee as low as $1,000, Figure 28-1 shows that a senior would need a gross pre-tax income of at least $16,700 a year to qualify. In 2003, about 62 percent of people 75-plus will be in this bracket. But this becomes largely an academic exercise, because sponsors cannot realistically offer assisted living for that $1,000/month figure.

Seniors Need Relatively High Qualifying Incomes

The magnitude of the challenge to make assisted living truly affordable is enormous. By 2003, only about 30 percent of those aged 75-plus will be able to afford typical assisted living offered for total monthly service fees starting at $2,000. To meet such fees, they would need pre-tax incomes of almost $35,000 (refer to Figure 28-1).

FIGURE 28-1

PERCENT AFFORDABILITY AT
VARIOUS MONTHLY SERVICE FEES

Required Monthly Service Fee	"Theoretical" Qualifying Income[1]	Percent of 75+ Households Who Qualify In 2003[2]
• $1,000/mo	$16,700	62%
• $1,500	$25,000	42
• $2,000	$33,400	30

[1]Assumes a 10% *average* tax bracket and spending 80% of their after-tax disposable income for the monthly service fee.

[2]These percentages would increase modestly for seniors selling their homes and putting their liquidated home equity to work.

Moore Diversified Services, Inc.

Figure 28-1 shows that the percentage of qualifying households might go as high as 35 percent for a $2,000 monthly service fee – assuming many assisted living prospects are current homeowners who could sell their houses, adding the net home sales proceeds to their existing income-earning savings portfolios. But that leaves approximately 65 percent of those 75 years or older – over 8 million seniors – unable to meet the $35,000-plus affordability criteria.

Some Surprising Aspects of Assisted Living Qualifying Income

Many sponsors and owner/operators are surprised when they conduct a thorough analysis of the required qualifying income for seniors with respect to their assisted living community. Some of the key issues they routinely overlook when generally referring to monthly service fees – absent of a more detailed analysis – include:

- **Discretionary Income Factor** – Seniors should be able to reserve approximately 20 percent of their *after-tax* income for discretionary spending; the remaining 80 percent can be allocated to the assisted living monthly service fee. Note that, as time passes, a typical assisted living resident's acuity level increases; at this point, they will be subject to increased/tiered pricing. When this happens, more of their discretionary spending shifts to pay the increasing obligations to the owner/operator for higher (tiered) monthly service fees.

- **Seniors Must Pay Taxes** – Many forget the common demographic sources we all access (including the U.S. Census) report senior incomes in *pre-tax* dollars. I conduct a detailed analysis each year with the help of professional accountants and have determined that the *average* (not marginal) tax brackets of seniors typically fall in the range of 10 to 15 percent. Since seniors can only pay for their obligations in *after-tax* dollars, this factor must also be considered.

Figure 28-2 shows a typical income qualified senior tax situation, while Figure 28-3 summarizes the "theory" of assisted living qualifying income. Note that, because of the above factors, qualifying income requirements escalate quite rapidly; frequently presenting surprises to both owner/operators and market analysts.

Qualifying Income for a Typical Assisted Living Community

Figure 28-3 shows the qualifying income for a typical assisted living community in 2003. Note that this qualifying income schedule is consistent with typical assisted living private pay pricing, along with the factors outlined in Figure 28-4. This is obviously before any spend-down, or help from children.

Income Qualified Seniors Have Surprising High Savings Portfolio

As Figure 28-4 indicates, many seniors must have pre-tax incomes in excess of $40,000 to qualify for today's private pay assisted living. Figure 28-5 indicates that, if such is the case, seniors must have an extensive savings portfolio or pension program to supplement their typical Social Security benefit. As Figure 28-2 illustrates, a senior requiring a $40,000 pre-tax income must have over $430,000 earning a 7 percent investment

FIGURE 28-2

TYPICAL SENIOR CONSUMER TAX SITUATION SUMMARY

Total Gross Income

● Interest and Dividends	$ 30,400[1]
● Gross Social Security	9,600
Total	$ 40,000
● Less Portion of Social Security Not Taxable ($9,600 - $5,520)	(4,080)
Adjusted Gross Income (AGI) (For Tax Purposes)	$ 35,920
Deductions:	
● Standard	(5,500)
● Exemptions	(2,800)
Subtotal	($ 8,300)
Total Taxable Income	$ 27,620
Taxes as a Percent of Total Gross Income	10.8%

[1]Reflects a needed savings portfolio of over $430,000 earning 7% annually.

Moore Diversified Services, Inc.

FIGURE 28-3

THE THEORY OF ASSISTED LIVING QUALIFYING INCOME

(For Assisted Living With a Base MSF of $2,500/Month)

	Qualifying Income Impact	
	Monthly	Annual
Required "Base" - *Net* MSF After-Tax Income Needed:		
• 80% for Base MSF	$2,500/Mo.	$30,000/Yr.
• 20% for Discretionary Spending	625	7,500
***After-Tax* Income Needed**	$3,125/Mo.	$37,500/Yr.
Gross Pre-Tax Income Requirement @ *Average* Tax Bracket of:		
• 15%	$3,675	$44,115
• 20%	$3,900	$46,875

Before any spend-down, a senior typically needs a gross pre-tax income of over $40,000 in order to have sufficient after-tax income to pay the monthly service fee and have modest discretionary income.

MSF = Monthly Service Fee

© Moore Diversified Services, Inc.

FIGURE 28-4

MINIMUM QUALIFYING CASH FLOW INCOME REQUIREMENTS FOR A TYPICAL ASSISTED LIVING COMMUNITY

(Based on Estimated 2003 Monthly Service Fees)

Assisted Living Unit Type	Required Base Monthly Service Fees		Annual Cash Flow	
	Monthly	Annual	After-Tax	Before-Tax
Assisted Living Units:				
• Studio/Alcove	$2,200-$2,400	$26,400-$28,000	$33,000-$36,000	$38,825-$42,350
• One Bedroom	$2,600-$2,800	$31,200-$33,600	$39,000-$42,000	$45,880-$49,410

Assumptions:

1. Rates based on single occupancy in 2003 dollars.
2. Senior's cash flow allocation for fees: 80.0%
3. Assumed average Senior's tax rate: 15.0%

Moore Diversified Services, Inc.

return. That's for a widow with a Social Security benefit of $800/month. Figure 28-5 provides additional information for a senior whose Social Security is $640/month.

Future Potential is Difficult to Predict

Of course, the *average* entry age in assisted living is 82, not 75, and not every senior household will need or want assisted living. What's more, seniors in the future may be willing to spend down some of the principal in their savings portfolios, although this is still a controversial issue and has not yet become a totally acceptable assumption when assessing *initial* project feasibility. It may even become common – or at least less uncommon – for family members to pitch in and help pay the fees.

But no matter how we count them, the underserved pool of seniors is still significant. Let's assume that 25 percent of the 8 million underserved seniors discussed earlier could benefit from assisted living at some point in their lives, *if* they could afford it. That would leave us with close to 2 million underserved seniors – enough to fill 25,000 80-unit assisted living communities, or a rough average of 500 additional communities per state.

To put some of these "macro statistics" into perspective, there are currently about 1.6 million seniors in nursing homes. About 70 percent of the bed census days are Medicaid reimbursed. This means the majority of seniors in nursing homes have very limited assets and income. Sadly, many entered as private pay residents, with reasonable financial resources. But with nursing home costs of $40,000 to $80,000 per year, many seniors are rapidly spending down the assets accumulated over their lifetimes at an alarming rate. Anticipated inheritances for their children are often wiped out.

I've labeled seniors opting for assisted living as *Distinguished Achievers* for many reasons. One is economic.

While reporting relatively modest incomes, a large portion of these incomes are typically realized by earnings from surprisingly significant assets.

Home equity plays a major role in a senior's personal balance sheet. Prior to making the difficult assisted living transition decision, a typical senior will likely own a home free and clear (no mortgage). Upon sale of the home, the senior will add approximately $100,000 to his or her personal balance sheet, significantly increasing his ability to private pay for assisted living. Chapter 26 deals in more detail with senior incomes.

Chapter 27 covered what sponsors typically need in their pricing of assisted living. This chapter defined senior consumer affordability. The affordability gap is enormous – but so are the potential opportunities. Read on – the next chapter addresses nine pathways to pursue in our long odyssey to crack the affordability nut.

FIGURE 28-5
INCOME QUALIFIED SENIORS MUST HAVE
AN EXTENSIVE SAVINGS PORTFOLIO

	Gross Pre-Tax Income *		
	$30,000	$40,000	$50,000
I. Gross Pre-Tax Income Typical Sources			
● Widow's Social Security Annual Benefit: $7,700 ($640/month)	$7,700	$7,700	$7,700
● Net Income Needed From Other Sources . . .	22,300	32,300	42,300
● In Order to Realize a Gross Pre-Tax Income of:	$30,000	$40,000	$50,000
● Less Income Taxes*	(3,000)	(4,800)	(10,000)
● After-Tax Income	$27,000	$35,200	$40,000
Average Tax Bracket	10%	12%	15%
II. Required Savings Portfolio**			
● Required Savings Portfolio Earnings (After-Tax)			
5.0%	$446,000	$646,000	$846,000
7.0%	$318,571	$461,429	$604,280

* Seniors typically have an *average* tax bracket of approximately 10% - 15% - considering deductions, adjusted gross income, etc. These examples are net after-tax disposable income of $27,000, 35,200 and $40,000 respectively ($30,000 with 10% tax = $27,000 net).

** Reflects a combination of conventional savings portfolio and pension proceeds (if applicable). The savings portfolio requirement might be decreased by an average of $100,000 to $150,000 for a current homeowner selling a home and moving into senior housing.

Moore Diversified Services, Inc.

CHAPTER 29

NINE PATHWAYS TO AFFORDABLE ASSISTED LIVING

There May be Light at the End of the Tunnel

Let's recap the complex issue of affordability. Chapter 26 provided a pragmatic definition of affordability. Chapter 27 addressed what prices sponsors and owner-operators typically need to charge to cover the costs of providing services to senior consumers. Chapter 28 examined the sobering realities of what various groups of senior consumers can really afford.

The task of achieving practical affordability is formidable. There are, however, ways this can be accomplished.

The Nine Pathways to Affordable Assisted Living

There are nine basic approaches to achieving practical affordability:

1. Reducing Capital Costs and Resulting Debt Service:

- Reduced All-In Project Cost:

    - Land
    - Building
    - Soft costs

- Lower the Cost of Capital:

    - Lower interest rates
    - Use of tax credits
    - More equity; less debt

- Use Fund Raising/Endowment Proceeds to:

    - Replace alternative debt

2. Permanently Reduce Operating Expenses:

- Expense avoidance
- Expense reduction

3. Provide Shared Occupancy Accommodations:

- For unrelated seniors

4. Deploy Rate Shifting – Blending the Rent Roll:

- Offer a mix of market and reduced rate units

5. Operating Subsidies, Scholarships and Endowments:

- Provide non-operating income
- Provide operating subsidies
- Offer reduced rate resident "scholarships"

6. Use Medicaid Waivers and Other Entitlements:

- Government entitlements
- Local/regional initiatives

7. Encourage Financial Support From Children

- Funding the dollar gap
- Dollar-matching incentive

8. Recognize Spend-Down of Assets:

- Requires prudent planning
- Creative/responsible use of home equity

9. Exploit the Potential of Tax Advantages

- Current opportunity: Medical deduction for the <u>complete</u> assisted living monthly service fees?

    - *Above* the 7.5 percent of adjusted gross income threshold?

- Future opportunity: *Complete* deduction *without* a 7.5 percent exclusion (a future tax reform issue)?

Each approach to affordability offers unique challenges and opportunities.

In Chapters 27 and 28, we started laying the foundation for seeking true assisted living affordability. This is best accomplished by matching senior consumer affordability with the real economic needs of the sponsor or owner-operator. Let's now look at these important challenges in more detail.

Two Major Economic Barriers to Achieving Affordability

Both for-profit and not-for-profit sponsors have two primary economic barriers to delivering affordable assisted living to primarily the Gap Income Group – those seniors with pre-tax incomes ranging from $12,000 to $25,000 per year:

1) *Funding your project's capital costs and covering ongoing debt service, or required return on investor equity.*

2) *Paying ongoing operating expenses for the life of the project.*

It's amazing how far some well-meaning organizations go in their affordable assisted living planning process before actually coming to grips with these fundamental, unavoidable financial hurdles.

Reducing All-In Capital Costs

Impact of Capital Costs – Some organizations with owned or donated land feel they are well on the way to realizing a truly affordable, low-income assisted living community. But raw land costs, depending upon your geographical location, will typically cost about $5,000 to $10,000 per unit. This represents only 5 to 10 percent of the total project's capital costs, and thus has only a nominal impact on reducing required monthly service fees. (See Figure 13-1 in Chapter 13 on capital costs.)

Reducing Total Project Costs – Capital costs are being reduced through donations of land, and, sometimes, through cash and in-kind contributions involving the reduction of development and construction costs for the community. Aggressive "value engineering" and the use of donated in-kind professional development and planning services are also typical initial capital cost reduction strategies.

Let's assume you can create an ideal *affordable* community with a very modest *total all-in* cost of only $85,000 per unit; clearly beating the typical capital costs of $120,000-plus outlined in Chapter 13. Figure 29-1 illustrates this comparison.

The $85,000 figure assumes the total turn-key project cost is divided by the number of units. This project will require a monthly debt service per unit of approximately $410, assuming a *very low* 6.0 percent interest rate/cost of capital. We can further assume (optimistically) that the land could be donated.

Making required adjustments for 7 percent vacancy and a debt service coverage ratio (safety margin) of 1.3 involves a cash flow/debt service requirement per *occupied* unit of approximately $410 per month. But, as Figure 29-1 demonstrates, debt service to cover these capital costs typically represents only 18 percent of the total required monthly service fee (also see Figure 22-1 in Chapter 22 on pricing).

FIGURE 29-1
TYPICAL OPERATING SCENARIOS

Costs to be Covered[1]	"Typical" $120,000 Unit Cost		"Affordable" $85,000 Unit Cost	
	Monthly Cost	Percent of Total Cost	Monthly Cost	Percent of Total Cost
• Operating Expenses @ $55 PRD[2]	$1,675	63%	$1,675	75%
• Debt Service Payment	785[3]	30	410[4,5]	18
• Cash Flow/Requirement - Investor Return on Equity and/or Debt Service Coverage	180	7	145	7
• Required Monthly Service Fee	$2,640	100%	$2,230	100%

[1]93% occupancy.
[2]Per Resident Day (30.4 days per month).
[3]@ 75% debt, 25% equity, 9% interest, 30 years.
[4]@ 75% debt, 25% equity/fund-raising, 6% interest, 30 years.
[5]Also provides acceptable and required debt service coverage ratio of 1.3x.

Figure 29-1 also presents a more "typical" assisted living operating scenario that is likely to exist in many markets in the 2003 time frame. This operating scenario drives the development of a pricing strategy – approximately $2,640/month for the "typical" scenario, and $2,230/month for the "affordable" scenario.

So, if you think you'd like to offer "more affordable" assisted living pricing in your market area, you first must face the reality of this financial summary. Where can you cut costs? And by how much?

Stretching the Affordability Envelope

Figure 29-2 presents *very best case* affordability scenarios. Note that *every* input assumption in Figure 29-2 has been stretched to its most optimistic limit – and it's still difficult to break the $1,800 monthly service fee barrier! Simply stated, reduced capital cost alone will not get the job done.

Creative Financing

Low-interest loans and tax credit incentive programs certainly help; but remember, the real challenge is in the area of operating expenses. You can deploy a higher concentration of equity, but the results don't have a very high payoff. Revisiting Figure 29-1 shows that debt service represents only about 18 to 30 percent of the total monthly service fee requirement.

FIGURE 29-2

REQUIRED MONTHLY SERVICE FEES
VS. REDUCED PROJECT COST

	Total (All-In) Cost/Unit - (The Very Best Cases)		
	$65,000	**$75,000**	**$85,000**
• **Debt Service (100% financing @ 5.5%, 30 yrs) Per Occupied Unit** [1,2]	$388/mo	$445/mo	$505/mo
• **Debt Service Coverage Factor@1.25x**	97	110	125
Subtotal	$485/mo	$555/mo	$630/mo
• **Operating Expenses @ $45 PRD** [3]	$1,370	$1,370	$1,370
Minimum/Best Case Required MSF [4]	$1,855/mo	$1,925/mo	$2,000/mo

[1]Assumes 95% occupancy
[2]Optimum debt service; 5.5%, 30 years, 100% financing
[3]PRD = Per Resident Day – an optimistic assumption
[4]MSF = Monthly Service Fee (Best Case)
Moore Diversified Services, Inc.

Permanent Reduction in Operating Costs

Reducing capital costs and deploying creative financing must be combined with lowering day-to-day operating expenses, *without* major compromises in services provided or quality of care.

Delivering affordable assisted living involves the long-run challenges of reducing operating expenses which are incurred by the community in perpetuity. In terms of operating cost reduction, progressive organizations have made substantial progress in lowering recurring operating expenses through property tax abatement or elimination, the selected use of volunteerism, utilizing the universal worker concept and realizing the advantages of ongoing in-kind service donations.

Others have considered the careful unbundling of selected services. Unbundling is a tempting strategy that does reduce costs, but it can also create other major affordability problems for many of the seniors being served. Large numbers of low-income seniors have escalating assistance needs with the activities of daily living, and, often, no funds to pay for this additional help. This situation will only intensify as time goes on, so it is not usually practical to provide affordable long-term senior housing by eliminating services to reduce costs.

Covering Ongoing Operating Costs

Independent Living – Operating costs are a fact of business life. Owner/operators have found it extremely difficult to offer basic, service-enriched congregate *independent living* for a cost per resident-day under $25, or $760 per month. Add these operating expenses to the previously discussed debt service cost of $755 per month and it's easy to see a <u>cost floor</u> for *very basic independent living services* of approximately $1,515 per month.

Assisted Living – Now, *assisted living* operating expenses could easily be $45 to $55 a day, or approximately $1,520 to $1,675 per month. Figures 29-1 and 29-2 covered various operating scenarios. The sobering reality is that serving the Gap Group is frequently limited by the inability to effectively cover basic, ongoing operating expenses, *even when* land and brick-and-mortar costs are reduced significantly.

Addressing Affordability Through Revenue Enhancement

A large number of the affordability options worth considering involve the revenue side of the financial ledger:

1. ***Shared Occupancy of Unrelated Individuals*** – While normally a dangerous marketplace assumption for market-rate assisted living, shared occupancy often works at the lower-end of the pricing spectrum in private pay assisted living. A moderately-priced assisted living unit charging market rates of $2,000 to $2,200 per month for *single* occupancy can typically offer that same unit for $1,550 to $1,650 per resident per month for *double* occupancy. While not the optimum living arrangement for most seniors, this option is being explored by

more and more sponsors as a practical alternative to serve the growing needs of those seniors with modest incomes. But remember, this is a *very* tricky business strategy (see Chapter 24 for more details).

2. *Blending the Rent Roll* – The blended rate approach typically involves *decreasing* the rates on 20 to 30 percent of the units in your assisted living community, while modestly *increasing* the rates of the remaining 70 to 80 percent. With this option, the rent roll retains a *revenue neutral* status while 20 to 30 percent of the units, in fact, serve at least a portion of the Gap Group.

The downside to this scenario is the sobering fact that market rate residents are partially subsidizing members of the Gap Group; you are shifting the burden to those seniors who can afford to pay more. Figure 29-3 depicts a typical rate shifting model. Note that "full pay" residents are paying a premium of over $300 per month, or funding a 12 percent subsidy, to keep overall revenues the same. This concept also requires the establishment of a pragmatic means-testing screening process to determine which residents are legitimately entitled to the below-market rate benefit.

3. *Using Endowments for Reducing the Monthly Service Fee* – Endowment, or "buying down" the rates, is a concept whose time may have come, especially for not-for-profits. But in order to reduce the monthly service fee for a Gap Income Group senior by $500 per month, a permanent endowment fund of approximately $86,000, earning an average seven percent annual *after-tax* return, is required. The endowments would obviously have to be increased if that interest income was taxable. Reducing the monthly service fee by $750 per month would require a tax-free interest earning endowment of approximately $129,000 for a single unit. Buying down the rate by $750 per month for 25 units would require a tax-free, interest earning endowment of $3.2 million. Figure 29-4 provides some typical endowment scenarios.

FIGURE 29-3
POSITIVE SPIN . . . "BLENDING THE RENT ROLL"
REAL WORLD . . . "RATE SHIFTING"!

I. *TARGET MARKET RATE PRICING*

| | Market Rate Monthly Fees | |
| | Monthly Service | Total Annual |
Assisted Living Units	Fee	Revenues
Studio	$2,300	$27,600
1-Bedroom	$2,760	$33,120

II. *BLENDING RATES WITH SUBSIDIZED PRICING*

| Assisted Living Units | Subsidized Units | | | Non-Subsidized Units (NSU) | | | Effective |
	%Mix Subsidized Residents	Monthly Subsidy Amount	Effective Subsidized Mo. Fee	Remaining NSU Resident %	Additional Monthly $ NSU	Adjusted NSU Mo. Fee	Total Annual Revenues
Studio	25.0%	($1,100)	$1,200	75.0%	$367	$2,667	$27,600
1-Bedroom	20.0%	($1,260)	$1,500	80.0%	$315	$3,075	$33,120

Moore Diversified Services, Inc.

While these numbers may seem daunting, many communities are gradually building endowments through fund-raising activities in order to better serve the Gap Income Group seniors of the future. Much of this endowment money frequently comes from existing, affluent residents of the community who either provide endowment funds while still living, or as part of their estate.

A variation of this strategy is to establish what I call a *"Family Member Matching Challenge:"* A not-for-profit sponsor tells a family they can offer their loved one a "scholarship" of $300 per month *if* the family can provide an equivalent amount. This leverages or stretches available endowment funds, and provides motivation and incentives for family financial participation.

4. *Spend-down of Liquidated Home Equity* – A modest-income senior selling a $110,000 home with net sale proceeds of $100,000 can place the proceeds in a portfolio earning approximately five percent after taxes, which would come to $5,000 a year. This would lower the senior's qualifying income level for a community requiring a threshold of $30,000 down to $25,000. In a typical primary market area, this would increase the number of income qualified 75+ households by about five percent.

```
┌──────────────────────────────────────────────────────────────┐
│                       FIGURE 29-4                              │
│                                                                │
│            BUYING DOWN THE MONTHLY SERVICE FEE                 │
│                                                                │
│                                                                │
│    Desired          Per Unit Endowment        Total Endowment  │
│   Reduction          Required at Various       Required to Cover│
│   in MSF¹           After-Tax Savings Rates    25 AL or IL Units│
│                        7%          5%                          │
│  ● $  500/mo       $ 86,000     $120,000     $2.2 mil - $3.0 mil│
│  ● $  750           129,000      180,000      3.2    -  4.5    │
│  ● $ 1,000          170,000      240,000      4.3    -  6.0    │
│  ─────────────                                                 │
│  ¹MSF = Monthly Service Fee                                    │
│  Moore Diversified Services, Inc.                              │
└──────────────────────────────────────────────────────────────┘
```

Desired Reduction in MSF[1]	Per Unit Endowment Required at Various After-Tax Savings Rates		Total Endowment Required to Cover 25 AL or IL Units
	7%	5%	
● $ 500/mo	$ 86,000	$120,000	$2.2 mil - $3.0 mil
● $ 750	129,000	180,000	3.2 - 4.5
● $ 1,000	170,000	240,000	4.3 - 6.0

[1]MSF = Monthly Service Fee

Moore Diversified Services, Inc.

A senior could also spend-down the newly acquired home equity at a pace that (statistically) does not exceed their expected life (see Chapter 30 on spend-down for a more complete discussion).

5. *Cash Flow from Other Projects* – A sponsor may tap into one of a growing number of private-pay service delivery business opportunities on their campuses to help underwrite another part of the community's overall mission. For example, an effectively designed and properly operated 80-unit assisted living facility on a retirement community campus, with independent units and access to skilled nursing care, can yield approximately $3,000 per unit of annual cash flow after paying all operating expenses and debt service. This adds up to a gross potential of $240,000 in annual residual cash, some or all of which can then be dedicated to serving economically-disadvantaged seniors.

6. *Government Involvement – Medicaid Waivers* – Experimental Medicaid waivers that essentially transfer nursing entitlements to assisted living have received much publicity in recent years. But let's look at the facts as recently published in *State Assisted Living Policy: July, 2000,* from the National Academy for State Health Policy. This definitive study reported there are approximately 58,500 participants in various state Medicaid waiver programs. Some 18,500 participants were in North Carolina, 7,900 in Missouri and 4,400 in Michigan. This leaves approximately 27,700 spread across the remaining 35 participating states. That reflected an average of 790 low-income seniors per participating state served via waivers. It's a start, but current waiver initiatives meet only about 2 percent of the total potential assisted living affordability need.

Some expect that assisted living Medicaid waivers will grow significantly. But can the Medicaid program, which is being scrutinized to hold down costs, really afford to provide universal funding for a whole new type of long term care – one that caters to many seniors who don't qualify for nursing home care today? If a major public entitlement program for assisted living were implemented, would seniors currently ineligible for today's nursing entitlements (because of lower acuity) literally "come out of the woodwork" to benefit from this expanded entitlement program? And, finally, will Medicaid provide sufficient, consistent and predictable *multi-year* funding to cover assisted living costs?

7. *Assisted Living as a Medical Tax Deduction* – It is highly likely that, for seniors receiving help with two or more activities of daily living, the *total* assisted living monthly service fee may be deductible. This, of course, would be subject to total medical expense deductions that exceed 7.5 percent of a senior's adjusted gross income. Chapter 19 deals with this very important issue.

Unfortunately, this initiative does not help low income seniors with little or no tax obligations. But it does represent about a 12 to 20 percent discount for income qualified, market rate seniors.

The Public Sector Dilemma

When I ask prognosticators how public-sector involvement in affordable assisted living really works, they typically respond, "Policies that *could* be put into place *might* work," or, "The state *could* realize that assisted living is more cost-effective than nursing and therefore they *might* allocate more money." True, the public sector could do these things, but it probably won't. Doing so would mean investing a considerable amount in the short term on the chance of realizing savings in the long run. No responsible state government I'm familiar with makes policy that way. It would be political suicide!

In the end, if we are to meet the affordability challenge, we must rethink our approaches to funding long-term care through entitlement programs. Families with sufficient financial means must be motivated to pay their fair share for long-term care services, perhaps with appropriate income tax incentives. Private-pay residents should not have to directly subsidize others through blended rent rolls, or other inequitable cost shifting initiatives.

Life is Full of Trade-Offs

There is one market dynamic that can assist greatly in developing Gap Income Group assisted living affordability strategies. A consumer's level of discretion, selectivity and sensitivity regarding the acceptance of available senior living options decreases as a function of decreasing income. Simply stated, there is no free lunch; as with all of us, senior consumers of varying economic status must accept tradeoffs based on their relative affordability. This in no way makes low-to-moderate income seniors second-class citizens. Rather, it is the economic reality of the marketplace that these seniors can be effectively served with selected tradeoffs that might not otherwise be acceptable to higher-income seniors who can afford a more upscale community. This situation goes on daily in the broad consumer marketplace.

A Look to the Future – A Step Outside the Box

In this new millennium, we must completely rethink both existing and new approaches to affordability. Some of the future changes will be painful, but necessary. Here are seven provocative ideas:

1. **Stop Asset-Shifting** – We have to stop the well-intended, but financially devastating, asset-shifting by seniors in order to qualify for Medicaid nursing entitlements. However, there are other forms of "asset strategies" that should be considered (see Chapter 19 for details).

2. **Pay Our Fair Share** – Those of us with the financial means (both seniors and our immediate families) must pay our fair share of either necessary nursing costs, or seek out other viable alternatives, such as assisted living.

3. **Putting Over $1 Trillion of Assets to Work** – Seniors' pent-up equity exceeds $1 trillion (that's with a T!). We should develop financial models that strike a delicate balance between optimizing a senior's autumn years and leaving a reasonable legacy to their children or heirs.

4. **Eliminate Unfair Subsidies** – Private-pay patients or residents should not have to directly or indirectly subsidize the care or sheltered living of others through blended rent rolls, or other inequitable cost shifting initiatives.

5. **Children Must Help Seniors** – Adult children who have the means must be financial participants. There should be reasonable, financially responsible tax incentives for families who supplement the cost of care for their parents. This would be the most effective next step in the "privatization" of the health care system. How about repeal of the 7.5 percent medical tax deduction exclusion for families helping seniors?

6. **Create Innovative Sponsor Financial Incentives** – Possibly through the dollar-matching challenges with families and operating profit tax incentives, for-profit operators could have more impact on individual consumer affordability than through tax credits associated exclusively with debt service and capital costs.

7. **Offer Financially Responsible Tax Incentives** – Seniors and their families should receive tax incentives to pay directly for the efficient delivery of health care and living options. Formal and official recognition should be given to the tax deduction of all assisted living monthly service fee (for service at two ADLs and above). Ideally, these deductions should not be subject to the 7.5 percent of adjusted gross income exclusion.

We are making progress – but we must attack difficult affordability issues with pragmatic, hard-nosed strategies rather than wishful rhetoric.

CHAPTER 30

SPEND-DOWN OF ASSETS

*Finding New Ways to Pay Through Creative Use
of Home Equity and Other Assets*

Caution – The concepts outlined in this chapter have not
been universally accepted by the industry, personal financial
planners or the consumer marketplace. But we must find
new approaches to solving old problems by sometimes
"stepping outside the box." If you utilize these ideas, do so
with *extreme caution* – perhaps initially on a limited,
experimental basis.

In the not-too-distant future, the following scenario will play
out hundreds of times each week across the U.S. In fact, it has
already started to happen:

*"Roy, this is Kim. Sorry to be calling you so late, but we
have a family crisis and an important decision to make. You
remember when you came home at Christmas, you said Mom
seemed to be getting quite frail. Well, her condition has gotten
worse and I've been searching for options. She just can't live
alone anymore. I'm almost over my head with my job and our
two kids, and Bill and I are going to need every cent we earn
just to cover our own expenses, at least for the next few years."*

334

"So we've got to figure something out. I've been looking around, and I'm positive the best choice for Mom is a place called The Gardens at Westridge. They have what's called 'assisted living,' which provides a nice residential setting with a strong medical foundation. But here's the problem. The Gardens costs $2,500 per month for all the care and services Mom currently needs. But she can only afford about $1,500 a month, unless she sells the house and uses some of the proceeds to help pay."

"I'm working on what some people call a spend-down model on my laptop, but Mom seems really concerned about hanging on to her money so she'll have something to leave us and the grandchildren. She said that when Dad was alive, they talked frequently about being sure to provide us all with an inheritance. I told her she needed to do what was best for her, and not to worry about us. Do you agree? If so, here's what I'm proposing . . ."

The great majority of the assisted living communities developed in the U.S. over the last ten years are structured to be private-pay. Most residents must rely on their Social Security, company pensions and interest earned on their lifetime savings – in other words, their after-tax annual incomes - to pay their bills. Some may also get help from their adult children, or other relatives. But other creative, prudent methods of payment must be found if our industry is to sustain its rapid growth rate and serve considerably more than just the 30 to 35 percent of age 80+ seniors who, currently, can realistically afford to *private pay* for assisted living.

In order to have enough money to pay for other discretionary purchases, a senior should ideally spend no more than 80 percent of his or her *after-tax income* on the assisted living monthly service fee.   At today's rate, that rules out approximately 65 to 70 percent of seniors aged 80 and over. But many of those same seniors could afford assisted living if the industry were to follow the lead of private pay nursing homes, or most for-profit and not-for-profit CCRCs. That means introducing innovative options like properly planned spend-down, or partially refundable entry fees.

The Case for Mrs. Barker

Consider Mrs. Barker, the 83-year-old widow introduced at the beginning of this chapter. She's living alone in a home she's owned for 30 years. A recent heart attack and osteoporosis have taken their toll and left her frail, occasionally forgetful, and in need of assistance with the activities of daily living. She has a modest after-tax income of $22,500 a year, or $1,875 a month. Figure 30-1 summarizes Mrs. Barker's situation.

After considerable homework and soul-searching, Kim concludes that *The Gardens at Westridge* assisted living community is the most suitable place for her – and her mother reluctantly agrees. But 80 percent of Mrs. Barker's after-tax income is only $1,500 per month; The Gardens charges $2,500 per month for basic services and a reasonable array of assistance with the activities of daily living.[1]

---

[1]Approximately 45 minutes of direct, hands-on care per 24-hour day.

Kim and her mother have certainly considered other options. Mrs. Barker could move in with Kim and Bill, find a more modestly-priced rest home (perhaps with semi-private accommodations). She could also stay in her current home (at relatively high risk) while accessing intermittent, marginally effective and costly home health services. Ultimately, she would undoubtedly end up in a nursing home, spending down the precious assets she and her husband had accumulated over a lifetime. Eventually, she would become a Medicaid recipient. All of these possibilities seem terrible to Mrs. Barker and her daughter.

FIGURE 30-1

MRS. BARKER'S CURRENT SITUATION

- **83-Year-Old Widow:**
  - **Statistical Life Expectancy: 6 Years**
- **Lives Alone in Her Home of 30 Years:**
  - **Current Home Value: $110,000**
  - **Mortgage paid off**
- **Current Health Condition:**
  - **Recent Heart Attack & Advancing Osteoporosis**
  - **Somewhat Forgetful & Frail**
  - **Needs Assistance With Approximately 3 ADLs**
  - **Considering Moving to an Assisted Living Community**
- **Current <u>After-Tax</u> Income of $1,875/Month, or $22,500/Year:**
  - **Social Security ($900/Month)**
  - **Savings Portfolio of $235,000 (earns $975/mo. at 5% after-tax savings)**
- **Can Afford to Spend 80% of Her After-Tax Income for Assisted Living:**
  - **$22,500 x .80 = $18,000/Year, or $1,500/Month**

Moore Diversified Services, Inc.

The Plan

Kim runs some numbers and comes up with a plan. Her analysis assumes that her mother's Social Security income of approximately $900 a month will increase at only two percent per year, while the *after-tax* interest rate on her existing savings portfolio of approximately $235,000 will continue to earn a conservative 5 percent annually. Kim also assumes that the Gardens at Westridge's required $2,500 per month assisted living service fee in 2001 will likely increase at about 4 percent a year. Figure 30-2 summarizes the situation.

Then Kim makes the most critical assumption – her mother's reasonable life expectancy. Based on life expectancy tables for a female age 83 and her personal physician's assessment of her current health, Kim estimates a life expectancy of six years. She realizes that, of course, her mother could either die sooner or outlive her statistical life expectancy.

Kim sets up her laptop on the kitchen table and, working well into the wee hours of the morning, develops a computer model that answers the question: ***"What additional principal assets, put to work as a declining balance fund earning five percent over eight years, could cover the gap between the required $2,500 assisted living monthly service fee and the $1,500 that represents 80 percent of Mom's after-tax income?"***

FIGURE 30-2

MRS. BARKER AND HER DAUGHTER LIKE "THE GARDENS AT WESTRIDGE"

The Gardens at Westridge

Mrs. Barker's Current Situation

- 2001 Monthly Service Fee (MSF): $2,500/Month[1]

- A $1,000/Month affordability shortfall (before any spend-down)

- Annual MSF Escalation: 4%

- Only her Social Security has a modest COLA[2] of approximately 2%/Year

Mrs. Barker's Options Appear Limited:

1. Do nothing
2. Access home health on a sporadic basis
3. Try to find lower quality, semi-private Assisted Living accommodations
4. Continue to live at home at increased risk

or . . .

GET CREATIVE!

---

[1]With reasonable allowance for assistance with Activities of Daily Living ADLs).
[2]COLA = Cost of Living Adjustment

Moore Diversified Services, Inc.

Putting Home Equity to Work – Prudently

Fortunately, Mrs. Barker owns her home free and clear. Its market value is approximately $110,000, so, upon sale, she would net approximately $100,000 after selling costs (see Figure 30-3). Kim rationalizes that her mother's existing $235,000 savings portfolio can still serve as her final estate or act as a financial buffer. In addition, through carefully planned spend-down of her *new asset* – the liquidated home equity – they can fund mom's affordability gap and help pay for an appropriate level of care, independence, dignity and quality of life in her final years.

FIGURE 30-3
MRS. BARKER AND HER DAUGHTER GET CREATIVE

1. **The Plan: (in round numbers)**
   - **Sell Home**   **$110,000**
     - **Selling Costs @ 9% - Approx.**   **(10,000)**
   - **Net Sales Proceeds**   **$100,000**

2. **Set-Up a "Declining Balance Fund" to Cover the Gap Between:**
   - **80% of Her Current After-Tax Income ($1,500/Month)**
     And . . .
   - **The 2001 Assisted Living MSF of $2,500**
     (This Fund covers the 2001 Gap of $1,000/month)

3. **Some Other Variables to Consider:**
   - **Fund Earnings: 5% (After-Tax)**
   - **MSF Annual Increase: 4%**

Moore Diversified Services, Inc.

Figures 30-4 and 30-5 illustrate Mrs. Barker's spend-down profile. If net proceeds from her home sale were $100,000, that would last for 8 years vs. her life expectancy of 6 years. If her home netted $150,000, the spend-down profile would last for about 11 years.

FIGURE 30-4

A PRUDENT SPEND-DOWN PROFILE CAN BE STRUCTURED TO EXCEED A SENIORS' EXPECTED LIFE

Required to Cover a $2,500 MSF[1]		Maximum Term of Seniors' Spend-Down Using Only Liquidated Net Home Equity of:[2]		
Payment From *Current Income*	*Spend-Down* Per Month[3]	$100,000	$125,000	$150,000
$2,000 Mo	$ 500 Mo	11 Years	13 Years	15 Years
1,750	750	9	11	12
1,500	1,000	8	9	11

Prudent and individually planned assisted living spend-down models can deliver affordability with time spans that will likely exceed the statistical life expectancy of many seniors.

Note: At the end of the spend-down time span indicated above, Mrs. Barker still has the original principal value of her existing savings portfolio (reference Figure 30-1).

Source: Moore Diversified Services, Inc.

---

[1]MSF = Monthly Service Fee
[2]Reflects "annuity model" that considers the time value of money (interest earned).
[3]Spend-down funding shortfall vs. required base MSF of $2,500/month.

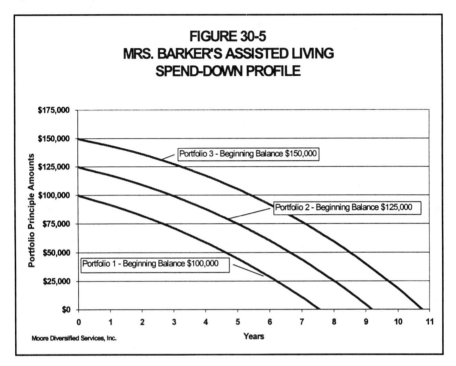

FIGURE 30-5
MRS. BARKER'S ASSISTED LIVING
SPEND-DOWN PROFILE

What Have The Barkers Accomplished?

To summarize Mrs. Barker's future prospects:

1. Mrs. Barker optimizes the quality of life for her remaining years – with dignity, proper care and optimum independence.

2. Kim and Roy and the grandchildren live essentially guilt-free, with reasonable peace of mind.

3. A largely benign asset (Mrs. Barker's home equity) is put to work *prudently, creatively* and *cost-effectively.*[1]

And . . .

4. Mrs. Barker still retains her original $235,000 savings portfolio for her estate legacy.

From a financial and market feasibility perspective, Mrs. Barker's required qualifying annual income threshold for market rate assisted living has effectively been lowered from the normally required $44,000 to her yearly income of $22,500.

The Devil's Advocate

Suppose Roy responds, *"Sounds like a good plan, Kim. You've designed a prudent spend-down plan with an 8-year term vs. Mom's life expectancy of 6 years. But what if Mom lives to be, say, 103?"*

Hopefully, Kim has already considered this contingency: *"Let's suppose Mom outlives the 8-year spend-down plan. At that point, her liquid financial situation will be exactly like it is today - predictable income from her Social Security and existing savings portfolio. Yes, she'd have to start spending down those assets. By then she would either still be in assisted*

---

[1]See Chapter 20 for more details on this $1.1 trillion national asset held by age 75+ seniors.

living or in a high acuity nursing home setting. The ultimate worst case is that she would become one of about 1.2 million seniors who are nursing home Medicaid patients. But that possibility doesn't make our current plan imprudent or any less feasible."

There's yet another option: Financial help from Kim and Roy. This might come into play after Mrs. Barker has lived in The Gardens for some time and encountered financial difficulty.

Is Spend-Down Financial Voodoo or a Dominant Trend?

How much of this kind of spend-down is going on? It's hard to know. Empirical and anecdotal evidence of spend-down or financial help from children is extremely difficult to obtain. It seems that many owner/operators are playing a "don't ask, don't tell," game. Rather than ask about income and asset qualifications, they simply inform seniors and their families what it costs to live at their community; letting them decide whether they can afford it.

Recent surveys have indicated many seniors may be spending all their available after-tax income on assisted living monthly service fees, and are also spending down significant amounts of the principal portion of their savings portfolio. This may be true, but beware of basing your *initial market feasibility* estimates for a new community on the assumption that residents will initially dip <u>significantly</u> into savings to pay their monthly fees. Instead, consider spend-down as initial project <u>safety margin</u>. Spend-down might be required to cover tiered pricing increases resulting from cost creep due to the increasing acuity and ADL needs as your residents age in place.

Is Spend-Down Really New?

Spend-down has been occurring in other senior housing settings for many years. It is universally accepted in nursing homes, where the government can be counted on to step in with Medicaid coverage if a resident becomes impoverished. In fact, about 70 percent of the 1.6 million nursing beds are funded by Medicaid.

Spend-down is also being used effectively in many CCRCs, although the practice goes by another name – *non-refundable entry fees.* Communities that charge entry fees often only partially refund them upon a resident's death or move-out. They retain a certain percentage of the original entry fee every month until reaching a refundability floor (usually 50 to 80 percent). Let's look at a common, real world example. If the entry fee for a particular unit in a CCRC is $100,000 and the non-refundability rate is 2 percent per month, residents are essentially *spending down* $2,000 of their assets every month until reaching a guaranteed refundability floor of about 50 to 80 percent. Some CCRCs allow residents to spend down the remains of their entry fees to make up the difference if rising monthly fees exceed their current incomes.

Putting Spend-Down in Perspective

Another way to look at this situation is to observe the *effective monthly service fee.* If a CCRC is charging $1,800 for a conventional monthly service fee, we can add to that the $2,000/month non-refundable portion of the entry fee (spend-down), for a total *effective fee* of $3,800 a month! Figures 30-6 and 30-7 compare typical CCRC "spend-down" with planned assisted living spend-down.

FIGURE 30-6

COMPARISON OF ASSISTED LIVING SPEND-DOWN RATE VS. TYPICAL CCRC ENTRY FEE NON-REFUNDABILITY RATE

Assisted Living Spend-Down/Month[1]	Assisted Living Rate of Monthly Spend-Down[1]		
	$100,000	$125,000	$150,000
● $ 500/month	0.5% / Mo.	0.4% / Mo.	0.3% / Mo.
● 750	0.8	0.6	0.5
● 1,000	1.0	0.8	0.7

Versus . . .

. . . A Conventional CCRC Entry Fee's
Non-Refundability (Effective Spend-Down) Rate
of 1.5% to 2.0% / Mo.[2]

Source: Moore Diversified Services, Inc.

---

[1]Typical source is liquidated home equity. (See Figures 30-4 and 30-5).
[2]In some situations, the non-refundable portion of the EF is purchasing limited life care benefits.

FIGURE 30-7

IS SPEND-DOWN REALLY A NEW CONCEPT?

Spend-down Has Been Taking Place in For-Profit and Not-For-Profit CCRCs for Years

Comparison of CCRC Entry Fee Non-Refundability vs. Assisted Living Spend-down

CCRC Entry Fee (EF): $100,000   (Typical Minimum EF)
Refundability Typically Declines at 2% per Month or $2,000[1]

	Guaranteed EF (Floor) Refundability Levels		
	80%	50%	0%
CCRC EF Spend-down Characteristics . . .			
• Non-Refundable Portion of EF	$20,000	$50,000	$100,000
• No. of Months of "Spend-down" @ $2,000/mo	10 months	25 months	50 months
	. . . Versus Assisted Living Spend-down Characteristics		
• Equivalent No. of Months @ $1,000/mo (Using MDS' Spend-down Model)[3]	36 months	52 months	84 months

Source: Moore Diversified Services, Inc.

---

[1]In some situations, the non-refundable portion of the EF is purchasing limited life care benefits.
[2]Average length of stay in assisted living: 24 months.
[3]Refer to Figure 30-4.

The Complexities of Qualifying Incomes

So how can you determine who really qualifies for your assisted living services? First, don't forget that census information or other demographic data usually provides *pre-tax* income data. But seniors must pay their bills with *after-tax* income. Most seniors who qualify for assisted living today are in the 10 to 15 percent *average* tax (not marginal) bracket.

Furthermore, seniors who don't want to spend down their assets should pay only about 80 percent of their after-tax income for assisted living, leaving the rest for other discretionary purchases. This modest discretionary income pool can be used initially for modest lifestyle expenditures in the early stages of a senior's residence in assisted living. Later, as their acuity increases and their lifestyle becomes more limited, these available funds can be shifted to pay for advanced levels of tiered pricing as additional ADLs are needed and provided.

Applying these tax and discretionary income factors yields the following calculations:

	Monthly	Annually
● Required Monthly Service Fee	$2,500	$30,000
● Adjust for 20 percent discretionary income	3,125	37,500

	Monthly	Annually

- Adjust for required *pre-tax* gross income:

  - 10 percent average tax bracket   3,475   41,700

  - 15 percent average tax bracket   3,675   44,115

So, someone who needed to pay $2,500 per month, or $30,000 per year – in *after-tax* dollars – for assisted living service fees and still have 20 percent for discretionary purchases (without spending down assets) would actually need $37,500 in annual after-tax disposable income. That comes to about $42,000 to $44,000 in *pre-tax* income, depending on their individual tax situations. The economics of prudent spend-down are summarized in Figure 30-8.

Expanding the Market With Prudent Spend-Down

Let's look how the market expands if Mrs. Barker and her family are willing to implement a prudent spend-down strategy. As Figure 30-9 illustrates, for someone with Mrs. Barker's fixed assets, the income needed to afford a $2,500 monthly service fee drops from a gross annual income before taxes of $44,000 (without spend-down) to about $25,000 (with prudent spend-down). Nationally, about 2.6 million households headed by someone age 80 or older have incomes of at least $25,000, while only 1.5 million report $44,000 annually or more.

FIGURE 30-8

THE ECONOMICS OF PRUDENT ASSISTED LIVING SPEND-DOWN

**(How a Senior Consumer Can Cover a Shortfall
Involving a $2,500 Base Monthly Service Fee)**

Monthly Payment From Current Income	Amount of *Spend-down* Per Month	Base MSF	After-Tax Requirements With 20% Discretionary Income	Available Discretionary Income @ 20% Annual	Monthly	*Pre-Tax* Income Required Before Spend-down[1]
$2,500 /mo	- 0 -	$30,000 /yr	$37,500 /yr	$7,500 /yr	$625 /mo	$44,115 /yr[2]
2,000	$500 /mo	24,000	30,000	6,000	500	35,300 [2]
1,750	750	21,000	26,250	3,700	310	29,165 [3]
1,500	1,000	18,000	22,500	3,175	265	25,000 [3]

MSF = Monthly Service Fee

Source: Moore Diversified Services, Inc.

---

[1]Using a prudent spend-down model, annual pre-tax income requirements are significantly reduced by as much as $20,000 . . . increasing the potential market.
[2]Using an *average* tax bracket of 15%.
[3]Using an *average* tax bracket of 10%.

If someone in every one of those additional 1.1 million age 80+ households with annual incomes between $25,000 to $44,000 qualified for assisted living, they would represent about 14,000 80-unit communities in the year 2003. Obviously, not all would have the qualifying home equity, or would even opt for assisted living if they did. But if just <u>10 percent</u> qualified and were interested, they would represent an additional 415 80-unit communities – meaning an increased demand of more than 33,000 units.

FIGURE 30-9
THE SHAPE OF THE FUTURE?

If spending down to pay for assisted living became widely accepted, a whole new market would open up for a typical community that required a $2,500 monthly service fee.

Monthly Payment From Current Income	Monthly Spend-Down	Qualifying Income Needed[1]	Additional 80+ Income Qualified Households	Additional 80-Unit AL Communities Needed in 2003[2]
$2,500	$0	$44,000	0	0
$2,000	$500	$35,500	373,400	140
$1,750	$750	$31,000	737,775	275
$1,500	$1,000	$26,500	1,102,150	415

[1] Pre-tax qualifying income, allowing 20% to be set aside for discretionary spending.
[2] Assuming that only 30% of the income qualified seniors would have a need for assisted living and only 10% would have sufficient assets for spend-down.

Moore Diversified Services, Inc.

Increased Savings Portfolio – Another Option

Instead of spending down her $100,000, Mrs. Barker could add it to her current savings portfolio. Assuming it earned five percent interest, it would produce an additional after-tax income of approximately $5,000 a year, or $417 a month. Added to her $1,500 budget, this additional income would allow her to spend approximately $1,917 per month for The Gardens at Westridge. Obviously, this would still leave her short of the necessary $2,500 by $583 per month.

Approach Assisted Living Spend-Down with Caution

The concept of spend-down in assisted living needs cautious, extensive market testing. The prudent approach would be to implement spend-down of the liquidated home equity, but not a senior's existing savings portfolio. Significant safety margins should be deployed. These concepts are not without challenges, but their potential to expand the market for assisted living is significant – and worth exploring.

Is spend-down a significant factor in assisted living today? Probably not. But it will likely become much more common over the next few years.

Operators will begin to encourage spend-down as they realize that, used prudently, it can significantly expand the market. More seniors and their adult children will agree to spend their assets as they become convinced it offers options that allow seniors to live out the final stages of their lives with more ambience, independence and dignity.

A Final Word of Caution

To a casual observer, the Barkers' story might seem an ideal solution to a family and industry dilemma. But experienced assisted living professionals know it's not that simple. Spend-down is universally accepted and works in nursing homes because the government can be counted on to step in with Medicaid coverage once a resident becomes impoverished. But this is often not the case in assisted living. Medicaid waivers for assisted living are limited in number, and most owner/operators consider Medicaid reimbursement rates to be too low.

Spending down too quickly could leave a senior destitute in the final stages of life. What's more, improper use of spend-down can misrepresent a project's true market feasibility and long-run viability.

It is my professional opinion that initial market feasibility determination should not rely heavily on spend-down assumptions. However, spend-down can have a positive impact on forecasting safety margins, overall market acceptance and enhanced unit absorption.

SECTION SEVEN

Special Market Niches
and "Carve-Outs"

CHAPTER 31

STRATEGIC CONSIDERATIONS FOR NICHE MARKETS

Zero-Based Thinking About Service Delivery

As assisted living moves through its product life cycle, many sponsors and owner-operators are asking, *"Is this all there is?"* The answer is clearly, *"No";* there are viable niche marketing opportunities to be exploited.

Increasing competition in the assisted living market is creating a need for providers to consider a more focused approach to caregiving. By targeting your services toward specialized market opportunities – or niches – you will be better able to play to your strengths, neutralize your weaknesses and establish a solid strategic foundation on which to expand your reach of caregiving. The idea is to seek synergy and economies between your existing systems, procedures, technology, etc. – using these resources in other areas where they make the right strategic fit.

Niche marketing generally can be viewed from three basic perspectives:

● *Line extension:* Offering a basic product to take advantage of other closely related market opportunities. An example is when an assisted living community is adjacent to an active adult retirement community so residents of that community – typically ages 50 to 65 – can live the good life and still be near their own aging parents. As time passes and the community matures, the active adult eventually becomes the assisted living resident.

- *Horizontal integration:* Applying some of your basic resources to offer different products or services, frequently aimed at different – but generally compatible – market segments or niches. For example, the addition of an Alzheimer's or dementia wing to an assisted living facility could broaden your community's business base by serving residents who require very specialized services.

- *Vertical integration:* Selling individual components of your existing products or services to fill a new need or reach a new market. An example might include adding an adult day care center to your assisted living community in order to maximize your investment in staff, physical plant, food service and other services. Another option would be offering assistance in living (AIL) into existing independent living units or as a form of home care; the *holistic* approach to serving seniors outlined in Chapter 33.

Partnering Opportunities

When considering market niche opportunities, you should begin by focusing on your current knowledge base and resources – what you do and know best. In the case of the residential-social model of assisted living, which involves a seamless delivery of shelter, services (food, living arrangement, housekeeping) and assistance with activities of daily living (ADLs – hygiene, eating, dressing, toileting, etc.), there are several major partnering opportunities.

<u>Note</u>: While partnering strategies may appear to make good business sense, you will frequently find that your potential partner may prefer to "go it alone" – capturing the financial rewards for their own internal operation. In any event, here are some typical opportunities.

• *Independent Living Communities.* Some assisted living providers are ensuring themselves a place in the continuum of care by working with established independent living communities. This market niche strategy not only enhances the marketing of independent living by providing a response to the future needs of its residents more effectively, but the niche strategy opens the way for assisted living providers to service a ready market.

• *Continuing Care Retirement Communities (CCRCs).* Assisted living providers can also benefit by partnering with CCRCs. Simply stated, CCRC residents can frequently fulfill their high acuity care needs at an adjacent assisted living community rather than at a higher-cost nursing home.

• *Nursing Homes.* Likewise, assisted living operators are finding synergy with nursing homes, whose core business is serving high acuity seniors by delivering quality care and attempting to provide optimum independence. This opens a viable market niche for assisted living providers as many nursing home sponsors see assisted living as a viable way to extend the average length of stay on their campus and to assist in sustaining otherwise declining private pay nursing ratios. Approximately 35 to 40 percent of seniors leaving assisted living are entering nursing facilities. Initially, most enter as private pay residents. (See Chapters 6 and 7 for more details.)

• *Hospitals.* Some assisted living developers are forming joint ventures with hospitals in order to realize revenue enhancements and to take advantage of significiant referral resources realized through the hospitals' social workers and discharge planners. (See Chapter 8.)

• *Active Adult Retirement Communities.* Another viable market niche opportunity for assisted living providers is to form alliances with active adult retirement communities. This market niche strategy offers two opportunities. First, newer retirement communities typically are attracting younger residents whose parents are still living. An adjacent assisted living community allows aging parents to live near their adult children. In addition, freestanding assisted living communities can find opportunities by partnering with active adult retirement communities where the existing residents are age 70 or older. When these residents require a higher level of care, they can essentially "age in place" by moving to an adjacent assisted living community as their "final step." The marketing offices of many active adult communities report that approximately 50 percent of their move-outs are seniors requiring higher levels of health care.

Other Niche Opportunities

Once you have explored the more obvious uses of your basic freestanding assisted living model, other market niche opportunities can be evaluated:

- *Special Care or Dementia Units.* In the 1990s, a number of assisted living providers unknowingly backed into niche marketing through their lack of a strategic vision. Upon entry into assisted living, they took the initial position that they would not serve residents with even early stage dementia, incontinence or high acuity needs requiring assistance with more than two activities of daily living (ADLs). But when these providers experienced annual resident turnover rates of 50 percent or more, they were forced to alter their strategies. Chapter 32 addresses this market niche in more detail.

- *Assistance in Living (AIL).* This model is actually a customized variation of traditional home health services. An example might be a CCRC in which AIL services are offered on an additional fee basis to independent living residents. Those residents typically have short-term needs. But excessive implementation of this strategy can be counter-productive; creating a naturally occurring assisted living community within an independent living building. Some providers are carrying this market niche one step further by offering AIL and other on-campus services off-campus within their primary market area neighborhoods – into single family homes and conventional apartments. (See Chapter 33 for more details.) In these situations, the AIL services usually take a form that is similar to licensed home health.

• *Respite Care.* This model provides short-term accommodations for two basic situations: seniors recovering from an episodic event such as a hip fracture or stroke and sheltered living for seniors to provide respite for the family caregivers. Respite care is basically short-term assistance living at premium pricing – frequently 15 to 20 percent above the prevailing longer term assisted living rates.

• *Adult Day Care.* This seems like a natural market niche, offering synergy by deploying existing physical plant and service delivery resources. But frequently this is not the case. Like affordable assisted living, adult day care represents a tremendous economic and social dilemma in which financially viable solutions can be an elusive target. The reasons are simple: The concept typically attracts clients with very high, complex needs and limited ability to pay privately for the necessary services rendered. When an assisted living community provider identifies the necessary resources and allocates their true cost, the numbers frequently do not produce a profit.

• *Rehabilitation.* This has always been a classic outsourcing decision for providers. Frequently, rehabilitation is subcontracted to specialized companies, but many assisted living providers are re-evaluating that strategy. Instead, they are choosing to directly offer these services as part of their continuum of care package. The number of clients likely to be served and prevailing prospective payment system reimbursement challenges must be carefully considered to ensure financial viability. In fact, Medicare reimbursement opportunities and limitations must always be carefully evaluated when developing market niche strategies that involve third party payor reimbursable services such as AIL and rehabilitation.

- *Catered Living.* This model is one step higher in resident acuity than independent living and one step lower than conventional assisted living services. It is typically a living arrangement offering measured or a la carte services that are slightly more comprehensive than independent living, but less intensive than assisted living.

- *Geographical Market Niches.* These would include rural or small markets wherein a smaller-sized assisted living market model would be appropriate. This is extremely difficult to accomplish because of the heavy fixed and semi-variable costs associated with delivering assisted living services. However, the need is significant if such a model can be effectively developed.

In evaluating market niches, you must exercise caution. Expansion into new areas makes little sense if it actually dilutes your current business opportunities. Focus on definitive success strategies. Successful expected outcomes include spreading your existing overhead and fixed costs over more revenue-producing units, developing new net revenue after additional operating costs and diversifying operations to further reduce your marketplace risk and expand your market area.

CHAPTER 32

SPECIAL CARE
ALZHEIMER'S/ DEMENTIA

A "Carve-Out" Market Niche
Whose Time Has Come

I frequently get calls from potential clients considering the development of assisted living. Some opening statements go something like this, ***"Jim, we're getting into the business, but we're going to be different. We won't be dealing with residents with dementia or incontinence."*** Oh, really.

The impacts of Alzheimer's and other related dementia is devastating for both the victims and their caregivers. It has been labeled by the national Alzheimer's Association as "the disease of the century." Most victims are over age 65, with a surprisingly concentrated number of those afflicted being in their late '70s and early '80s. Because of this, the disease is obviously becoming an integral part of the sheltered living, aging-in-place challenge that is facing both independent and assisted living sponsors and owner-operators.

Levels of Incidence

The estimated incidence levels of the disease by age cohort vary by reporting agency but empirical evidence suggests the following ranges:

Age Cohort	Incidence Level or Percent Needing Assistance[1]
• 75-84	16% - 19%
• 85+	47% - 50%

Weighted Average, Age 75+Cohort: 26%

In response to this challenge, many progressive assisted living community sponsors are considering the introduction of a special care assisted living; state-of-the-art Alzheimer's living arrangements as yet another component in the complex and growing continuum of care for seniors. For many sponsors, the growing incidence levels of dementia is perhaps the most complex issue they face as they develop effective responses to resident aging in place.

Much has been published about the dreaded disease and the debilitating impact on its victims. Innovative living arrangements are evolving that are striking a delicate balance between reasonable freedom and appropriate security. These specialized Alzheimer's facilities place a high priority on minimizing chemical and physical restraints in order to attempt to enhance living and optimize comfort and dignity while lowering the excitement level of the resident.

---

[1]Alzheimer's Disease and Related Disorder Association

There Are No Quick Fixes

There is a potential trap as owner/operators accept the reality that Alzheimer's and other related dementia are challenges that cannot be avoided in assisted living. Merely calling an area that has physical security a "special care unit" is not enough. Special care units of the future must address at least three very important issues:

1. Recognize that Alzheimer's/dementia involves a unique care level and is a distinct market niche
2. Have a *purpose-built design* to respond to special needs
3. Develop *strong programmatic content* aimed at the unique needs of each resident

Achieving these necessary objectives requires direct care staffing levels considerably higher than conventional assisted living. For example, typical direct care staffing on a day shift for assisted living would likely be one direct care FTE for every 17 to 20 residents. In a special care/Alzheimer's unit, that staffing ratio could be one FTE for every 7 to 9 residents. See Figure 16-1 in Chapter 16 for more details.

The ideal market positioning for the new millennium is two-fold: 1) to convince the marketplace that you understand special care and 2) you, in fact, provide *the* special care/Alzheimer's living environment of choice.

Two Market Models

As special care units are becoming better defined, two basic market models are emerging:

- **Residential/Social Model** – For those seniors with early stage dementia who are in relatively good physical health, but need sheltered living combined with low to moderate level assistance with the activities of daily living. The physical product is a special design variation of assisted living.

- **Medical Model** – For seniors with more advanced stages of Alzheimer's and other related dementia who also have more complex health problems.

There will be complex market overlaps between today's assisted living models and traditional nursing. These overlaps are addressed in Chapter 2 and illustrated in Figure 2-4. Special care/Alzheimer's units may well become the "carve-out" market niche of the new millennium, but this trend will not evolve successfully without addressing complications that will require considerable attention to necessary details.

The Mind-Set of the Alzheimer's Caregiver

While major emphasis is being placed on the victim, relatively little has been published about the specific market dynamics and the mind-set of the caregiver. But the adult child caregiver is really *the* market. All of the characteristics of the caregiver addressed in Chapter 34 apply, plus other need-driven motivations. Keep in mind, that in many cases, the Alzheimer's caregiver is not an adult child; but the elderly spouse of the victim.

Our focus group research and experience has indicated that there are a number of perceptions, misconceptions, emotions and unmet needs involving the Alzheimer's caregiver:

● *Caregivers have strong need-driven motivations* – The adult children or spouse caregivers of victims clearly demonstrate strong need-driven emotions. They are constantly on a search for options to improve both the quality of *their* life and that of their Alzheimer's victim. In describing their unmet needs in focus groups, caregivers frequently mention that their search for alternatives has delivered less than satisfactory results. However, most are pleasantly surprised when they ultimately become aware of special care Alzheimer's assisted living arrangements that are evolving around the United States.

● *Caregivers complain about delayed diagnosis* – While conclusive Alzheimer's medical diagnosis is complex, many caregivers claim that their loved one's actual condition was diagnosed later in time than was acceptable. This delayed diagnosis creates considerable frustration and hardship on the part of caregivers and their families.

● *Caregivers experience diagnosis denial* – Many caregivers, when actually presented with the initial diagnosis, refuse to admit that this malady could exist in *their* family. A common question: *"Isn't dad just getting old?"*

● *Alzheimer's has been described as a closet disease* – The caregiver's initial reluctance to accept the fact that a relative or loved one has the disease, coupled with society's current level of discomfort regarding dementia, has caused individual Alzheimer's situations to be "covered up" for a period of time. Many respondents in focus groups felt that, in retrospect, this phenomenon has a distinct negative impact on effectively addressing dementia in a timely manner; both medically and through service and outreach programs. It has certainly caused family pressures and social problems with friends and neighbors.

● *Caregivers have mixed emotions about support groups* – Most indicate that support groups are clearly helpful in providing emotional support and developing the mental and physical stamina needed to face their tremendous personal challenges. But many comment that support groups do not offer sufficient specific assistance in dealing with the wide spectrum of their unmet needs.

● *Experienced caregivers demonstrate a nursing home frame of reference* – While many caregivers put up a courageous fight to avoid thinking of ultimate custodial nursing care for their loved one, most are aware of the nursing home option. To them, the nursing home is considered a most difficult, expensive and marginally acceptable alternative due to their perceptions and misconceptions of this living environment. For many, this alternative is clearly perceived only as a future reality – and they try to delay the decision as long as possible. With this state of mind, the special care, assisted living option becomes increasingly attractive.

● *Caregivers ultimately display limited guilt regarding difficult decisions* – In retrospect, caregivers report that they experienced surprisingly little long term guilt with regard to the ultimate difficult decision to place their loved one in some form of sheltered living or custodial care. They gradually reached the realization that the decision was both prudent and necessary – both for their loved one and for their own personal health and well being. Simply stated, if they knew *then* what they know *now,* they would have made the difficult sheltered living decision sooner.

Economic Realities

The economic realities of special care/Alzheimer's presents a good news/bad news situation. The good news is that, from a *business perspective,* special care units are characterized by being premium priced with good operating margins. You can probably count on a broader primary market area with deeper market penetration because of the strong need-driven response of caregivers and other referral services.

From a *consumer's perspective,* the sobering news is that, unlike conventional assisted living, many situations involve two person senior households. In these situations, the decision to move into your special care unit involves incurring the ongoing costs of maintaining two households.

THE MIND-SET OF THE ALZHEIMER'S CAREGIVER

1. Have very strong need-driven motivations
2. Complain about delayed medical diagnosis
3. Diagnosis denial – initially
4. Describe dementia as a "closet disease"
5. Demonstrate a nursing home frame of reference
6. In a continuing search for options and alternatives
7. Experience limited guilt regarding ultimate difficult custodial care decisions
8. Have mixed emotions about support groups

For many sponsors in the 1980s and early 1990s, it was a traumatic experience to consider and eventually offer what has become known as conventional assisted living within their independent living retirement communities.

But in the late 1990s, many of these same sponsors were expanding their continuum of living arrangements by offering innovative living arrangements and a wide spectrum of services that will serve the growing needs of both Alzheimer's victims and their caregivers. For continuing care campuses, these new initiatives will also meet the rapidly expanding needs of their independent and assisted living residents as they continue to age in place.

EXPECTED OUTCOMES OF DEMENTIA CARE

- **Minimize excitement levels**
- **Facilitate adaptation to changing needs**
- **Maximize awareness and orientation**
- **Ensure safety and security**
- **Provide opportunities for socialization**

Sources: Moore Diversified Services, Inc.
Kirby Pines Retirement Community

The newer concepts of special care are emphasizing a special adaptation of the integrated, yet subtly separated, residential/social model of assisted living.

CHAPTER 33

A HOLISTIC APPROACH
TO SERVING SENIORS

Achieve Market Diversification by
Offering Community-Based Services

The overall health of your assisted living or CCRC community can be improved if you constantly seek out practical strategies that either enhance revenues or reduce fixed expenses. One approach is to expand your spectrum of services offered. This is best accomplished right on your campus by implementing four important initiatives: 1) optimize occupancy of existing revenue-producing units; 2) add alternative forms of care and service delivery; 3) improve departmental efficiency; and 4) by renovating common areas and individual living units to moderately enhance revenues.

Many of these strategies will continue to be relevant well into the future. But many sponsors are now realizing that meeting strategic goals in the future also includes taking a serious look at what I call a more *holistic approach* to serving seniors. This includes new approaches to community-based services and a careful evaluation of other outreach services.

The Strategic Umbilical Cord

These programs benefit both seniors and sponsors; seniors gain access to an array of new services while allowing you to realize extra income. You will also be creating strategic "umbilical cords" between the seniors currently living at home and your campus. These connections can also make a senior living community much more visible; especially to potential future residents.

To avoid unnecessary repetition, refer to important issues involving the holistic approach to service delivery addressed elsewhere in this book:

- Assistance in Living Services   Chapters 4 & 22
- Home Health Care   Chapter 9
- Special Care/Alzheimer's   Chapter 32
- Relevant Niche Markets   Chapter 31

Many of these services have been generally referred to as "community-based services." I prefer to call them "strategic products and services for the future."

The Top Ten Community-Based Services

The top ten more commonly offered community-based services are:

1. Formal Home Health Care
2. Homemaker and Companion Services
3. Adult Day Care
4. Meal Preparation/Delivery
5. Personal Emergency Response Systems
6. Transportation
7. Case Management and Geriatric Assessment Center
8. Alzheimer's/Dementia Information Clearing House
9. Rehabilitation and Therapy Clinics
10. Respite Care - on Demand

Some senior living communities are using their food service operations to prepare and deliver meals off campus – sort of a "meals on wheels" concept. Still others are using their own transportation vehicles to transport non-resident seniors, for a reasonable fare, to civic centers, medical practitioners, community events and shopping areas. Respite care (on demand) is being offered as part of assisted living and adult day care.

Five Important Planning Questions

Before offering community-based services, answer five crucial questions. Not every community has the resources, activity levels or incentives to embark on a formal program of community-based services. Before deciding whether to jump on the community-based services bandwagon, answer these five crucial questions about any service you may be considering:

1. *Is the new initiative really consistent with your mission or strategic plan?* Even a "great idea" will fail if it is incompatible with your existing operations or organizational culture. The most frequent incompatibilities with existing operations are in the cost-efficient use of space and staff for the new endeavor. If existing space is already used to its full potential, or if there is no reasonable staff time availability, then the financial rewards may be insufficient to justify the planned venture's new expenses. The optimum community-based services outcome is a synergistic situation that derives additional net income *after* covering all new costs from otherwise underutilized space or staff time or other resources.

2. *What business volume or market penetration is required to make your new service really profitable?* Many times, the business plan and financial pro forma are correctly structured, but the critical input assumptions are either unrealistic or flawed. For example, the financial viability of home care services breaks down into the basic difference between the hourly charge to the client (incremental revenues) and the salary expenses and other direct and indirect expenses (variable and fixed costs) you will incur. The key question to answer is: *How many visits are required to produce sufficient revenues to cover your fixed monthly expenses and variable costs per visit; yielding an acceptable profit?* The results of this simple exercise can be very revealing.

3. *Based on existing and future competition, how likely are you to succeed in the competitive marketplace?* Compare your answers to the previous questions with the amount of business you are likely to generate, taking into account both existing and future competition as well as the estimated size of the total target market. The chances are you might find that the total business volume you and your competitors would really need may not be available in your marketplace.

4. *Have you identified all of the direct and indirect operations costs associated with the new venture?* Many new community-based service ventures fail or are ultimately discontinued because of unrealistic initial estimates of future financial performance. Frequently, the total operations costs are surprisingly high and the rewards are lower than expected. The initiative may be a well-intended, *technical success* but the venture fails basic financial tests. The market to be served may appear large, but does it have both the willingness and ability to pay?

5. *Will the new service effectively exploit or utilize existing resources and will there be an acceptable return on required new investment?* New investment examples include the space and staff required to support Adult Day Care, the cost of responding to new licensing or certification requirements for a Home Health Agency or the normal but sometimes significant start-up costs of other community-based services initiatives.

Even if the early answers to some of these questions are discouraging, you shouldn't necessarily give up on offering community-based services. Instead, consider forming an alliance with another service provider that would normally be a competitor. For example, a co-venture with a licensed home health agency or rehabilitation service might allow you to expand the range of services you offer without investing a great deal of money. It also allows your provider partner to access your campus, which offers them a guaranteed customer base at a central location.

Ten Steps to Developing the Community-Based Services Financial Model

The following simple financial model is an approach to quickly determine the preliminary financial viability of your community-based project:

1. Develop a short list or spectrum of services to offer

2. Establish scope and intensity of offering those services

3. Construct an isolated financial pro forma for each individual service (where practical)

4. Determine <u>direct labor</u> concentration[1]

- Position, titles, skill levels, etc.
- Number of hours or events billed per calendar period:
  - Week   - Quarter
  - Month   - Year

---

[1]Those actually delivering services for a fee.

5. Identify the fixed cost/overhead structure for the venture

6. Allocate *all* appropriate fixed, indirect and direct costs to the new venture

7. Develop a realistic rationale for any planned write-downs/subsidies:

  - Use of existing resources during start-up without full cost allocation or recovery
  - Exploiting unused existing capacity or resource whose cost is already covered
  - Etc.

8. Spread your fixed cost/overhead over expected billing hours or service event or "unit" sales:

  - Uniformly
  - Stratified based on appropriate criteria and rationale

9. Determine "loaded" hourly/event rate (price) for labor which is the sum of:

  - Direct compensation/hour or event
  - All overhead, fixed, and variable costs allocated to each hour or event

10. Set ultimate pricing based on previous steps; including profit/entrepreneurial rewards

This pragmatic process will deliver appropriate financial results if your marketplace assumptions are correct and costs are accurately projected and covered with a pragmatic pricing strategy. The use of a sensitivity analysis and added contingency factors can provide additional effective hedges against future risks.

Synergistic Spin-Off Benefits

Going through the community-based services strategic planning process has a number of spin-off benefits. These include, but are not necessarily limited to, the following:

1. Optimizing and leveraging your existing or potential resources.

2. Creating a sharpened, strategic focus for your future operations.

3. Creating potential to expand the continuum of services offered.

4. Enhancing your revenues synergistically.

Finally, the resulting service and image "umbilical" between the marketplace and your campus could lay a new foundation for the future success of your operations.

CHAPTER 34

THE ADULT CHILD/
DECISION INFLUENCER

The Sandwich Generation Caught in a Squeeze

Let me get right to the point; the decision *influencer* was clearly the most overlooked seniors housing and health care market segment of the early to mid 1990s! These adult children were not adequately targeted or properly educated with respect to assisted living options. Now, some ten years later, there is still significant, untapped, pent-up market potential with this important target market group.

As most experienced assisted living operators now know, adult children between the ages of 55 and 64 are not only the decision *influencers* for their parents, they are frequently decision *makers*. Savvy owners and operators are now selling directly to this crucial market. In order to properly assess and tap this market you must first understand their demographics, psychographics and past migration patterns. Demographics can tell us the size of the potential market. But a study of psychographics gives us keen insights on emotions and motivations – how and why influencers make important decisions.

Demographics

Today, we size up the adult children as the age and income qualified "gatekeepers" for their parents. Assuming their parents' average childbearing age was about 25, the age 55 to 64 cohorts represent the primary decision influencers for today's age 80+ senior consumers. It is important to note that the leading edge of the baby boomers started turning 50 in 1996. Today more than 14 million households are headed by adults between 55 and 64. What's more, in excess of 4 million of these households report annual incomes exceeding $75,000 (refer to Figure 34-1). This is important for two reasons:

1. Decision influencer involvement appears to be enhanced with higher income adult children. The reasons are unclear, but a definite trend is emerging.

2. Financial support by some adult children in the form of supplementing their parent's income in order to help them private pay for assisted living. This is especially true some time after move-in if the parent gets into financial difficulties. I've done some important strategic research into tax incentives for assisted living. Simply stated, many adult children might be able to realize *significant* tax benefits when providing financial assistance to their parents. See Chapter 19 for details.

However, these favorable trends should not yet be factored directly into formal market feasibility studies, as empirical information on this important issue is still very limited and not statistically significant.

FIGURE 34-1

DEMOGRAPHIC PROFILE OF THE AGE 55 TO 64 DECISION INFLUENCERS IN THE UNITED STATES

Year	Total Age 55 to 64 Households	Total Age 55 to 64 Households With Cash Flow Incomes of:	
		$50,000+	$75,000+
• 1990	12.4 Million	3.6 Million	1.6 Million
• 2000	14.2	7.0	4.0
• 2005	17.5	9.4	6.1
Absolute Growth in Age 55 to 64 Households:			
• 1990-2000	1.8 Million	3.3 Million	2.4 Million
• 2000-2005	3.3	2.4	2.0
Average Annual Percent Increase:			
• 1990-2000	1.41%	6.79%	9.76%
• 2000-2005	4.27%	6.22%	8.52%

Source: Claritas
                 MDS Data Base

Important Psychographics

The real key to marketing to these decision influencers is understanding what motivates them. In conducting several hundred decision influencer focus groups, I have discovered that they have a very high propensity to consider and favorably embrace assisted living for their parents – assuming they clearly understand the service delivery concept and related costs. Many do not.

For example, when we assemble 10 to 12 adult children for a focus group, more than half usually tell a "need-driven" story involving significant concerns about their parent's current health status. Most are concerned about their parent's ability to continue to live independently. These focus group respondents have been screened for only one characteristic; having at least one living parent anywhere in the U.S. The parent's relative health status was *not* a screening criteria. Yet these randomly selected respondents frequently tell stories about the increasing frailty and declining health of their parents.

Many express frustration that their parents either fail or refuse to recognize these subtle changes, and most children find it difficult to delicately discuss or counsel their parents about their changing health and declining independence. Many confirm that a role reversal has taken place. As one adult child put it, *"Mom is giving me fits like I'm sure I did to her when I was a teenager."* Another said *"My husband and I are conducting a loving conspiracy in seeking what is best for my mother."*

Decision Influencer Frustrations and Emotions

Caregiver frustrations fall into five major categories as summarized in Figure 34-2:

**FIGURE 34-2
DECISION INFLUENCER FRUSTRATIONS
WITH THEIR AGING PARENTS**

1. Observe increasing frailty & declining health

2. Parents failure to recognize the inevitable

3. Difficult discussing alternative living options with parents

4. Parent/child role reversal takes place

5. Facilitating the difficult move decision gets very emotional

---

In discussing this dilemma, most adult children express love, guilt, frustration, a sense of helplessness, and economic concern. These emotions are intensified when the senior and the adult child are geographically distant. This is especially true for those families dealing with Alzheimer's or other related dementia. See Chapter 32 for more details on the Alzheimer's caregiver.

FIVE EMOTIONS OF DECISION INFLUENCERS

1. **Love**
2. **Guilt**
3. **Frustration**
4. **Helplessness**
5. **Economic Concern**

*Marketing & Sales must respond
to these five emotions*

Impact of Influencer Migration Patterns

Decision influencers can expand your primary market area's potential! There are predictable geographic factors that set the stage for adult children playing a very significant role as decision influencers in your marketplace. Their role, properly recognized, can have a major impact on expanding the effective depth of your local primary market area. This is accomplished by encouraging the migration of their parents who currently live outside of your market area to consider moving to your community.

Migration patterns and employee mobility trends of the past quarter century have geographically separated many parents from their children. Many of these parents sought the warmer climates of Florida, Arizona and California. Meanwhile, the children went just about everywhere chasing the brass ring and the golden handcuffs offered by Corporate America. In a typical assisted living market area today it is not unusual to discover that many adult children do not currently reside in the city or town where they grew up. To a lesser degree, but certainly significant, many of their parents have also moved to other locales.

Later in life, there is a basic motivation for a permanent reunion of the aging senior with at least one of the adult children. Trends have indicated that, in many cases, one child takes most of the early initiatives to re-establish that link. Hence, the appropriate label of *decision influencer*.

The demographic stereotype is typically a married female balancing the roles of homemaker while frequently working outside the home. Many are still raising children, some are heavily involved with grandchildren *and* growing increasingly concerned about her or her husband's aging parents.

This geographical displacement between adult children and their parents presents another challenge for influencers and an opportunity for assisted living sponsors. Children are highly motivated to move their parents closer to them as health complications increase. If you are in a metro market that has experienced corporate relocations involving a large influx of new employees in the past 10 to 15 years, chances are you can significantly expand your local market by attracting seniors who also did not previously reside in your primary market area.

Some seniors will be attracted to your area so they can be near their children. The adult children are the *gatekeepers* but if you can capture only a *one-half of one percent* of this gross potential you can typically realize a theoretical absorption of 50 units. Obviously, no single community can be filled in this way alone, but the migration potential for assisted living is clearly significant, and frequently overlooked. It is not unusual for a typical assisted living community to have 25 to 30 percent of their residents moving in from outside the community's defined (local) primary market area.

The Sandwich Generation Caught in the Middle

These decision influencers of today are facing other challenges. Because of delayed marriages, many are putting their children through college while also trying to save for retirement. Now many are receiving a major wake-up call involving the unplanned-for task of caring for their aging parents. Many are dual income households with both spouses working outside of the home. The number of households facing these multiple challenges will only increase in the future.

So just about the time they become traditional empty nesters, many face the almost immediate challenge of caring for their parents. And some experts predict the sandwich generation may spend almost as much time and money caring for their parents as they did raising their children.

THE GENERATION CAUGHT IN THE MIDDLE
Three Major Challenges

1. **Putting children through college**
2. **Saving for retirement**
3. **Caring for their parents**

Family patterns are changing. Mother does not traditionally move in with married children as in past generations. Seniors tell us consistently that they do not want to move in with their children and become a burden. Most would prefer not living with them, even if invited.

Caregivers and the Work Force – Major Conflicts

Recent surveys by major employers clearly indicate that an alarming number of their employees, primarily female, are struggling with a caregiver responsibility to the extent that it is affecting their workplace productivity. And the labor force participation rate of females has soared past the 60 percent level in recent years.

In 1998, the Labor Department's Women's Bureau released the results of a study on work and caregiving. Some of their findings were:

1. A significant proportion of American households provides care for an elderly relative.

2. Approximately 72 percent of the caregivers are women and 64 percent work full or part time; 41 percent are also caring for children.

3. More than half reported taking time off from work or coming in later because of caregiver conflicts.

With unemployment rates in the year 2000 at typically the lowest level in 25 years, major employers are starting to see similarities between the needs and benefits of senior care and child care. The future of senior care may see some significant involvement in elder care initiatives by Corporate America.

Marketing to the Decision Influencers

To appeal to the adult children/decision influencers, you must develop a credible and ethical market positioning strategy that acknowledges their emotions while addressing their parents' specific needs and concerns. The ideal message to convey is that many adult children have discovered that assisted living is a surprisingly affordable living alternative offering ambience, dignity and maximum independence for parents in later stages of life.

Time-Distance Dynamics

The primary market area for your new assisted living community should be defined or at least heavily influenced by time-distance clusters of adult children. Frequently it is the adult child/decision influencer who really shapes a community's primary market area. Wherever possible, apply the following time-distance rule when defining your primary market area:

Time-Distance Rule

Working adult children/decision influencers will typically travel up to 30 to 35 minutes from their home or place of employment to visit their parent in assisted living.

Benefit-driven marketing strategies must offer the best of two worlds, for both the senior and the adult children. This means that assisted living must be designed and positioned in the marketplace for two types of prospects or decision makers; the adult child and the ultimate senior resident. The decision influencer must feel good about supporting and, in many cases, initiating the parent's decision to move. This can best be accomplished by developing strategies aimed at the top five emotions of the decision influencers mentioned earlier in this chapter.

Strategies must be developed with both markets in mind. Market to the seniors in the primary market area using conventional techniques, but also communicate with adult children in the same area using innovative target marketing strategies. The decision influencer's significant role in marketing assisted living to seniors will continue to grow. Properly targeted, the decision influencer can be the center piece and catalyst that enhances all of the other sales and marketing strategies.

SECTION EIGHT

Strategic Considerations

CHAPTER 35

THE AGONY AND ECSTASY OF PROJECT FILL-UP
How to Prepare for an Assisted Living Launch

Like a space shuttle lift-off at Cape Canaveral, an assisted living project launch can represent the most critical, high risk phase of the entire development process. As with a rocket launch, the cost of preparation and actual launch is significant, yet frequently underestimated. But the cost of a failed launch is enormous, and would have a long-term impact on both your reputation and your financial statement.

Absorption Defined

The simple definition of assisted living absorption is the time it will take a new project to reach stabilized occupancy of 93 percent from initial opening or Certificate of Occupancy (COO). Absorption is typically viewed in two major phases:

- *Pre-opening marketing phase* – This is typically a period of six to eight months <u>before</u> Certificate of Occupancy that is used to lay the foundation for a successful opening. It involves a critical countdown that is discussed in more detail later in this chapter.

● *Fill-up/net absorption phase* – This phase begins immediately upon Certificate of Occupancy with the first resident move-ins. Technically, the phase ends when the project reaches a stabilized occupancy of approximately 93 percent. But realistically, marketing of assisted living is an ongoing process. With turnover frequently exceeding 40 percent annually, you will *always* be in a proactive marketing phase.

Within the fill-up phase, there are actually two major components - the initial arrival of residents who were actually waiting for your project to open its doors, and then a moderately sloped "ramp up" of increasing move-ins and occupancy after opening.

Referring to Figure 35-1, let's look at the typical expectation for a new 80-unit, freestanding assisted living community. Initial "in-rush" occupancy upon opening will usually range between 12 to 15 percent, or approximately 10 to 12 move-ins upon achieving a Certificate of Occupancy. After the initial move-ins, you might expect future move-in rates to average between 4 to 6 units per month *net of turnover.* The operative words are "net of turnover." That's because, while you're initially filling up your project, you're already experiencing resident turnover. Annually, this turnover can exceed 40 percent. If you perform within these fill-up parameters, you will reach 93 percent stabilized occupancy in about 16 to 19 months from first opening your doors.

FIGURE 35-1

TYPICAL ASSISTED LIVING ABSORPTION PROFILE

I. **The Basic Absorption Challenge**

- Total units to be absorbed   80

- "In-rush" absorption upon opening @ 12%   10

- Net remaining units to be absorbed @
  93% stabilized occupancy   65

  but . . .

- Annual turnover ratio for assisted living during
  initial fill-up/absorption   25%

  leaving . . .

- Total assisted living units to be <u>sold</u>   94

- Actual net units to be *absorbed*   65

II. **Most Likely Absorption Scenarios**

	Units/ Months	Fill-Up Period: Assumption of Initial Turnover	
		<u>None</u>	<u>25%</u>
• Conservative	4	16 mos.	24 mos.
• Expected *	5	13	19
• Achievable *	6	11	16

* Most likely project absorption experience under normal market conditions

The absorption rates reflect <u>averages</u> over the entire fill-up period - from an early "in-rush" of residents to the slower fill-up as the project approaches stabilized occupancy.

Source: Moore Diversified Services, Inc.

Factors Impacting Absorption

There are a number of factors that will affect your actual absorption profile. These include, but are not necessarily limited to the following:

1. The degree of sophistication of your consumers in your Primary Market Area.

2. Consumer awareness – that is, the level of understanding of assisted living as a viable option.

3. Relative intensity of viable competition.

4. Degree of living options and services currently being offered within your Primary Market Area.

5. The appropriate site layout and size of your project.

6. A state-of-the-art design implemented by qualified industry experts.

7. A significant, dedicated sales and marketing budget.

8. Quality, intensity and effectiveness of your sales and marketing program.

9. An experienced marketing team with a specific understanding of the unique position of your project in this particular market area.

10. Sophisticated pre-market testing with Senior consumers, and with decision-influencer involvement.

11. Competitive pricing that communicates high value.

12. Level of perceived *benefits;* not *features!*

13. An experienced, professional management operation.

14. Finally, an adequate fill-up budget.

Invest for Success

To insure a successful project, your capital budget must include significant dollars to fund a sophisticated sales and marketing program, and to cover some substantial negative cash flow deficits that will occur during the critical fill-up period. This investment for success is a two-step process:

- **Step #1** – Sales and marketing should be initially budgeted at $3,500 to $4,500 per unit – which rounds out, for an 80-unit community, at $280,000 to $360,000! And that's just to get to 93 percent stabilized occupancy, so your normal operating budget can kick in.

- **Step #2** – Once you allocate this block of dollars for your sales and marketing budget, you must *immediately* prepare a detailed budget, line item by line item.

In order to properly execute a cost-effective sales and marketing program, you should embark on a program that involves a "six month pre-opening countdown".

Absorption time for a project of this nature will vary as a function of marketing intensity, experience and image of the Development Team. Other factors include specific marketplace conditions such as size and depth of age and income qualified market, level of existing competition and the senior's ease of selling their home.

The preceding must be augmented by an aggressive pre-marketing effort and networking/outreach program, which will involve appropriate advertising and marketing aids.

Financial Buffers and Safety Margins

Working capital/fill-up reserve funds are necessary because, in the early months of initial project fill-up, it is normal to experience negative cash flow. This reserve fund is necessary to cover the anticipated cash flow deficits (both net operating income shortfalls and debt service) because modest, but growing, revenues are not yet large enough to cover necessary fixed and semi-variable expenses already being incurred.

Just like a new retail shop or restaurant, you must have an impressive opening with absolutely no flaws in your product presentation or service delivery. For a new assisted living community that means most of your staff (Executive Director, community that means most of your staff (Executive Director, Cook/Chef, Activities Professional, Direct Care Personnel, etc.) must already be part of your operating budget – even though there are not yet adequate revenues to cover all of these fixed expenses.

Most projects will already be making significant mortgage payments on either their project's construction or permanent loans. For an 80-unit project, the typical (negative) cash drain from covering debt service can average $45,000 per month. Peak or cumulative negative cash flow (expenses <u>and</u> debt service) can total at least $360,000 during the entire fill-up period. Under normal fill-up conditions, this is to be expected, and should be presented as a distinct line item in your project's initial capital budget.

The sales and marketing and working capital budgets are carefully designed to underwrite the successful launch of your project. Without these resources, your project could experience a costly, unstable and potentially disastrous launch into the competitive marketplace. Many sponsors tell their lenders and investors that their subpar community financial performance was not their fault. They blame unpredictable market conditions, or irresponsible competitors. In fact, many may not have funded their start-up project adequately, while others did not properly allocate and deploy available cash that was provided in their initial capital budget.

Let's face it: The worst that can happen if you *overbudget* sales and marketing and working capital is that you have successfully. Not a bad problem to have in the early history of your project!

Three Strategic Initiatives

Like that space shuttle liftoff, your assisted living project launch is a very complex endeavor. There are three basic strategic initiatives that must be executed – consider them a "countdown" to successful launch:

1. *Develop and Execute a Six- to Eight-Month Pre-Launch Program* – Sophisticated operators hire key staff (Executive Director, sales and marketing professionals, etc.) well in advance of the official project opening date. They actually execute a detailed, pragmatic "countdown to opening" to insure a successful project launch.

2. *Build a Strong Back Pressure of Market Demand* – A successful project launch requires significant pre-opening (we'll call it "pre-sales") efforts in order to realize the critical initial move-ins upon opening. This "sweet smell of early success" is very similar to the initial favorable reviews of the opening of a new restaurant or hotel. As mentioned earlier in the chapter, ideally you should have about a 12 to 15 percent "in-rush" of move-ins upon obtaining your Certificate of Occupancy (COO). For an 80-unit project, that's about 10 to 12 residents.

Many projects suffer sagging sales momentum after the initial in-rush because they did not properly plan to sustain their projected ongoing fill-up ramp of 4 to 6 units per month. We're frequently so preoccupied with the grand opening and euphoria of initial move-ins that we lose sales momentum in the months immediately afterwards. While actual industry sales closing ratios are difficult to track and a closely guarded competitive secret, you will probably need 1,600 to 2,000 solid, qualified leads to initially fill an 80-unit community.

3. Finally, Conduct a Pragmatic Fill-Up Sensitivity Analysis – The earlier you get the proverbial wake-up call, the better! Most new sponsors dream of an initial absorption rate of 6 units per month – or better. For some, the dream turns into a nightmare when – *after* turnover and the impact of emerging local competition – their actual absorption rate comes in at about 3 units per month. Figure 35-2 summarizes the impact of sub-par absorption. With that downside scenario, you'll probably conclude that: 1) the initial fill-up period to stabilized occupancy almost doubled from 16 months to 31 months; 2) the sales and marketing budget was not invested in an optimum manner; 3) the required working capital/fill-up reserve (because of negative cash flow) has ballooned from approximately $350,000 to $685,000; and 4) the equity investor's annual internal rate of return (IRR) – with a 5-year stabilized holding period – decreased from about 17 to 4 percent.

FIGURE 35-2

SLOW FILL-UP CAN BE *VERY* EXPENSIVE

	80-Unit Project Fill-Up/Absorption Rate[1]	
	6/Units/Mo	3/Units/Mo
I. Months to Stabilized Occupancy of 93% – Assumes a15% In-Rush Upon Opening	16 months	31 months
II. Required Fill-Up Reserve/ Working Capital:		
• Total Dollar Cost	$324,675	$685,080
• Cost per Unit	$4,058/unit	$8,564/unit
III. Additional Debt Payments Required to Service Added Costs of Fill-Up of $360,400[2]		
• Annual	$ 36,290/year	
• Over 10 Years	$362,900 (10 years)	
IV. Internal Rate of Return (IRR) Change (With a 5-Year Holding Period)	17.1%	3.8%

Source: Moore Diversified Services, Inc.

_____

[1] Net of turnover

[2] 9% interest, 25 years

Cluttered, Saturated Markets

Some sponsors complain they are victims of cluttered or temporarily saturated markets. If you find yourself in that unpleasant situation, it is time to execute some sound project recovery fundamentals. This typically involves a quick-reaction analysis of the true size and depth of your market (maybe it is not really saturated). You must realistically compare your project to the competition in terms of product, price and value. You also need to re-emphasize proactive sales and marketing initiatives. A market could be considered "permanently saturated" when, in fact, your project may actually be experiencing the short-run challenges of what I call "the velocity of simultaneous project fill-up". This is a situation where two or more nearby competitive projects are entering the marketplace at the same time, both trying to capture the attention and business of a finite number of potential age-, income- and acuity-qualified assisted living residents. In most cases, this does not mean that the market is impossibly saturated. The truly focused owner/operator can still achieve success, albeit at a slightly slower pace.

As some markets mature and competition intensifies, the successful launch of a new assisted living project will become an even more critical element of that project's life cycle. There are still many good opportunities for properly conceived and effectively launched assisted living communities.

CHAPTER 36

MANAGING ASSISTED LIVING
Internal Resource or Third-Party Contract?

Consistent and effective management is one of the most important and critical elements driving the success of both new and existing assisted living communities. In theoretical business terms, determining how to execute the management function of an assisted living community is a classical "make or buy" or outsourcing decision taught in leading business schools for the last 50 years. In today's terms, it's a strategic decision with two options:

1. Build a strong permanent internal resource

or . . .

2. Outsource to a qualified third party firm

Short-run, the decision to "go internal" or engage an external third party management company appears relatively easy, but the long-run view introduces a number of variables suggesting that the "make or buy" decision is far more complex. And it is the long-run view of total assisted living management needs that is critical to the future success of both senior living communities and professional management companies in the 21st century. One thing *is* clear - you need a defined and structured management function. You should always assess about a 5 percent management fee (discussed in detail later) as part of your normal operating expenses.

Third Party Management Rationale

The possible selection of an external management company should be viewed as a beneficial, value-added strategy – both short-run and long-run. When evaluating the pros and cons of going internal versus entering into a third-party management contract, many issues must be considered. The initial issues that come to mind as potential disadvantages of engaging outside expertise are losing direct control, autonomy and incurring more costs. But a closer look at this important decision leads to identifying the top five project management needs to be satisfied – and the possible rationale for considering a third party contractual arrangement.

Top Five Project Management Needs

These top five needs are:

1. Extensive industry knowledge and comparable database

2. Sophisticated, yet practical and cost-effective systems, procedures, and controls

3. Potential for delivering significant ongoing economies of scale that directly benefit your community

4. The ability to stay on the leading edge of the state-of-the-art in an ever-changing industry

5. Cost-effective, consistent, focused and continuous creative input

These and other objective criteria should really drive the critical internal staffing versus outsourcing project management decision.

If you're planning a new, start-up community and you have limited industry experience, your lender or underwriter may require the retention of a nationally recognized third party management company. Your friendly lender wants you to be successful, but he must always consider potential foreclosure and a graceful exit strategy.

Management Company Pitfalls

In spite of their obvious strengths and advantages, some apparently sound third party management companies fail to deliver full potential to their clients. There are typically four potential weaknesses that must be avoided in any selection decision:

1. The lack of consistent, ongoing involvement and oversight by the same key, experienced individuals who initially sold you the contractual relationship .

2. Inconsistent quality of contract services and sub-par performance of on-site personnel permanently assigned to your community.

3. The inability to effectively communicate and work with owners, sponsors, and boards of directors.

4. They don't get the job done; ineffective sales and marketing results and/or excessive operating costs.

Consistent monitoring and progress reporting systems can serve as effective early warning signals.

Fire the Manager!

Progressive management companies recognize these potential challenges and most work very hard for their clients, trying to avoid what has been termed in the business as the "baseball manager syndrome." This is a frequently erroneous business rule of thumb that says, *"When successful community performance is in doubt, fire the manager!"* True, it's a proactive move – but it may not be the right one.

Stabilized Occupancy and Ongoing Operations

Management contracts are sometimes terminated when a community reaches stabilized occupancy of 93 percent. The owner frequently thinks the job is done – **"We don't need you**

any more." Yet this could be one of the most beneficial periods to actually have a professional manager providing ongoing guidance and leading-edge strategies. Net operating income and cash flow increase dramatically beyond break-even occupancy and becomes extremely attractive if you can operate in that rarified zone above 93 percent stabilized occupancy. The difference between 93 percent *stabilized* occupancy and 97 percent *optimized* occupancy can frequently justify the *cost* of a professional management company. *Value* would be a more appropriate term.

Maintenance marketing and ongoing management strategies at stabilized occupancy certainly include a continuation of existing initiatives that were implemented during initial project fill-up. But now these initiatives require increased focus and intensity. The ongoing initiatives include but are not necessarily limited to the following: 1) maintenance marketing; keeping the community full, 2) a detailed capital replacement and cosmetic upgrade program with both short- and long-run implementation goals, 3) execution of the fine points of subtle, but effective, revenue enhancement and expense reduction and 4) sustaining and optimizing resident satisfaction, quality of life and perceived value. Extraordinary management of service, cost, quality and convenience leads to high perceived value by both existing and future residents.

Indeed, management initiatives leading to operational enhancements at or above stabilized occupancy may be difficult to identify and execute, but the pay-offs can be significant. For every dollar earned or saved, the financial value of a community increases by a factor of almost ten dollars[1].

Value Considerations

Third-party management companies can appear to be, and sometimes are, very expensive. But the financial pay-off for extraordinary community management and the resulting performance puts many of these costs into proper perspective. One of the best ways to evaluate the relative costs of going internal versus using a professional management company is to seek answers to three key questions: 1) What obvious overhead costs would exist under *either* scenario?, 2) What are the tangible and intangible cost-benefits of the potential relationship? and 3) Can existing or restructured internal management realistically achieve the same objectives and performance levels as a professional management company? The final question to ask is how can you *most effectively* provide a wide array of leading edge management services in a cost-effective manner.

Management Fees

Basic management company fees can vary for a number of valid reasons, but typically range from approximately 4.5 to 5.5

---

[1]Net income is typically capitalized using a rate of approximately 10.5 percent; meaning investors are willing to accept (initially) a 10.5 percent return on their investment.

percent of adjusted gross operating revenues. This is frequently defined as net revenues collected – considering the impact of vacancies. The "industry standard" is about 5.0 percent – that is the figure lenders typically look for as an expense line item when they evaluate your financial pro forma or loan package. Management fees of six to seven percent of revenues exist; but only in cases where extraordinary benefits and value are delivered by the management company to the owner.

Performance Incentives – Risk sharing incentives are starting to emerge in the industry. Under the risk sharing concept, both the owner and the management company agree on a budget with a defined net operating income (revenues minus expenses) or net cash flow target. If actual performance exceeds budget expectations, the management company receives an added incentive fee.

A typical incentive arrangement might be where the additional incentive management fee is 25 percent of any *increase* in net cash flow above the budgeted amount for a definable period (usually one year). Keep in mind there is no free lunch; the practical rules of risk vs. reward factor into all of these negotiated relationships.

And if minimum expectations are not met, the management company's fees are impacted accordingly. Sometimes a management company agrees to subordinate at least some of their earned management fees to available cash flow after normal operating expenses and required debt service.

If you're thinking of getting into the third party management company business, the rewards can be attractive, but the business is very complex. If you're successful, you can expect an operating margin of approximately 50 percent if you are managing ten or more communities. That means it will likely cost you $.50 for every management fee dollar you collect.

Typical Management Services Provided

For newcomers to the assisted living industry, there are frequently some misconceptions and misunderstandings regarding the specific services actually provided by management companies in exchange for their fees. For example, the third party management company will hire certain personnel and incur other costs at your community – *in your behalf* and based on your prior approval. That means these costs are passed through to your normal operating expense budget and are not covered as part of the typical five percent management fee. This is normal, conventional and common throughout the industry. In addition, a new project that has not yet reached stabilized occupancy will require some fixed cash retainers; fixed monthly payments to the management company as they help you bring your project to stabilized occupancy. The amount of these fees vary with the size of your project and other characteristics, but can range from approximately $5,000 to $10,000 per month during the initial start-up phase.

As in any other purchasing or outsourcing decision, it is best to receive competitive inputs from several quality management companies with long-standing industry experience and good reputations. You must carefully evaluate a number of important services that are typically included in a very comprehensive management contract relationship. Some of these services include, but are certainly not limited to, the following:

1. Management Services

- Provide oversight and expertise
- Supervise daily operations
- Implement policies and procedures
- Establish qualitative and quantitative objectives
- Implement pre-opening "countdown"
- Develop and implement licensure and regulatory compliance program

2. Sales and Marketing Initiatives

- Select and install lead tracking systems
- Develop a strategic sales and marketing plan and budget
- Manage/supervise all operations and activities
- Report status; weekly, monthly, quarterly
- Deliver appropriate results to agreed-to budgets and forecasts
- Coordinate marketing collateral development
- Conduct periodic competitive analyses

3. Provide Operating Systems and Procedures

- Develop ⎫
- Install ⎪   Accounting systems/software, Policy and Procedures Manual, Residency Agreements, Employee Manual, external agency compliance reporting, etc.
- Execute ⎬
- Maintain ⎭

4. Staffing/Human Resources

- Develop job descriptions
- Compensation and benefit plans
- Recruit and interview candidates
- Hire
- Train
- Supervise
- Implement payroll

5. Overall Financial Management and Controls

- Establish
- Maintain
- Monitor
- Report
- Prepare billings/collect receivables; disburse payables

6. Budgets and Financial Management

- Prepare annual budget
- Obtain review and approval
- Capital expenditure plan

7. Monthly Financial Statements

- Develop
- Prepare
- Report monthly
- Compare actuals vs. budget
- Issue variance reports
- Balance sheets
- Income statements
- Cash flow statements
- General ledgers

8. Resident Care

- Develop overall care plan
- Create resident assessment criteria
- Define/maintain appropriate standards of care
- Define and monitor resident expected outcomes

9. Risk Management

- Recommend adequate insurance coverage
- Keep appropriate insurance coverage in force
- Monitor and minimize current and future costs

These are typical services provided. Keep in mind the management company is typically incurring significant costs in your behalf. However, individual management contract terms and conditions can vary over a wide spectrum. Note that effective third party management involves a two tier seamless process. The resources of the management company's *home office* must be integrated with initiatives that take place on your *campus*.

Short-Run & Long-Run Relationships

Some sponsors new to the business will retain a third party management company for their initial project and then gradually develop a strong, permanent internal resource. In these cases, let your management company know in an honest and straightforward manner about your long-run strategic objectives. In order to retain the right quality level of services, you must allow the management company an adequate budget and a reasonable time period to get the job done. You will not get top talent and focused attention if they think you are likely to be an unfair, "short-term client."

The ideal approach may be a multi-tier strategy involving continuous access to top-level industry expertise and experience, while developing a strong, permanent internal resource base – constantly keeping up with the ever-changing state-of-the-art in the assisted living industry.

Clearly, third-party management arrangements are not appropriate for every situation. But the inherent challenges and potential downsides of such a relationship can be eliminated or neutralized. And the significant advantages can sometimes lead to new levels of superior performance and lender confidence benefitting both residents and sponsors.

CHAPTER 37

"I *WAS* SOMEBODY ONCE"

The Real Issue is Resident Quality of Life . . .
Not Just Resident Satisfaction

In my 30 years of working with seniors, I try to *live* in as many senior living communities as possible. So far I've had short stays in over 40 independent and assisted living communities - with many of them being repeat visits. As I was having dinner one evening with a distinguished senior in an assisted living community he said, *"You know, I was somebody once."* A lady at the next table chimed in, *"The young people who help us are just delightful – but they really don't understand us."* This community had all the right services and amenities. It was also staffed abundantly, and all the staff members knew residents on a first-name basis. Yet, something very important was lacking – a true understanding of seniors' inner emotional needs.

Over the past few years, people who provide senior living environments, from independent living through assisted living and nursing homes, have talked a great deal about developing a *seamless continuum* of care. But our sharp focus on the "continuum" is sometimes no more than a business strategy. The real issue for determining success in the 21st century involves an area where many have accomplished very little; delivering true *quality of life* for residents.

What Seniors Want and Need

Most seniors define a high-quality life as including a comfortable living environment, relatively good health, independence in their daily routine, the opportunity to express themselves and to experience life satisfaction and fulfillment. These desires can be translated into ten quality of life attributes as outlined in Figure 37-1.

Five of these are delivered by any good senior community. They are: 1) health maintenance, 2) security, 3) comfort, 4) peace of mind, and 5) services offering quality, value, and utility. But the next five present some real challenges. Senior housing owners and operators *must* provide ways for residents to: 1) enjoy experiences, adventures and nostalgia, 2) maintain relative independence and control of their daily lives, 3) socialize with others, 4) be intellectually stimulated, and 5) express themselves and enjoy self-fulfillment.

Changing "Birthmarks"

A new breed of seniors in the 21st century will expect more from our communities. We all recognize the importance of *demographics,* but we must also recognize seniors' changing *psychographics.* Let's assume the typical seniors considering your community will be 80 years old in the year 2003. As teenagers during the Great Depression and young adults during World War II, they reached maturity during the post-War boom. By the time of the Vietnam War and the rebellions of the 1960s, they were in their forties. By the 1970s, many were members of "The Establishment," and they were nearing retirement age during the boom/bust cycle of the 1980s. All those turbulent times created a series of *birthmarks*, making many of these seniors more demanding, less complacent, and more pragmatic in their search for self-fulfillment than their predecessors. These birthmarks are depicted in Figure 37-2.

FIGURE 37-1
TOP TEN QUALITY OF LIFE ATTRIBUTES

Seniors are on a constant search for quality of life in the following areas:

1. **Experiences/adventures/nostalgia**

2. **Comfort/peace of mind**

3. **Security**

4. **Convenience**

5. **Quality and value**

6. **Health maintenance**

7. **Individual recognition**

8. **Socialization**

9. **Intellectual stimulation**

10. **Self-expression and fulfillment**

The Real Issue is Resident Quality of Life . . .
Not Just Resident Satisfaction

Moore Diversified Services, Inc.

FIGURE 37-2
BIRTHMARKS OF AGE 83 SENIORS
IN THE EARLY 21ST CENTURY (2003)

"Birthmark"	Year	Age of Senior
Great Depression	1933	13
World War II	1943	23
Post War Boom	1950	30
Vietnam War/ Rebellions of '60s	1965	45
Boom and Bust of the '80s	1985	65
Prosperity of the Mid '90s	1995	75
Your Potential Resident	*2003*	*83*

A new breed of seniors will expect more
from senior living communities.

Moore Diversified Services, Inc.

These birthmarks are further complicated by gender. The men will have experienced the *"gray flannel suit"* era of Corporate America – along with the transition from that period of conformity to a more entrepreneurial time that made modern day pioneers and adventurers popular. The females will have made the transition from being primarily homemakers to joining the skyrocketing numbers of women in the outside work force, making them less passive, more worldly and less apt to settle for someone else's definition of the status quo.

Five Quality of Life Initiatives

To give tomorrow's seniors the quality of life they want, you must seriously consider five initiatives:

1. *Answer the question: What do my residents really want out of the remainder of their lives and how can we best deliver it – even if it involves shared risk?*

2. *Focus clinical and medical care plans more on supporting and enhancing quality of life rather than heavily regimented and institutional medical routines.*

3. *Add an increased emphasis on geriatrics and holistic approaches to wellness and health care to your existing traditional health care procedures, which tend to emphasize just treating health problems.*

4. *Make sure your assistance with activities of daily living truly supports each resident's needs, wants, and capabilities – in a flexible resident-centered manner.*

5. *Focus your operations on the <u>individual</u> resident's daily life, not a general group setting or high-tech care plan.*

It may not be easy to determine how well your efforts are working, but it's important to try. Resident satisfaction surveys are useful, but they frequently don't tell the whole story. Many respondents soften their assessments, some actually fearing *retribution* from management if they criticize their communities. Providers must learn to monitor another vital sign of each resident – paying close attention to how well each resident's quality of life needs are really being met.

Our "Distinguished Achievers"

If one were able to inventory and make use of the aggregate knowledge, experience and resources that exist with seniors in a typical senior living community, the results would be staggering. The unique capabilities, intellect and inner drives of these seniors that were developed over a lifetime of productive work and community contribution suddenly do not fade away as they "retire" and move into senior living communities. But sadly, in many cases, they are inadvertently suppressed – never surfacing again during the autumn years of their lives. Senior living communities have a tremendous opportunity (and responsibility) to provide a truly stimulating lifestyle for the senior. Today's seniors are not just survivors or older Americans – they are our most *Distinguished Achievers!*

Quality of Life - Both a Challenge & Obligation

Resident panels, focus groups and satisfaction surveys all indicate that most seniors report being generally happy living in retirement communities. But these results do not necessarily mean that they have achieved *optimum* self-fulfillment.

The primary obstacles to improving quality of life will be creativity and cost. Implementing the new quality of life discipline will require increased staff time and innovative programming strategies, which would increase operating expenses. But there could also be financial advantages. In the long run, increased quality of life may lead to decreased institutional health care needs and related costs. Although this is only a theory, it's a plausible one that deserves to be tested.

Providers who don't take resident privacy, dignity, optimum independence, and the seniors' search for self-fulfillment seriously may pay for it in the end. In the not-too-distant future, a new breed of seniors may demand key quality of life elements, seeking out communities of choice that are truly focused on improving quality of life.

To personalize the quality of life challenge, those of us involved in the senior housing and health care industry might consider ourselves "achievers." By the time we reach 80 years of age, we will probably want to be called *"distinguished achievers."* In order to sharply focus on this complex issue of quality of life, project yourself into the future 30 or 40 years and ask the defining question, ***"What would I really want out of life*** *at age 80?"* It's safe to say that the answer for many of us would be, *"Not exactly what I see today."*

The quality of life challenges are tremendous as we attempt to optimize senior's lifestyle in a cost-effective group setting but with individual privacy, dignity, optimum independence and self-fulfillment.

CHAPTER 38

EVERYBODY NEEDS AN EXIT STRATEGY

"You've Got to Know When to Hold 'em, and Know When to Fold 'em"

There are times when everybody needs an exit strategy. Most of us have wills, estate plans and life insurance; all important parts of a personal exit strategy. This doesn't mean we plan on exiting any time soon, but we also realize it's sensible to be ready for anything.

Yet when I tell clients that even if they don't plan to sell, they need an exit strategy, many act uncomfortable. Some for-profit owner/operators tell me they're not about to leave the assisted living market sector and plan to ride out the current business cycles, thank you very much. Not-for-profit sponsors often assure me they've been serving seniors for many years, and plan to be around for many more.

But developing a sound exit strategy doesn't mean you're actually planning to get out of the senior living business. Evaluating your community's value and competitiveness and strengthening its weak points to make it more appealing to a hypothetical prospective buyer is a valuable exercise. It doesn't matter whether you intend to get out of the business next year or stay in it until you retire. It's the acid test and the best insurance for survival, success and financial viability in the 21st century.

Start by answering these five basic questions:

1. How competitive is your campus in two time frames: Now, and over the next five years?

2. If a knowledgeable observer was scoring you and your competition on scales of 1 to 10 for product, service, price, and value, how would you measure up?

3. If you were on the other side of the negotiating table and about to purchase your community, what concerns would you have about the business being acquired?

4. As a potential buyer, would you reduce your offering price because of some flaw or shortcoming?

5. Based on your answers to the first four questions, what should *you* change over the next 18 months?

Some for-profits remain situation-driven, rationalizing that their shortcomings are either not really significant or that they will certainly be understood and readily accepted in the marketplace. Not-for-profits frequently think their humanitarian goals more than compensate for any flaws in product value. Both industry sectors are in for major wake-up calls as product life cycles shorten, consumers become more demanding and savvy competitors (with sound exit strategies) move ahead with market-driven capital improvements.

Little Things Mean a Lot

Little things will make a big difference as our industry matures, so your operations must be based on sound fundamentals. Refine your exit strategy planning by answering five more questions:

1. Do you have a proactive sales and marketing program, or are you just waiting for prospective residents to show up?

2. Are there any emerging trends that could alter your current resident referral patterns?

3. How is the aging-in-place of both your residents and your physical plant likely to affect your competitiveness over the next five years?

4. Are you using appropriate reserve funds to improve living units and public spaces while maintaining equitable pricing?

5. Do you have a detailed capital investment plan – accumulating replacement reserve dollars to allow your community to remain in "like new" condition?

Keeping up with the changing market means also investing constantly in such things as advanced computer software, training and education, and capital equipment. Whether you are a self-contained, internally operated for-profit or not-for-profit organization, charge your community a management fee of approximately 5 percent of net revenues. This won't hurt your financial profile, as lenders expect to see such an assessment as a normal line item under operating expenses.

But execute investments wisely. You can't afford to spend too much, or charge residents too little. Financial guidelines can help you decide how much is too much, but use them with caution: Different communities have different accounting systems, and prices will vary according to your location, target market, and competition.

Use the Resident-Day Concept to Evaluate Your Expenses

To run a quick check on your financial ratios, compute your total resident days by multiplying the number of residents you have times 365 days. Divide your total operating expenses (not including interest, taxes, depreciation, or loan amortization) by the total number of resident days to compute operating expenses per resident day. Compare this number to the industry average of about $50 to $55 per resident day, which applies to most markets across the U.S. Refer to Figures 38-1 and 17-1 in Chapter 17 for some valuable quantitative benchmarks.

Operating Expense Ratio

Now divide these same total operating expenses by net revenues collected from occupied units. This yields your *operating expense ratio,* which should be approximately 60 to 65 percent. The inverse of this ratio would now be operating margin.

FIGURE 38-1

SEVEN VITAL SIGNS FOR A SOUND ASSISTED LIVING EXIT STRATEGY

<u>How are you doing</u>?

1. Expenses per Resident-Day $50.00 - $55.00

2. Operating Expense Ratio   60% - 65%

3. Operating Profit Margin:

   • EBITDA[1]   35% - 40%

4. *Minimum* Debt Service
   Coverage Ratio   1.25x - 1.30x

5. Total Staffing – FTEs/Unit:

   • Assisted Living   .45 - .55

   • Special Care Dementia   .55 - .65

6. Reserve for Replacement $225 - $250/Unit/Year

Approximately 75 percent of the assisted living projects in the U.S. fit this profile. If yours is off, take a closer look: Is there a good reason or does something need to be fixed?

Source: Moore Diversified Services, Inc.

---

[1]Earnings Before Interest, Taxes, Depreciation and Amortization (also referred to as Net Operating Income).

If your operating expense ratio is higher than 65 percent but your operating expenses per resident day are "normal," chances are you are collecting abnormally low revenues, and it may be time to rethink your pricing strategy.

If both your operating expense ratio and your expenses per resident day are above the high end of the range, take a long, hard look at your operating expenses, department by department. To conform with industry norms, your *total* staffing should average approximately .45 to .55 FTEs per unit for assisted living, and somewhat higher for special care/dementia (see Chapter 16 on staffing).

Develop cost accounting and pricing systems to compensate for cost creep. That's profit erosion resulting from the steadily rising cost of providing care to residents as they age in place. Make sure that each department or service is a stand-alone cost/profit center, developing accounting systems and pricing strategies that treat each resident and their families fairly, while fully recovering the total cost of their care. (See Chapter 14 on operating expenses and Chapter 15 for a treatment of cost creep.)

And if operating expenses and revenues are in line and revenues are appropriate, you should realize an operating profit of approximately 35 to 40 percent for an efficiently operated assisted living community of at least 80 units. All of these ratios should continue to improve the longer your assisted living community has been in operation with stabilized occupancy.

Operating profit margin – an elusive target – It should be noted that even the most sophisticated assisted living operators in the United States today are still chasing the elusive 40 percent (EBITDA) operating profit margin mentioned earlier. It's become a frustrating target because of operating cost creep.

Debt Service Coverage

If you have a typical debt on your community of about 75 percent of its total value, your lender is likely to require a debt service coverage ratio of approximately 1.25 to 1.30 (to determine this figure, divide your net operating income by your annual debt payment). This means that after paying all of your annual operating expenses, you must have $1.30 in available cash for every dollar of required annual debt payment (both principal and interest).

Capitalization rate determines value – The key value indicator for your community is your net operating income. As an exit strategy, a buyer will generally look at your community as an income producing "black box." In today's market, these potential buyers (or lenders) are likely to value your community using a capitalization rate of approximately 10.5 to 11.0 percent. This means that, in the short run, they are willing to initially realize a 10.5 to 11.0 percent return on their cash invested. Thus, dividing your net operating income by between .105 to .110 tells you and potential buyers and lenders how much cash they can afford to invest for these appropriate returns. The actual determination of value is more complex, but these are the basics. Refer to Appendix C for more details on cap rates.

This simple exit strategy rule of thumb for value indicates that, for every extra dollar of annual net operating income you realize, the value of your community increases by almost $10. This can be accomplished by either enhancing revenues or decreasing expenses. Remember, cash flow is the "lifeblood" of your community; whether you are a for-profit having to answer to lenders and investors or a not-for-profit struggling to fund an ongoing charitable mission.

Are exit strategies useful only for improving your operation so you can hold onto it longer? Not necessarily. There are many operators who don't realize that, all things considered, it would be appropriate to enact an exit strategy. Kenny Rogers' advice in "The Gambler" – **"You've got to know when to hold 'em, and know when to fold 'em"** – is sound advice for senior housing operators. Sometimes your smartest move is to get out of the game.

But whether you plan to fold your cards soon or hold them for a very long time, a sound exit strategy is your ace in the hole.

SECTION NINE

The Future is Not
What It Used to Be

CHAPTER 39

THE INDUSTRY IS AT A CRITICAL MARKETING CROSSROADS

The Future is Bright if We Focus on Today's Sales & Marketing Opportunities

There was plenty of bad news in assisted living in 2000 and early 2001: public company stocks were depressed, some major metropolitan markets appeared to be saturated, new project fill-up was slowing and pricing concessions were becoming commonplace. But don't be fooled about the industry's future.

An entire book could be written about senior living sales and marketing (I'm writing one). This chapter lays the strategic foundation for fresh approaches to sales and marketing.

Some Sobering Assisted Living Sales & Marketing Realities

Let's start with five provocative and sobering facts of life:

1. Many sponsors and owner-operators have been largely "order takers" with well-intended, but largely passive, sales and marketing programs.

2. The industry has not effectively responded to serious and long-lasting senior consumer misconceptions.

3. The adult child decision influencer has been largely taken for granted and frequently under-exploited.

4. Assisted living could become the most significant new and beneficial element of a senior's orderly and prudent estate planning strategy.

5. Finally, by accurately interpreting demographics and effectively responding to the above issues, we will realize that the real growth potential for the industry is *now* – rather than hanging our hats on vague and general references to *future* demographic growth.

It would obviously be unfair to state that *everyone* is seriously overlooking these five marketplace realities. But it would also be irresponsible to ignore them as industry shortcomings and opportunities. Let's take a look at the facts and opportunities.

The industry outlook is more favorable than many indicators seem to imply – *if* you embark on 10 strategic initiatives:

1. *Get out there and market your product.* Many professionals are already working hard to achieve fill-up in seemingly overbuilt markets. But before you panic, ask yourself eight tough questions:

- Have you developed a qualified lead base deep enough for the number of units you need to absorb?

- Do you have *quantitative* goals and initiatives to execute daily?

- Do those daily initiatives lead to defined results and specific expected outcomes?

- Do you have an easy-to-use computerized lead tracking and sales status system?

- Are all your sales professionals appropriately trained and armed with technical sales knowledge, closing techniques and listening skills?

- Do they really understand the quantitative and qualitative strengths and weaknesses of your product and your competitor's offerings?

- Have you developed a subtle but strategic response to exploit your community's strengths and mitigate your weaknesses?

- Do you regularly conduct detailed surveys of your lost prospects?

- Remember the 80/20 rule: approximately 80 percent of our productive results came from only 20 percent of our efforts. The challenge is to focus on the right 20 percent.

2. *Focus on the here and now.* When evaluating market potential, we typically look at two broad sets of demographics – seniors who are currently age 75-plus and income-qualified, and the future growth in that age and income cohort. While the total number of quality assisted living units is difficult to track, there are an estimated 400,000 quality units nationally. This represents an implied absorption of about 12 percent of the 3.4 million age 75-plus, $35,000-plus households.

Given numbers like these, it's easy to see substantial untapped potential in achieving a deeper market penetration. The potential over the next five years based on demographic growth projections is approximately 650,000 age 75-plus, $35,000-plus households. But keep in mind that much of that new potential will be absorbed in *refilling* existing projects experiencing about a 40 percent turnover.

Considerable future growth in assisted living could take place if new – and sometimes controversial – assisted living initiatives were implemented. For example, a policy of prudent and practical spend down of assets would result in an added potential of approximately 1.9 million units or approximately 2,400 80-unit communities. Similarly, if shared accommodations could be effectively created and accepted by consumers, an additional 1.3 million units or 1,600 80-unit facilities would be needed to meet demand. These projections assume a very low capture rate for assisted living. (These initiatives are not mutually exclusive.)

3. *Don't overlook the adult child decision influencer, age 55 to 64.* Consumer research indicates that more than half of these members of the "sandwich generation" – a group of about 42 million are caught in an economic squeeze between their children and their aging parents. They report significant concerns about their parents' current health and ability to continue to live independently. And they respond favorably to the assisted living concept when it is objectively presented to them in simple, straightforward terms.

More than 8 million of these households report annual incomes in excess of $70,000. This is significant in light of growing evidence that some adult children are supplementing their parents' income in order to pay privately for assisted living. Have you positioned your product to capture the attention of these buyers? Have you clearly communicated that message?

4. *You must effectively respond to some very deadly senior consumer misconceptions.* These misconceptions lead to procrastination and sales objections representing major challenges for sales and marketing professionals to overcome.

Here is a real world exchange between a mother and daughter. *"Kim, I appreciate your concern but, really, I'm just fine. Sure, I have an occasional 'spell,' but I can always rely on you and, if necessary, call 911. That assisted living brochure from The Gardens at Westridge looks just like a glorified nursing home to me."*

"I'm not ready yet, but when it's time, my Medicare coverage will cover all of the costs of a nursing home as long as I need it. If not, there's that other program called Medicaid which also provides coverage. I don't know the cost of a nursing home, but I'm sure it's all covered. You know, The Gardens at Westridge will probably raise their prices as soon as I move in. And besides, there's no way that I could afford the $2,300 a month 'rent' that's in their brochure – my current cost of living is only about $700 a month."

Kim responds, "Mom, you're really not looking at this situation objectively. I've done some homework and have some startling different results. Your Medicare covers only nursing care costs under specific and very limited conditions. The Medicaid coverage would not apply unless you have spent down essentially all of your savings including the equity in your home."

"The cost of an institutional nursing home, compared to the very nice Gardens at Westridge, is about 20 to 25 percent higher. The Gardens at Westridge have told us that they have increased their fees by only about 3-1/2 percent per year since 1990. And they reminded us that their inflation is not unlike the inflation that we all experience with food, utilities, real estate taxes, etc. And, mom, your cost of living is really not $700 a month when you factor in real estate taxes, home repairs, insurance premiums and other bills that you don't pay every month; it's really more like $1,800 per month."

"I know you want to leave the home and your savings portfolio to us children – but, if we sold the home today and put that extra money into your existing savings account, you could afford to live at The Gardens at Westridge and still leave most of your savings portfolio to us. We only want what's best for you at this point in life."

If there's anything unrealistic about the above scenario, it is the fact that a typical daughter also has similar misconceptions and is not usually armed with a high degree of accurate information. They, too, are caught up in the emotion and frustration of the situation.

5. *Promote assisted living as a new consideration in prudent estate planning.* A senior's desire for preservation of assets can represent either a major sales objection or a significant opportunity for assisted living sponsors. It all depends on your willingness and creativity in helping seniors and their families plan for the later stages of life. Keep in mind that many seniors seriously underestimate both the potential health care costs that arise in the later years, their current cost of living, and the true value of their pent-up home equity.

In response, put together an ethical and credible financial plan as if you were counseling your own mother. Show seniors how they can put their newly liquidated net home equity to work now, and still leave most of it to their estate. Convey that monthly fees are competitive and predictable and will not likely deplete savings.

Seniors and their families have hang-ups and misconceptions – but so do many dedicated industry professionals. With a more detailed game plan, we can substantially improve the performance and acceptance of assisted living.

6. *Selling assisted living to seniors, their adult children, and other referral sources is becoming less of an art and more of a science.* As competition heats up in some markets, assisted living fill-up rates will likely decline. Or as higher than expected turnover creates worrisome vacant units in projects across the country, some owner/operators will likely tell their professional staffs, **"We need some move-ins; let's sell something!"** I refer to that as the Hail Mary Touchdown Syndrome.

The game-saving touchdown sometimes happens in sports, but most winning situations involve game plans consisting of carefully-planned and appropriately-sequenced strategies and initiatives. Panic should not be the order of the day. It is time to get back to basic fundamentals and develop and execute a marketing and sales game plan for assisted living.

7. *There is a critical distinction between marketing and sales.* Many projects languish because of a basic lack of understanding of this difference. Marketing is a series of initiatives that delivers prospects to the community. Sales then works these prospects and converts a reasonable percentage of them to actual resident move-ins.

Marketing is typically a four-step process. First, you must position your project, explaining who you are, what you do, and who you serve. Then you must communicate with appropriate target markets, including seniors, their adult children, and other referral sources. Next you create a direct response call to action, encouraging people to request information by calling you, sending in a coupon or an RSVP for an event, or scheduling an appointment. And finally, you must deliver qualified prospects to the sales staff.

Sales must then further qualify the senior prospect and close the sale with a reasonable percentage of these prospects, thereby creating new residents for your community.

In football terms, you might consider this analogous to the quarterback (marketing) setting up and calling the play before handing the ball off to the fullback (sales/execution).

8. *Activities do not equal results.* Show me a project with low occupancy and I can probably show you reports of myriad marketing and sales *activities* and impressive planning, but with very limited *results*. The mark of success is to apply a laser focus to an orderly sequence of initiatives rather than using the shotgun approach or suffering from the Hail Mary Touchdown Syndrome.

9. *Marketing directed at seniors works best if you keep it simple.* There are a number of ways to communicate with seniors and caregivers. Brochures and collaterals, direct mail, and advertising are three of the most common. Focus on the benefits potential residents will value. Features and warm and fuzzy platitudes about your community are nice, but benefits are what seniors and their families are really looking for during one of the most difficult periods of their lives.

To stress the benefits that matter most, you must clearly understand the mind-sets of the two key target markets that will be the subject of your marketing communications. Potential residents typically feel vulnerable and have significant concerns about their health and their future. They are also concerned about dignity, independence, control, affordability, and ambience. Their adult children are torn between feelings of love, guilt, frustration, helplessness, and economic concern.

10. *An effective sales and marketing program is expensive, but it is probably one of the best investments you can make.* Plan to spend at least $4,000 per unit for your sales and marketing program. This includes all collateral and brochures, program development, media costs, and sales office overhead expenses. It also includes base compensation and performance incentives for the sales and marketing staff: essentially, everything needed to get your project to a stabilized occupancy of approximately 93 percent in a reasonable time frame.

Figure 39-1 shows the significant (lost) opportunity cost of just one vacant unit. That's the bad news. The good news is that there are a number of modest cost strategies that can have a very high payoff. Figure 39-2 summarizes the strategic positioning of effective sales and marketing professionals.

Now more than ever, sponsors and owner/operators have a mandate to execute appropriately sequenced marketing and sales initiatives to ensure the success not only of their communities but of the industry as a whole.

FIGURE 39-1
THE OPPORTUNITY COST OF A VACANT UNIT

	Fixed Cost (For Both Vacant & Occupied Units)	Truly Variable Costs	Total
Operating Expenses @ $55 Per Resident Day	$ 1,255/mo	$420/mo	$ 1,675/mo
• Vacancy Factor (7%) Contribution	200	0	200
• Debt Service Payment Per Unit ($120,000/unit@ 9% Interest)	725	0	725
TOTAL	$ 2,180/mo	$420/mo	$ 2,600/mo

Annual (Lost) Opportunity Cost:
- *One Unit = $26,160*
- *Five Units = $130,800 !*

© MOORE DIVERSIFIED SERVICES, INC.

FIGURE 39-2

THE MARKETING & SALES PROFESSIONAL

- "Overkill" Product Knowledge
- Empathy
- Credibility
- Listening Skills
- Selling Skills
- Closing Skills
- Understand Financial Implications
- Counter Misconceptions
- Neutralize Sales Objections

Develop *Two* Unique Benefit-Driven Strategies

The Potential Resident

- Fear
- Insecurity
- Denial
- Procrastination
- Misconceptions

The Decision Influencer

- Love
- Guilt
- Economic Concern
  – Sometimes Actual Greed !
- Product Confusion

© MOORE DIVERSIFIED SERVICES, INC.

CHAPTER 40

21ST CENTURY SURVIVAL, GROWTH AND PROFITABILITY
A "Back to Basics" Checklist for Success

As we race into the 21st century, assisted living continues to be a high profile service delivery system. Publicity about the robust 85+ population growth trends and senior living options appear almost daily in both the business press and consumer publications. The previous new development activity and recently announced marketplace adjustments by both public and private companies has created a very high industry noise level. But aside from all this activity and communications hype, there are some basic issues that require strategic focus by existing sponsors and operators in order to achieve survival, growth and profitability in assisted living. Here is a simple, but very important, ten point checklist for success as you plan for the future.

1. *Create laser - focused market positioning* – Start by answering the defining question, *"What business are we really in?"* If you do this you will avoid a disease called *market myopia*. Think in a broad context when you answer this question, and use terms that are understandable and respond to the needs and concerns of potential residents and their families. Some 50 to 60 years ago the railroad industry contracted the market myopia disease – narrowly positioning themselves as being just *railroads* rather than being in the *transportation business.*

You have at least three attractive options to choose from when positioning your product.

The first is to say that, *"Assisted living is a surprisingly affordable living alternative, offering ambience, dignity and maximum independence for seniors in the later stages of life."*

The second is to point out that, *"Our assisted living community has a strong, but largely invisible, medical basis as the foundation for our assisted living operating philosophy."*

Third is to assert that, *"Although achieving high scores on resident satisfaction surveys and third-party facility inspections is very important, our primary concerns are the quality of life of our residents and the peace of mind of their caregivers."* Chapter 3 addresses market positioning in detail.

2. *Develop a market responsive, cost-effective design* – This involves balancing *long-run operational efficiency* with *short-run high perceived value* in the eyes of the consumer. There are currently three major design issues: 1) total project size, 2) design and efficiency of the public spaces and 3) the mix of studios versus one-bedroom units. While it may appear desirable to maximize the number of units in order to optimize revenue and spread fixed capital and operating costs efficiently, it is equally important to avoid unacceptable marketplace risk by introducing too many units into your competitive market.

Industry experience indicates that the *minimum* size for a stand-alone assisted living community should be approximately 60 units. The *optimum* size is 80 or more units. This assisted living unit count can be lower if these units are truly integrated with other revenue-producing entities such as independent living, nursing, etc. Elaborate public spaces such as "neighborhoods" or the cluster concept in each wing are nice, but such space can be relatively expensive. These design features certainly facilitate marketing and should be given serious consideration – but their relative cost must also be factored into the decision, particularly as it impacts monthly service fees in a very competitive market.

Assisted living unit design has evolved from modest studios of 275 to 300 s.f. to larger studios or alcove units of approximately 350 s.f. Within the past five years, there has also been a definite trend involving the growing demand for one-bedroom units with modest living areas averaging between 450 to 550 s.f. Current unit mixes can include up to a 60 percent concentration of these modest-sized, one-bedroom units. (See Chapter 10 for more details).

3. *Get creative with affordability issues* – Strike a delicate balance between the situation-driven financial needs of your project and market-driven dynamics. Affordability will become an increasingly difficult issue to address in the future. Some progressive sponsors and owner/operators are even considering practical and prudent approaches to assisted living spend-down and they are evaluating the practicality of selective use of semi-private accommodations. Some are implementing innovative staffing models trying to make the universal worker approach really work from a practical standpoint. You can count on labor being one of the most significant challenges of the future. As Chapter 16 points out, staffing can represent over 60 percent of total operating costs and can become a scarce commodity at both the entry and upper management levels.

4. *Look for ways to enhance revenues* – Most assisted living communities are truly profitable at an acceptable level of performance only when the occupancy rate is at least 93 percent. Although many operators are satisfied with somewhat lower occupancy levels, you shouldn't be. And don't ignore the revenue potential of rehabilitation services, geriatric assessment and creative home health services. Even if it was wise to outsource these services in the past, it might be prudent to take some of these services in-house as resident acuity levels intensify and case loads increase.

5. *Operating costs must be constantly value engineered with a passion* – And all of this must be accomplished without major compromises to what the consumer perceives as high value when comparing your costs with the products and services offered by the local competition. Chapters 25 through 29 address critical affordability issues.

6. *Sharpen your resident profile definition* – This will become an imperative in the next 12 to 18 months. With some resident turnover rates exceeding 40 percent, many operators are getting the proverbial wake-up call. They now realize that the assisted living business represents higher acuity care than they had originally bargained for – and providing such care has become absolutely necessary for their continued success.

Many sponsors are redefining admission and discharge criteria; resulting in increasing encroachment on the traditional skilled nursing care market sector (where licensing and regulations permit). Owner/operators must be prepared to provide higher levels of care and develop methods to proactively identify and address operations cost creep – the inevitable increase in staffing and operating expenses resulting from higher resident acuity levels.

7. Control as much of the continuum and the assisted living referral pipeline as possible – If you don't, someone else will. Resident referral patterns can change dramatically as other health care providers enter your turf. Your primary focus for gathering referrals should be:

- Hospitals/subacute
- Nursing
- Rehabilitation
- Home health
- Adult children
- Referral professionals

If you don't presently "own or control" many of these referral sources, you'd better expect that some of your current resident origin patterns will change in the not-too-distant future. (See Chapter 8 for additional detail).

8. *Explore market niche "carve-outs"* – The more common types of carve-outs include special care Alzheimer's/dementia units, respite care and "catered living", which is a form of assisted living with added flexibility and a la carte service options. If you offer Alzheimer's/dementia care, make it legitimate, coupling appropriate, purpose-built physical designs with special programming and customized resident care plans that have been proven effective. Refer to Chapter 32 for more details.

9. *Create optimum consumer pricing structures* – Make the plans easy to understand, equitable, flexible and market-responsive. Obviously, these pricing structures must be designed to cover both current and future costs while being competitive in the marketplace. Higher acuity levels are leading to operations cost creep creating a new set of challenges for many owner/operators. These sponsors are reluctantly implementing – or at least considering – various forms of tiered pricing to compensate for cost creep. Pricing is covered in detail in Chapters 22 and 23 and should exhibit the following attributes:

- Understandable
- Equitable
- Cover current and future costs
- Flexible
- Market responsive

As you revisit your pricing structures, you will likely find that the affordability issue represents a very significant future challenge for your operations.

10. *Establish best practices and benchmarking initiatives* – Determine how your community really stacks up when compared to both your immediate competitors and similar communities on a regional and national basis. Benchmarking is a relatively new discipline involving a comparative analysis of industry operating factors, financial ratios and overall best practices.

The benchmarking discipline can provide an early warning system; identifying impending problems while determining how you rank with your industry peers. Financial benchmarks can be found in Chapters 13 through 17.

How to Turn Four Key Challenges Into Opportunities

In this increasingly complex marketplace, it's becoming harder for providers to achieve survival, growth and profitability. What's more, some sectors of major markets are already approaching an overbuild condition as developers and providers rush to stake their claims in scores of "hot" markets. But savvy assisted living providers who take a realistic look at market trends have a unique window of opportunity to turn four distinct challenges into opportunities – and distinguish themselves from the competition.

Challenge #1: *Resident turnover is higher than expected.* Many owner/operators are surprised to encounter resident turnover of 30 to 40 percent a year. True, some residents live at their communities for extended periods, but the *average* length of stay is approximately two-and-a-half years. Refilling existing units vacated by turnover is consuming available demand at a faster pace than most people expected; amounting to the demand equivalent of several "phantom" projects in a typical metropolitan market area.

Opportunity: *Explore ways of expanding your market.* Some owners and operators are extending the resident stays by changing admission and discharge criteria while increasing the intensity of health care services. Others are attempting to lower affordability thresholds. This is difficult because significant portions of assisted living cost structures are largely fixed. Semi-private accommodations have met with mixed success in most markets.

Other owners and operators are considering offering residents new ways to pay, including the option of spending down assets. This is a controversial issue, but one that deserves serious consideration. For more details on this concept, see Chapter 30.

Still others are redoubling their efforts to market to the adult child decision influencer. Such efforts can expand a provider's reach in two ways. First by accommodating those seniors who currently live outside the primary market area and are encouraged by their children to move close to them. Second, by bringing in seniors who fall below acceptable private pay income thresholds, but could qualify through the financial assistance of their children supplementing the senior's income and ability-to-pay resources. For example, in Atlanta's Fulton

County there are over 23,000 households headed by adult children between the ages of 45 and 64 with current incomes in excess of $75,000. If just *one percent* either provided some financial assistance to income qualify their parent or attracted a parent back to the Atlanta area, the market would gain 230 new assisted living prospects.

Challenge #2: *Labor is rapidly becoming the most critical assisted living resource and cost issue.* At the turn of the 21st century, unemployment is at its lowest level in well over a decade. This does not bode well for the assisted living industry, whose operations, strategies and economics are based largely on the availability of low-cost, entry-level employees. In a typical 80-unit assisted living community, labor accounts for approximately 65 percent of operating expenses, and over 70 percent of the 40 full-time equivalent employees (FTEs) are at or near entry level. Even at entry-level base hourly rates, their average cost, loaded for direct and indirect payroll expenses and fringe benefits, can exceed $20,000 per year.

Labor unions see senior housing and health care as one of their last hopes of stabilizing their declining membership, or even regaining lost ground. Their demands typically include more pay, increased staffing requirements and more benefits. In a market with labor unions, a typical project might be required to increase by three FTEs; resulting in an entry level worker wage increase of 10 percent. This would increase operating expenses by approximately $66,000 annually or $2.50 per resident-day. To recover this cost increase at 93 percent stabilized occupancy, the owner would have to increase each resident's monthly service fee by about $75 a month.

Labor unions are not the only force that can cause payrolls to swell. Many assisted living operations are experiencing cost creep resulting from an increased need for assistance with the activities of daily living. As residents age in place, gradually needing more care, labor costs increase (see Chapter 15).

Opportunity: *Fine-tune your operations so you can tolerate increases in the cost of labor.* Recognize these labor threats now and conduct a financial sensitivity analysis of your operation to see how well you can tolerate potential labor cost changes in the future. Look for operational efficiencies and ways to realize economies of scale. Determine how to become financially competitive in your local labor market. Create a positive work culture that enhances employee morale. Finally, consider a pricing structure that can accommodate both cost creep due to aging in place and increased labor costs.

Challenge #3: *Hospitals are diluting assisted living's market share.* More and more hospitals are experiencing declining census and depressed acute care revenues. Hospital CEOs and CFOs see assisted living as a legitimate way to capture revenues they are currently *giving away* through referrals to other providers. Traditional referral patterns will inevitably change as hospitals create their own continuums, developing not only the so-called social model of assisted living, but possibly offering skilled nursing, home health, and rehabilitation services as well. This is discussed in detail in Chapters 6 and 7.

Opportunity: *If you can't beat 'em, join 'em.* Many hospital administrators are smart enough to realize that their acute care business culture may not work as well in the highly competitive, complex assisted living market sector. For example, hospitals who let their traditional culture drive the development of a new assisted living project might green-light construction costs of over $130 per square foot and operating expenses of up to $70 per resident day. With appropriate advice and counsel, these hospital CEOs and CFOs will quickly realize that, to be competitive in assisted living, they need to keep construction costs no higher that $95 to $120 per square foot and operating costs at no more than $50 to $55 per resident day. Joint ventures and synergistic relationships are being given serious consideration by many progressive hospital administrators, who would rather get 50 percent of properly earned assisted living financial rewards than 100 percent of the serious problems they could encounter without a partner who understands the business.

Challenge #4: *How to properly use home health* **care.** Properly used, home health is a viable way to service ADL needs, but problems are emerging in this industry. Several years ago a GAO report indicated that a surprising number of Medicare reimbursed home health transactions involved misuse of the entitlements. The "seamless" integration of housing and shelter services provided by the owner/operator and care by a qualified, licensed home health agency is a viable service delivery system. The operative word is *seamless*.

Some assisted living owners and operators are unrealistically attempting to use home health as their primary method of providing assistance with the activities of daily living. But many are ignoring the added financial burden placed on the senior. Home health in assisted living becomes inappropriate when owner/operators allow home health providers to provide fragmented services at premium prices or by charging extra for things that should be an integral part of a facility's normal spectrum of services to the residents.

Opportunity: *Exploit home health's legitimate strengths – but avoid its weaknesses.* Use home health to augment your own array of services, ensuring that outcomes are competitive, seamless, consistently high in quality, and in compliance with local licensing and regulations.

It's time to get head and shoulders above the increasing assisted living marketplace noise level. Responding to these four challenges now is an excellent way to plan for success in the 21st century.

The Odyssey of Survival, Growth and Profitability

Finally, you must answer seven important strategic questions. These questions are:

1. How much is enough – really?

- Development of product
- Profits
- Risk
- Etc.

2. What business am I *really* in?

3. Where do I want my community to be in three years?

4. How, *specifically*, will I get it there?

5. What could possibly threaten my project in the future?

6. What should I do *now* to mitigate that future risk?

7. Do I have an acceptable exit strategy?

Implementing these seven initiatives will sharpen your strategic focus, provide a hedge against downside risks and help you realize survival, success and profitability in assisted living as we race into the 21st century.

CHAPTER 41

TURNING AROUND TROUBLED COMMUNITIES
What to Do When Things Go Wrong

This chapter is for those readers who, unfortunately, missed taking advantage of many of the strategies discussed in the other chapters of this book.

In today's market, no senior housing community is immune to the sub-par performance virus. Markets are maturing and competition is intensifying. A better-educated, more demanding consumer presents additional challenges. Indeed, the sector itself, which is not merely alive and well but growing, is contributing to the performance problems of some communities. Rapid advances in the state of the art favor the latest and greatest communities over even well-established ones with good reputations.

Troubled assisted living projects are likely to plague the industry in the future. They will, in all probability, include both for-profit and non-profit communities. Some newly developed communities are clearly situation-driven rather than being focused on the true needs of and benefits to seniors. Existing assisted living communities in maturing market areas are succumbing to their own aging-in-place challenges and the forces of new, well-conceived competition. Many markets are becoming more complex and individual project primary market areas are shrinking due to evolving market saturation resulting from increasing competition.

Yet, in spite of these challenges, assisted living is still clearly a growing industry – and certainly not one that is mature and on the decline. One of the most significant problems associated with troubled assisted living communities is the lack of early recognition that the facility, in fact, needs help – and change. Many communities fail for all the wrong reasons. Sometimes fundamental and focused corrective actions are the answer. In other cases, the honest pursuit of a worthy mission for non-profit communities is now incompatible with the way the real world marketplace evaluates the value of, and the need for, their community. Inappropriate site locations and design flaws can be serious and may not be correctable but, for the most part, the majority of troubled assisted living communities can be "saved."

One of the most significant challenges for the owner of a troubled community is recognizing that the community is, in fact, sick. As with one's own health, early symptoms can be either ignored or addressed. Lack of early detection causes communities to fail when appropriate corrective action could have saved them.

Troubled communities are similar to personal health emergencies in other ways as well. Negative cash flow is like uncontrolled loss of blood. Unstable operations are similar to irregular heartbeats. The actions needed to turn around a community in the throes of a fiscal crisis are strikingly similar to how EMS would respond to a personal medical emergency.

Five Basic Actions to Take

There are five basic actions that must be taken to turn around a community that is experiencing an economic emergency – and these actions are strikingly similar to a medical response to a personal medical emergency. Here are five "ER" strategies that work:

1. *Stabilize the patient* – Many owner/operators are so caught up in the problem that they cannot find the time to stop and take a fresh objective look at their situation. Problems at a community will not get better without appropriate changes. Frequently there are multiple problems and conducting a triage analysis will help you decide which to attack first. This usually means implementing pragmatic strategies that make sense.

2. *Check for eight vital signs* – The following eight vital signs to monitor in order to start to determine the nature of the problem and provide the earliest clues for successful corrective action are:

> 1) Is your age and income qualified market size and depth sufficient?
>
> 2) Have you realistically defined your primary market area?

3) Has your market area changed due to the passage of time and the encroachment of new competition?

4) What is the level of relevant competition, both now and in the foreseeable future?

5) Does your community have a sufficient number of potential marketing leads that, properly exploited, can translate into closed sales?

6) Are there serious misconceptions about your community that are having a negative impact on fill-up?

7) What are your community's tangible strengths and weaknesses?

8) What are your competitors' obvious strengths and weaknesses?

3. *Go back to basics* – One of the most difficult challenges facing owner/operators is their reluctance to change the original plan or pro forma. In many cases, the *original* plan was seriously flawed or the pro forma financially unrealistic. Unless the owner/operator is willing to recognize these flaws based on the current facts at hand, recovery is doubtful. In short, you must break your bad habits.

4. *Prescribe a solution* – Troubled communities need both short-term medication and a change in long-term operating strategies. Negative cash flow for an operating community is similar to uncontrolled bleeding in a patient. The first step in turning around a troubled property is to identify the source of the bleeding and attempt to curtail its flow. While easier said than done, focusing on this critical issue aids materially in developing the long-run changes that are necessary.

For every community there can be up to 50 worthwhile strategies that can be used as part of the turnaround approach. Approximately one-half of these strategies can be implemented with relative ease. The other half are likely to be difficult, painful, and expensive, although in some cases, bitter pills may be necessary for survival. Among the strategies are:

- Engaging in laser-focused market positioning by asking, *"What business are we really in?"*

- Trying not to lose control of your referral pipeline as new players enter your market.

- Exploring additional sources of revenue such as tiered pricing, rehabilitation, home health satellites, and expanded campus and outreach services.

- Extending average length of stay by redefining admission and discharge criteria or adding other components of the continuum.

- Exploring market niches such as Alzheimer's, respite care, and "catered living."

- Creating an understandable, equitable, flexible, and market responsive pricing structure.

- Getting creative with affordability, including resident spend-down and semi-private rooms.

- Establishing best practices and benchmarking initiatives across the board, making detailed comparisons on a local, regional, and national level.

- Repositioning your community through cosmetic changes or modifying the physical plant. Adaptive re-use from one product type to another sometimes may be the only solution to a product that is no longer appropriate in a changed marketplace.

- Establishing a proactive sales and marketing program. It's a must if you want to spur new, qualified traffic to your community. And remember to conduct lost-prospect surveys; they can yield invaluable marketplace intelligence.

5. *Have regular check-ups* – New or revised systems and procedures are typically needed for long-term consistency and quality control. There are a number of fundamental strategies that can be applied to troubled properties. These include enhancing first impressions (cosmetically and physically) and repositioning the facility in the marketplace. In addition, installing systems and procedures associated with cost control, marketing tracking and quality control are sometimes part of the overall corrective action strategy. More severe action such as modifying the physical plant through adaptive re-use/conversion from one product type to another is sometimes the practical solution to an inappropriate product or changing marketplace conditions.

There are situations where formal sales and marketing programs are virtually non-existent. In these cases, a complete marketing effort must be developed to jump start new, qualified traffic to the community, resulting in increased sales potential.

One of the most difficult adjustments that sometimes must take place is the decision to change pricing. In many cases, the original pricing was clearly situation-driven rather than oriented towards the needs and preferences of the competitive marketplace.

Lost prospects are an excellent source of "miracle cure" information. The two percent of the senior consumers who move into your community are obviously very important – but understanding more about the *98 percent* who got away can yield invaluable marketplace intelligence. Properly structured, lost prospect surveys provide a very useful tool in prescribing a success strategy for the future.

Old Habits are Hard to Break

Just like changing harmful personal lifestyle habits, troubled communities must adopt permanent changes in operating style.

One serious impediment to turning around a troubled property is the "original pro forma trap." Most operators are unwilling to change their original plan, even though it now appears that it was ill-conceived and unrealistic. Success in turning around troubled assisted living properties involves recognizing that the present situation may not be compatible with achieving the original dream.

Measuring the gap between the original pro forma and the current situation can be painfully revealing. It can also provide the courage and conviction to recognize the need for change. Operators who have the business acumen and courage to change are the ones who will be able to turn troubled assisted living properties into bona fide success stories.

CHAPTER 42

WHAT HAPPENED TO
THE GOOD OLD DAYS?

Assisted Living is <u>Not</u> What It Used to Be

It's time for a reality check. In my last book, *Assisted Living 2000*, published in July of 1998, I stated that one of the major questions sponsors and owner/operators were asking privately in boardrooms and publicly at trade association meetings was, ***"Can it get any better than this?"*** Assisted living communities and CCRCs across the U.S. were enjoying high stabilized occupancies, often in excess of 95 percent. Conventional debt was readily available for growth and expansion, and new sources of equity capital were emerging. Wall Street and the public markets had embraced senior housing – particularly assisted living – as a viable investment option.

But I also observed that despite these positive signs, the pressure to improve performance was relentless. A number of for-profit assisted living and independent living companies had gone public since 1996 by launching Initial Public Offerings (IPOs). Every 90 days presented a new challenge for these companies as investors and security analysts pressed the question: ***"What have you done for me in this calendar quarter?"*** For these public companies, relentless growth and maximum activity was the name of the game as they sweated out their next quarterly earnings report.

The pressure is equally intense for not-for-profits as the senior housing and health care business becomes more complex, making it necessary for them to do more just to keep up with the changing market. Boards of directors are sharpening their focus on their growing fiduciary responsibilities, and recent refinancing of some communities is putting more pressure on meeting specific bond covenants and overall financial performance ratios. There is also a growing desire to generate significant cash flow after operating expenses and debt service in order to fund other missions.

In 1998, I asked the question, *"Can it get any better than this?"* My answer was, *"Probably not – and it could get worse."* It didn't take a rocket scientist to draw that conclusion. Warning signs were already on the horizon. In fact, today it may be time for some owner/operators to ask, *"Is my property or portfolio about to hit the wall because of market saturation?"*

The types of players who were attending overflowing seminars and conferences to gain insight about assisted living typically fell into three major categories: 1) existing, experienced freestanding assisted living developers and established owner/operators who were completing their continuum and expanding their campuses; 2) owner/operators and administrators of hospitals, nursing homes and other related businesses who saw assisted living as a natural extension of what they do and; 3) people who have not been directly associated with senior housing or health care, but saw assisted living business opportunities from their particular business perspective or company culture. The operative words for that third category are "company culture."

Many seasoned professionals attempted to explain assisted living market realities to newcomers, but the frequent response was, *"You don't understand – we're going to be different."* Many said, *"We're going to roll out 20 or 30 of these projects each year all over the country."* Sounded like the same story we heard in the 1980s when many relatively new industry players, including some of today's industry leaders, were surprised to discover that their well-intended senior housing strategies would ultimately go against the grain of the marketplace.

When confronted with these warning signs, some sponsors offer the rationale that the *tremendous* future growth in age and income qualified households will surely rebalance senior housing markets that become temporarily oversupplied. This rationale brings back memories of the 1980s real estate bust, when future inflation was supposed to compensate for any mistakes or overbuilding in real estate markets. Inflation was *not* the answer in 1988, and future senior household growth will *not* necessarily be the solution in the early 2000s.

The rhetorical question of the late 1990s, *"Can it get any better than this?"* has been replaced by some serious – but necessary – real world questions.

1. *What could happen in the next five years to threaten my assisted living community or portfolio of properties?* Is a major new competitor likely to move into your market, offering better quality, price, or value? Might an oversupply of new units lead to increased vacancies or price wars? If you can imagine any plausible scenario that could create future problems, *now* is the time to implement corrective action to mitigate or eliminate those problems.

2. *Am I really satisfied with my current financial returns?* These returns should be measured in a number of ways: cash flow, cash-on-cash return on investment, return on total equity, return on cost and internal rate of return over a reasonable holding period. For a mature, stabilized project, available cash flow *after* debt service should be at least 30 percent of the annual debt payment and cash-on-cash return should be 10 percent or higher. Internal rate of return (for mature, stabilized projects) should be 15 to 25 percent, depending on how long your community's been operating. Don't wait for a financial crisis to emerge; look for ways to enhance your financial positions now.

3. *How does my community stack up against general industry ratios and benchmarks?* Benchmarking, currently a popular business discipline, can be very useful but must be applied with caution. Using broad industry ratios as guidelines can be both helpful and misleading for your specific project. It's not unlike saying: ***"My blood pressure is this, doctor. I've never met you before, but is that okay?"*** On the other hand, the simplistic rationale, ***"we're just different and benchmarks don't apply to us,"*** is usually unacceptable and an early symptom of future problems.

4. *Do I have a proactive revolving five-year strategic plan?* The key word here is "revolving." Each year, your five-year plan should be sharpened, refocused, and rolled out for an additional 12 months. This allows you to always keep a clear five-year time horizon in front of you. Key items you should evaluate every year include capital improvements, value engineering, competitive repositioning, net operating income enhancement, increased resident satisfaction, and quality of life improvements.

5. *Do I have an acceptable exit strategy?* This applies to you even if you plan to hold your property indefinitely. Why? The reason is simple. Your long-term holding strategy will not be successful if it doesn't include an acceptable exit strategy.

Simply stated, an exit strategy asks the hypothetical question: ***"If I sold my community based on current market conditions, would I be pleased or disappointed by the results?"*** If you'd be disappointed, ask yourself an additional question: ***"What can I do in the next 12 to 18 months to improve the outcome of this hypothetical transaction?"*** The "hypothetical" exit strategy is the *acid test* for project viability.

6. *Is next year the appropriate time to step outside the box and consider unusual innovation?* Is it time to experiment with some changes that could yield positive results but are not yet fully supported by empirical evidence? Initiatives such as selective unbundling of services or providing expanded assistance with the activities of daily living to residents in independent living units may seem radical, but, like a good farmer or rancher, you can learn a lot by walking your boundaries and fence lines looking for current weaknesses and future potential problems.

As the assisted living business becomes more of a science and less of an art, we can no longer rely exclusively on the past to develop a realistic vision of the future. The following story was in my previous book – but it's worth repeating.

I had just completed a series of focus groups at a community in Chicago and, as usual, I was on a tight schedule, headed for another airplane. As I attempted my graceful, but hurried exit, one of the focus group respondents, an 85-year-old man, walked up to me, put his arm around my shoulder and said, ***"You know Jim, the future is not what it used to be. But if we can see the future, we can get there before it happens."*** I smiled politely and thanked him for his wisdom as I left the building. But the significance of his simple comment didn't hit me until I was driving to O'Hare airport.

Here was a man, supposedly living a relatively sheltered life, who in one simple statement, articulated how we must approach our industry as we plan for the future. We face some very challenging and exciting times in the assisted living industry. **And we must anticipate and plan for the future before it actually happens.** Failing to believe that the future will be different is perhaps our industry's biggest threat – and also our greatest opportunity.

I wish you much success in your assisted living and senior housing endeavors.

Jim Moore, March, 2001

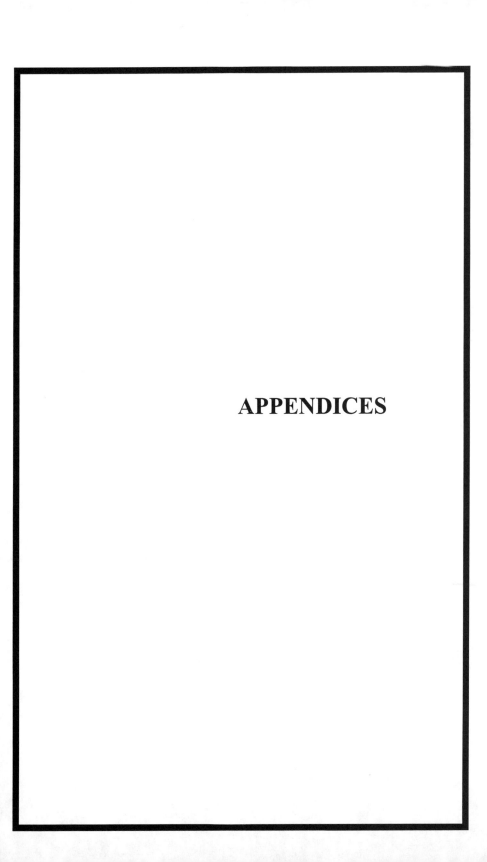

APPENDICES

APPENDIX A

OVERVIEW OF MARKET & FINANCIAL FEASIBILITY

An entire book could be devoted to just market and financial feasibility. The purpose of this appendix is to provide the outline or structure for this very important part of the project planning process.

Market and Financial Feasibility As a Closed Loop

Feasibility methodology is gradually evolving from an art to a science. But the process still requires a tremendous application of professional judgement and conventional wisdom. The days of, *"If I build it, they will come"* are over. Some of the classical feasibility analysis mistakes of the 1980s were:

1. Inadequate, improper and erroneous input assumptions
2. Faulty methodology
3. Some theories or hypotheses not supported by sound empirical data
4. Insufficient competitive analysis and field investigations
5. Flawed data analysis and conclusions
6. No direct linkage between market feasibility *outputs* and financial pro forma *inputs*
7. Failure to keep up with the ever-changing market

8. Using the rationale that inflation (growth of senior households) would compensate for any mistakes or overbuilding
9. Relying on incorrect age cohorts, income levels and annual turnover projections, etc.
10. Failure to effectively address "Aging in Place"

Item six is one of the most critical elements of the overall planning process. As Figure A-1 illustrates, market and financial feasibility must be *closely integrated using a closed loop philosophy*. Initially the market feasibility study outputs must drive the inputs to the financial pro forma. The pro forma, in turn, is heavily influenced by the initial design and overall development business plan. Any future changes, such as project cost increases, must be immediately transmitted back to the pro forma. If the pro forma requires increased revenues, the market feasibility study must be reworked to determine if all of these changes and their impacts are still acceptable in the marketplace.

Market Feasibility Study Outline

It is important to have a detailed, definitive work plan for market feasibility; with tangible and specific expected outcomes. The following outline can be used as a guide if you are conducting an in-house market feasibility study or preparing a Request for Proposal (RFP), for engaging a consultant.

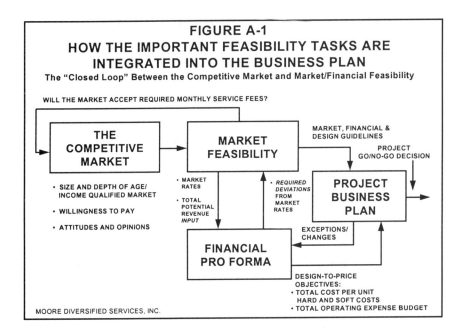

FIGURE A-1
HOW THE IMPORTANT FEASIBILITY TASKS ARE
INTEGRATED INTO THE BUSINESS PLAN
The "Closed Loop" Between the Competitive Market and Market/Financial Feasibility

MOORE DIVERSIFIED SERVICES, INC.

1. *Determine Relevant Market Areas*

- Define the primary, secondary and tertiary market areas
- Estimate impact of population mobility trends on seniors
- Determine impact of decision influencers (adult children)
- Obtain resident origin profiles of competition, where available

2. *Conduct Demographic Economic Base Study*

- Determine total number of age & income qualified households
- Conduct age cohort segmentation and growth projections
- Establish senior consumer qualifying income criteria
- Determine level of incidence for need for assistance with activities of daily living (ADLs)
- Determine impact of home equity on consumer affordability
- Identify relevant and prudent forecasting safety margins

3. *Conduct Competitive Analysis*[1]

- Assisted living/personal care
- Independent living/congregate care/CCRC
- Special care Alzheimer's/dementia facilities
- Nursing homes
- Acute care, subacute care
- Home health agencies
- Other senior housing products and services (senior apartments, subsidized elderly housing, etc.)
- Estimate managed care impacts – where relevant

---

[1] Must include both existing and announced projects

4. *Conduct Specific Site Analysis*

- Subject site description
- Access/egress characteristics
- Drive-by visibility/traffic counts, etc
- Surrounding development/adjacent property owners
- Potential buffers and set-backs
- Appropriate zoning
- Supporting amenities, benefits and features
- Evaluate/rank alternative sites - where applicable

5. *Estimate Overall Project Capture Rates and Market Share*

- By age cohort
- By qualifying income threshold criteria
- By need for assistance with Activities of Daily Living (ADLs)
- Primary versus secondary market area
- Consider annual resident turnover
- Adjust for competitive impacts (existing and planned)
- Weighting of competition – where applicable

6. *Conduct Unit Absorption Scenarios*

- Estimate time to stabilized occupancy (including pre-marketing efforts)
- Adjust for unit turnover during fill-up

7. *Recommend Final Product Mix*

- Unit types
- Number of units/unit mix
- Individual living areas/unit size
- Pricing by unit type
- Consider special market/product segmentation
    - Special care dementia
    - Catered living
    - Etc.
- Identify common area amenities
- Recommend services, amenities, benefits and features

Figure A-2 depicts the typical sequence to follow when evaluating your project's market feasibility.

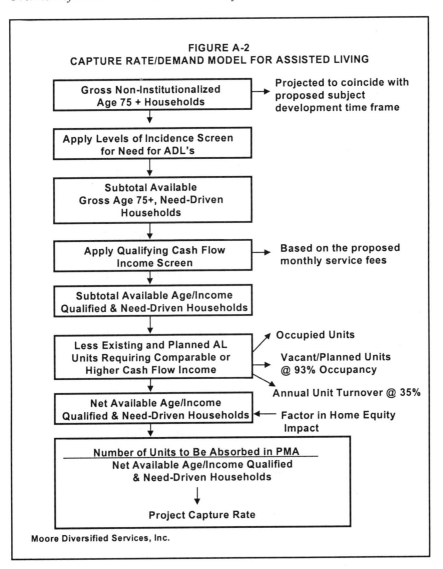

FIGURE A-2
CAPTURE RATE/DEMAND MODEL FOR ASSISTED LIVING

Gross Non-Institutionalized
Age 75 + Households
→ Projected to coincide with
proposed subject
development time frame

Apply Levels of Incidence Screen
for Need for ADL's

Subtotal Available
Gross Age 75+, Need-Driven
Households

Apply Qualifying Cash Flow
Income Screen
→ Based on the proposed
monthly service fees

Subtotal Available Age/Income
Qualified & Need-Driven Households

Less Existing and Planned AL
Units Requiring Comparable or
Higher Cash Flow Income
→ Occupied Units
→ Vacant/Planned Units
@ 93% Occupancy
→ Annual Unit Turnover @ 35%

Net Available Age/Income
Qualified & Need-Driven Households
← Factor in Home Equity
Impact

__Number of Units to Be Absorbed in PMA__
Net Available Age/Income Qualified
& Need-Driven Households
↓
Project Capture Rate

Moore Diversified Services, Inc.

"Bottom-Line" Answers Provided by Market Feasibility

The ultimate outputs of the market feasibility study must answer the following five questions:

1. What percent of the *net* supply of the age and income qualified market (allowing for turnover, competition, etc.) must I capture in order to fill my project?

2. How is the competition doing and is there enough demand elasticity in the market for my project?

3. Is my site really as attractive as I think it is – or am I really situation-driven when I should be market-driven?

4. How fast will my project fill-up – realistically?

5. Does my final product mix meet the following criteria:

   - Responds to market wants and needs
   - Compares favorably with both the existing competition and new potential projects in the future
   - Pricing is consistent with reasonable affordability levels of my target market and offers good value compared to local competition

There is another important question which requires much more analysis: **"Will my market-responsive project concept be financially feasible?"**

Financial Feasibility/Pro Forma Outline

1. *Develop Key Inputs to Realistic and Accurate Capital Budget*

   - Raw land cost allocation
   - Site development costs
   - Preliminary construction cost estimates
   - Contractor general conditions factor
   - Construction contingency
   - Construction interest
   - Construction time period
   - Development fees
   - Architectural and engineering fees
   - Furniture, fixtures & equipment
   - Legal and accounting fees
   - Financing costs
   - Market and financial feasibility studies
   - Initial absorption/fill-up reserve fund
   - Detailed marketing budget
   - Project contingency

2. *Establish Total Capital/Debt Structure Requirements, Mix and Sources*

   - Equity
   - Debt
   - Other capital sources
   - Credit enhancement

3. *Establish and Plan for Required Lender/Underwriter Criteria*

- Debt to equity ratio
- Debt service coverage ratio:
  - Initial
  - At stabilized occupancy
- Debt service reserve fund
- Cash to debt ratio
- Average debt per unit

4. *Set Design-to-Price Objectives*

- Implement the closed loop concept (see Figure A-1)
- Conduct cost containment/value engineering effort

5. *Project Realistic Operating Expense Scenarios*

- Actual experience (if existing community)
- Industry data base benchmarks
- Specific project analysis

6. *Determine Pricing Options*

- Flat monthly service fee
- Monthly service fee with tiered add-on charges for increased ADLs by:
  - Levels of care/case work-up
  - Additional minutes per day for added ADLs

- Develop preliminary menu of pricing options
- Implement cash flow impact scenarios for various pricing options
- Make final pricing policy recommendations

7. ***Implement Multiple Scenarios of Pricing Options Short List***
   - Based on quantitative results of previous tasks
   - Insure adequacy of:
     - Net operating income
     - Cash flow
     - Debt service coverage
   - Implement computer-driven sensitivity analysis of critical financial variables and assumptions

8. ***Estimate Total Revenues, Expenses, Net Operating Income, Debt Service, Cash Flow and Debt Service Coverage Factor***

   - During fill-up
   - At stabilized occupancy
   - 5 and 7 years in the future

9. ***Conduct Discounted Cash Flow Analysis***

   - Use appropriate capitalization and discount rates
   - Present value
   - Internal rate of return
   - Cash flow
   - Cash-on-cash return

10. *Run a Financial Sensitivity Analysis*

- Interest cost at +/- 1%
- NOI sensitivity at +/- 5%
- Fill-up rate at +/- 2 units/month

The critical questions that the completed financial pro forma should answer include, but are not necessarily limited to the following:

1. Have I included *everything* in the capital budget that will provide adequate funds to bring my project to stabilized occupancy?

2. Are there reasonable and adequate contingencies in the pro forma?

3. Are the debt, equity and interest rate assumptions realistic?

4. Will I meet all the criteria likely to be required by lenders?

5. Have I realistically projected revenues and conservatively estimated operating expenses?

6. Will my pricing strategy cover not only my current costs; but also my best estimate of future costs – including potential cost creep?

7. Is the overall project financially prudent; delivering appropriate financial safety margins and entrepreneurial returns – after all expenses and debt service payments have been covered?

The final critical question to ask is, *"Have I updated my market and financial feasibility study to accurately reflect all of the changes that have taken place during the planning and development process?"*

APPENDIX B

MORTGAGE LOAN
CONSTANTS

A loan constant is an easy way to estimate the total debt service payment for an assisted living community. The loan constant provides *one number or multiplier* that takes into consideration three key characteristics of an installment loan:

- Principal payment
- Interest payment
- Amortization (term) of loan

Example:

Referring to Figure 17-1, what is the debt payment per unit for an assisted living community where the average total (all-in) cost per unit is $120,000; with 75 percent debt ($90,000), 25 percent equity ($30,000) @ 9 percent for 30 years?

Referring to Figure B-1:

$90,000   x   .0966 = $8,694 /unit/year
Or
$ 725 /month

In Figure 17-1, the debt for 80 units is shown as:

$$\$8,694/\text{unit} \quad x \quad 80 \text{ units} \quad = \quad \$695,520$$

You can use the debt constant table in Figure B-1 to quickly and easily calculate your debt (mortgage) payments for various combinations of loan characteristics.

FIGURE B-1
MORTGAGE LOAN DEBT CONSTANTS

MORTGAGE TERM [1]

Interest Rate	20 Years	25 Years	30 Years	40 Years [2]
5.00%	7.92%	7.02%	6.44%	5.79%
5.50%	8.25%	7.37%	6.81%	6.19%
6.00%	8.60%	7.73%	7.19%	6.60%
6.50%	8.95%	8.10%	7.58%	7.03%
7.00%	9.30%	8.48%	7.98%	7.46%
7.50%	9.67%	8.87%	8.39%	7.90%
8.00%	10.04%	9.26%	8.81%	8.34%
8.50%	10.41%	9.66%	9.23%	8.80%
9.00%	10.80%	10.07%	9.66%	9.26%
9.50%	11.19%	10.48%	10.09%	9.72%
10.00%	11.58%	10.90%	10.53%	10.19%
10.50%	11.98%	11.33%	10.98%	10.66%
11.00%	12.39%	11.76%	11.43%	11.14%

Moore Diversified Services, Inc.

---

[1] Based on monthly loan amortization.
[2] Typical HUD Financing

APPENDIX C

THE CAPITALIZATION RATE CONCEPT

For some experienced operators, the concept of capitalization rates is very familiar and useful. For others, it may be a very foreign technical term. But like the loan constants discussed in Appendix B, capitalization rates can play a useful role in your strategic planning.

As used in this book, *the capitalization rate ("cap rate") is typically the annual debt-free (unleveraged) <u>cash return</u> that prudent and experienced investors would expect to realize from a specific cash investment.* Currently cap rates for assisted living typically range from 10.0 percent to 11.5 percent; a 10.5 percent *typical* cap rate is used throughout this book.

Example:

In Figure 15-2, the annual unleveraged change in cash return (net operating income) is $103,386. If an investor expects a 10.5 percent return, what might he or she be willing to invest (or in this example lower their purchase offer) in order to yield that return?

$$\frac{\$103,386}{.105} = \$984,630$$

In a similar manner, you can evaluate the incremental *imputed* increase (or decrease) in your project's value for any situation that would impact net operating income (NOI).

Example:

A capital investment of $50,000 is expected to save $12,000 per year in operating expenses; increasing NOI by a similar amount. How will my intrinsic project value be impacted (increased) at a 10.5 percent cap rate?

$$\frac{\$12,000}{.105} = \$114,285$$

This means that the $50,000 capital investment that saves $12,000 in annual operating expenses has increased the intrinsic value of your community by approximately $114,285.

Cap rates are used throughout this book to quantify the dollar impact or financial sensitivity of certain strategies.

About the Author

Jim Moore is president and founder of Moore Diversified Services, Inc. For over 30 years, Jim's company has been heavily involved in market feasibility studies, detailed financial pro forma analysis, marketing consulting, strategic planning and investment advisory services.

Jim has over 40 years of industry experience and has personally conducted over 1,800 major Senior housing and health care consulting engagements in over 650 markets in 47 states – experience that is unmatched in the industry today. He has also conducted major consulting engagements in 26 international markets encompassing Japan, Australia, Canada, Europe and Mexico. As part of his consulting practice, he has lived in over 40 retirement and assisted living communities. His clients include a broad spectrum of national leaders and small organizations – with a balanced mix of both for-profit and not-for-profit clients.

As a recognized national expert, his courtroom testimony as an expert witness is frequently in demand across the U.S. He has provided expert witness support and testimony in over 40 cases at the local, state and national levels. He is the author of several hundred industry technical papers and trade journal articles. Jim has also authored a regular weekly business column for two major newspapers and for over 10 years has authored a monthly column entitled, **"Assisted Living/Senior Housing"** for *Contemporary Long Term Care Magazine* – a leading industry trade periodical. He is the author of numerous books on assisted living, senior housing and health care including his previous industry best seller *"Assisted Living 2000."*

Jim is past president of a major industry trade association. He is active in five other industry trade associations and serves on the Advisory Boards of ten senior housing and health care organizations. He is on the Executive Committee and Board of Directors of a public senior living company traded on the New York Stock Exchange. Jim holds a Bachelor of Science degree in Industrial Technology from Northeastern University in Boston and an MBA in Marketing and Finance from Texas Christian University in Fort Worth, Texas.